Doing social psychology

Doing social psychology

Laboratory and field exercises

Edited by

GLYNIS M. BREAKWELL
University of Surrey

HUGH FOOT
University of Wales Institute of Science and Technology

ROBIN GILMOUR
University of Lancaster

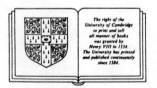

The right of the
University of Cambridge
to print and sell
all manner of books
was granted by
Henry VIII in 1534.
The University has printed
and published continuously
since 1584.

CAMBRIDGE UNIVERSITY PRESS
Cambridge
New York   New Rochelle   Melbourne   Sydney

THE BRITISH PSYCHOLOGICAL SOCIETY
Leicester

Published by the Press Syndicate of the University of Cambridge
The Pitt Building, Trumpington Street, Cambridge CB2 1RP
32 East 57th Street, New York, NY 10022, USA
10 Stamford Road, Oakleigh, Melbourne 3166, Australia
and
The British Psychological Society
St. Andrews House
48 Princess Road East
Leicester LE1 7DR

First edition published by The Macmillan Press, Ltd., 1982, as *Social Psychology: A Practical Manual*

Printed in the United States of America

Library of Congress Cataloging-in-Publication Data
Doing social psychology.
Includes index.
1. Social psychology – Problems, exercises, etc.
I. Breakwell, Glynis M. (Glynis Marie)   II. Foot,
Hugh C.   III. Gilmour, Robin.
HM251.D626   1987   302   87-6348

British Library Cataloguing in Publication Data
Doing social psychology: laboratory and field
exercises. – [2nd ed.]
1. Social psychology
I. Breakwell, Glynis M.   II. Foot, Hugh
III. Gilmour, Robin   IV. British Psychological Society   V. Social psychology
302   HM251

ISBN 0 521 34015 2 hard covers
ISBN 0 521 33563 9 paperback
ISBN 0 521 33564 7 instructor's manual

Contents

Contributors

Peter Ball
Department of Psychology
University of Tasmania

Glynis M. Breakwell
Department of Psychology
University of Surrey

Ray Bull
Department of Psychology
Glasgow College of Technology

Antony J. Chapman
Department of Psychology
University of Leeds

Mark Cook
Department of Psychology
University College

Hugh Foot
Department of Applied Psychology
University of Wales Institute
  of Science & Technology

Howard Giles
Department of Psychology
University of Bristol

Robin Gilmour
Department of Psychology
University of Lancaster

Rom Harré
Linacre College
Oxford University

Mansur Lalljee
Department for External Studies
University of Oxford

Bram Oppenheim
Department of Social Psychology
London School of Economics

Paul Robinson
Department of Psychology
Hollymoor Hospital

Robert Slater
Department of Applied Psychology
University of Wales Institute
  of Science & Technology

Mike Smith
Department of Management
  Sciences
University of Manchester Institute
  of Science & Technology

Peter B. Smith
School of Social Sciences
University of Sussex

Geoffrey M. Stephenson
Social Psychology Research Unit
University of Kent

Peter Trower
The Central Hospital, Warwick

Maryon Tysoe

Frances M. Wade
Department of Applied Psychology
University of Wales Institute
  of Science & Technology

Preface

This volume is a collection of research exercises in social psychology. They are designed to give students practice in using a range of research methods and techniques to investigate a series of problem areas central to modern social psychology. The description of each exercise includes the theoretical background, the processes of data collection, and the methods of analyzing and interpreting results.

A broad range of exercises is included: both field and laboratory studies are covered. The exercises encompass experimental, quasi-experimental, and ethnographic research designs. Such an eclectic choice of exercises is necessary if the object is to reflect something of what is happening in social psychology now. Increasingly, social psychologists are seeking to integrate different methods of research and to use them in concert to examine social phenomena. Each method has its weaknesses, and where one is weak another is strong: experimentation offers control but is confounded by artificiality; ethogenic methods offer realism but no control. Used together sensibly, methods that are each individually flawed can generate a more satisfactory picture than any could alone; hence the need to teach a broad range of methods and hence the eclecticism in the selection of exercises.

The exercises can be ranged along a continuum from those primarily concerned with a method or technique to those essentially concerned with a problem or phenomenon that needs to be researched. In a way, the continuum reflects the needs of a research methods course: the course has to teach specific methods and techniques in all their abstract purity, but it must also show how they relate to particular research problems. Of course, some research problems become almost totally identified with a particular method or technique, just as some techniques always seem to be used to explore one sort of problem. This book is divided into three parts, which represent distinct points along the continuum between technique and problem-orientation. Part I contains exercises that exemplify how some techniques are especially well suited to certain problems. The second part illustrates some specific applications of basic techniques. The emphasis in the third and final part lies in exploring particular problem areas in social psychology.

Part I consists of five chapters, each of which describes a technique that is standard in social psychology. In Chapter 1, Robert Slater describes an exercise that introduces students to questionnaire design. This is followed by an exercise by Mike Smith on how to conduct a selection interview, describing how to open the interview and how to end it; how to cover the important issues systematically; how to get the interviewee to talk; and what must be considered when drawing conclusions from an interview. The exercise in Chapter 3, by Bram Oppenheim, is a classical description of attitude measurement, an activity central to the research goals of innumerable social psychologists. Chapter 4, by Hugh Foot, is based upon the use of a modified version of the Bales Interaction Process Analysis, which gives students a route to interactional analysis in the context of group discussion. Rom Harré, in Chapter 5, portrays something of the epistemology and applications of "ethogenic" approaches.

The five chapters in Part II contain exercises that each illustrate how a particular method or technique can be especially suited to the study of a particular social psychological problem. In Chapter 6, Peter Ball and Howard Giles demonstrate the Matched Guise Technique, a method that has come to be associated with the study of the social psychology of language. In the following chapter, Antony Chapman and Frances Wade employ nonparticipant observation to examine the recreational use of the street by children; it is difficult to imagine what other technique would be effective in studying this phenomenon. Paul Robinson and Peter Trower, in Chapter 8, take us into the realms of applied social psychology, using role-play exercises to show the importance of social skill in interpersonal relations. Mark Cook presents in Chapter 9 an exercise specifically designed to show how results can be influenced by the techniques employed in a study of person perception. Chapter 10 concludes Part II with a study on negotiation processes by Geoffrey Stephenson and Maryon Tysoe. This exercise illustrates the commonly used technique of role play in studies in bargaining.

Part III represents the "problem" end of the continuum. These five chapters present exercises designed to introduce the student to specific problem areas in social psychology. Chapter 11, by Ray Bull, is concerned with the problem of gathering eyewitness testimony and examines some of the factors that influence the accuracy of an eyewitness's recollections in a field setting. Mansur Lalljee describes a study whose object is to test certain central tenets of attribution theory. In Chapter 13, Glynis Breakwell delineates an exercise that tests how group membership influences the expression of intergroup prejudices. The theme of group psychology is continued in Chapter 14 by Robin Gilmour, who outlines a study of co-operation and competition in groups. The concern with groups continues in the final chapter by Peter Smith, in which the emergence of group roles and norms is explored.

The structure of each chapter is obviously dependent upon the peculiarities of the subject matter covered. As far as possible, authors have used the tried and tested format of

- Theoretical introduction
- Procedure
- Forms of analysis and dimensions of discussion

With such a large range of topics, there has occasionally been some divergence from this straight and narrow path. Some of the exercises need to be done at particular times during the academic year if they are to work (e.g., Peter Smith's and part of Rom Harré's), and the specification notes give these sorts of details too.

It should be borne in mind when choosing exercises that they can be regarded as prescriptive and comprehensive patterns for a piece of research, *or* they can be treated as suggestive. The exercises have a certain amount of built-in flexibility. In most cases, they start with a simple design for a study that can be used as a foundation for more complex designs. Extensions and modifications of exercises are facilitated, because each chapter contains suggestions on various types of analysis that might be used on the data generated and includes a body of self-criticism on epistemological or methodological grounds.

The exercises can be seen as building blocks. Each stands alone, and yet they can be cemented together. Together they become a representative part of the edifice of social psychology, reflecting its methods and its problems.

Glynis M. Breakwell
Hugh Foot
Robin Gilmour

Part I

Technique demonstrations

1   Questionnaire design

Robert Slater

Introduction

Surveys are now found everywhere. We are bombarded with information based on surveys – for example, from Gallup or Harris opinion polls – almost every day of our lives. Research on purchasing behavior occupies many people in commercial agencies that do consumer research. Universities have their own survey centers – for example, the Survey Research Center at the University of Michigan, the Survey Research Laboratory at the University of Illinois, and the National Opinion Research Center at the University of Chicago. Much of the research that is done in the social sciences in general, and in psychology in particular, utilizes survey methods, but the widespread use of surveys brings with it a problem. People tend to think anyone can put together a few questions to make up a questionnaire – and they do. These then get sent to busy people who may have neither the time nor the desire to respond, especially to questions that to them perhaps appear unclear, nosy, irrelevant, rude, uninteresting, or that concern a topic of little apparent importance to them.

The primary aim of the exercises in this chapter is to help you understand the procedures involved in producing a valid questionnaire to be used as a scientific research instrument for collecting psychological data. A secondary aim is to give you practice in decision making in groups and in using your fellow students as a feedback mechanism (instead of pretesting the material on strangers). A third (and minor) aim is to use the survey and obtain "results" from it. The central aim, then, is to improve your skills in designing questions and questionnaires.

To arrive at a final questionnaire it is necessary to obtain the reactions of the target population to various drafts of questions and questionnaires. In this exercise the choice of survey subject area has been explicitly made, so that you yourself are part of the potential target population.

The survey topic has been chosen because it is an area of general

3

concern. In a directory of ongoing research concerning smoking and health worldwide, published by the U.S. Department of Health and Human Services in 1980, 648 of the 1,129 projects listed were based in the United States. For examples of such projects see Botvin and Eng (1982), and Arkin, Roemhild, Johnson, Luepker, and Murray (1981).

The exercises in this chapter are designed to give you the experience of deciding upon the areas of importance when constructing a questionnaire on a topic of potential interest to psychologists, health educationalists, politicians, cigarette manufacturers, and, it is hoped, you yourself. Why do teenagers (and younger children) start, continue, or stop smoking cigarettes? The "problem" of why people start smoking has, until recently, seemed to be insoluble, but in the context of *laboratory* studies in social psychology, the survey research question "Why do they start?" is comple- mented by more experimentally based work on what sort of communica- tions will influence them to stop (see Evans et al., 1981, for example). Research on what makes them stop necessarily must draw on research about what makes them start. Thus the topic demonstrates the inter- dependence often found in social-psychological research between field- work-based studies and laboratory-based studies.

Theoretical and methodological background of survey methods

In the nineteenth century, newspapers in the United States were already making informal surveys, and in 1912 Charles Coolidge Parlin, of the *Saturday Evening Post*, set up marketing research surveys.

The first systematic *social* survey ever made was a study of living conditions and poverty among the working classes in Britain (Booth, 1904), which greatly influenced the economic and social policies of sub- sequent British governments. Other "poverty surveys" followed rapidly, but A. L. Bowley is credited with being the first to seriously take into account such technical matters as how "selection effects" influence the generalizability of the data: that is, the possibility that "refusers," or those who are "not at home," may in some important way be different from the people from whom data *are* obtained (Bowley & Burnett-Hurst, 1915). The need for rigorous sampling, if generalizations were to be at all accurate, was increasingly recognized from Bowley's time on, although debate continues about the necessity for, and the cost-effectiveness of, random sampling techniques. The year 1935 saw the start in the United States of the Gallup Poll and of government surveys for the Department of Agriculture. Various British government surveys – on nutrition, cost of living, and illnesses – were brought together under the umbrella of the

Government Social Survey, which was set up in 1941, and this was matched by the setting up of the Current Population Survey in 1947 in the United States. Rigorous sampling methods were developed by the U.S. Census Bureau but were fought vigorously by commercial researchers, who wanted to keep the costs down. Only after the polls failed to predict Harry Truman's victory in the presidential election of 1948 was there a rapid shift to more sophisticated sampling methods by commercial organizations. In the United States, after the Second World War, survey research methods came into their own in the field of public opinion polling and in advertising. Since these fields were monopolized by commercial agencies, always cost-conscious, the development of sophisticated sampling procedures was rapid; poorly selected samples had been seen to produce inaccurate results, sometimes accompanied by high costs and slow turnaround of the data. With the arrival during this period of major nonprofit research centers at University of Chicago under Clyde Hart and at the Survey Research Center at the University of Michigan, survey research techniques began to be evaluated empirically. Today – for example, after a presidential debate – some market research agencies are able to conduct 3,000 short interviews during the same evening (when most working adults are at home) and have simple frequency tabulations of the data ready by the next day.

Besides market research surveys and opinion polls, most surveys carried out today are probably for research and policy purposes: to establish the prevalence of, say mental illness in a community; to establish norms of human performance or characteristics, as in the development of intelligence and personality tests; and to examine social attitudes and relate them to biographical data. Many such surveys are intended to be descriptive rather than analytical – that is, to produce an accurate picture of the state of affairs in a population by surveying a sample, rather than explicitly setting out to examine hypotheses. In such descriptive surveys, the clustered and stratified random samples must be large enough to permit an accurate description for the entire target population. Otherwise the conclusions – about what percentage of the voters say they will vote Democratic in an election, for example – may be so broad – i.e., the sample percentage "plus or minus 15%," meaning that between 25% and 55% of the voters say they will vote Democratic – that the information is hardly worth having.

Other research surveys are intended to provide the data with which hypotheses can be tested. Even here, though, you might want to demonstrate that a relationship between two variables observed in a sample was likely to hold in the population from which the sample was drawn. Thus, if you want to test hypotheses that are framed in general (i.e., population) terms – such as the statement "There is a relationship between income level and child-rearing patterns, in which the higher the parental income, the more the parents' instructions to children are accompanied with rational explanations" – then sample size becomes as important as it was in the descriptive survey, since one is trying to describe a *relationship* in the population that is hypothesized to exist.

The more confident you are that the standard deviations of the variables under investigation are small (for example, the more confident you are that "man" can stand for "men"), then the less need there is for large samples. On the other hand, the more varied you think the behavior, attitudes, and opinions under investigation are, the more necessary are random sampling methods, with relatively large samples. Since survey sample sizes are frequently in the 500 to 4,000 range, you can see at once that surveys can make heavy demands on resources. As a result, most surveys with large samples, as with censuses, confine themselves to relatively few, simple questions, although others may need interviews lasting over an hour, using extremely complicated branching patterns of questions.

Important survey data of interest to psychologists have been collected in the past to answer such questions as "Is there a relationship between family size and intelligence of children?" and "Is the average intelligence of the nation declining?" (Maxwell, 1969). And although it is a truism to say that a survey has undoubtedly been conducted (probably badly) somewhere on almost any topic you care to name, since the early 1950s little in survey research methods and techniques has changed substantially, except for the advent of computer-readable questionnaires, computer-assisted telephone interviews, and multivariate analysis of data by computer and on-line cable television systems. The future may well see us all pressing buttons on our television sets in response to some question asked "over the air," with nearly instantaneous playback of results, but the central problem for most survey research will still remain: namely, asking questions that produce reliable and valid data.

Specific background to this exercise

As suggested earlier, studies of the effectiveness of persuasive communications in general, and of antismoking propaganda in particular, require information about why some teenagers (and, of course, children) take up smoking whereas others do not. What differences are there between the reasons for starting smoking and the reasons for continuing and for wanting to stop? Are smoking patterns changing? For example, are women becoming more like men in their smoking patterns, and is this connected with aspects of women's liberation? A whole gamut of sensible questions, some largely sociological, can be posed in order to explicate smoking attitudes and behavior. Surveys by the Survey Research Center at the University of Michigan suggest that daily smoking among American high school seniors peaked at nearly 29% in 1976–7 but that between 1978 and 1979 the prevalence of daily smoking declined significantly, from 27.5% to 25.4%. The percentage of seniors smoking half a pack or more per day declined from 19.4% in 1977 to 16.5% in 1979, and during this period a shift in sex differences occurred, with 17.1% of females smoking half a pack or more per day, compared with 15.4% of male seniors. Surveys such as these suggest that there has been an increase in personal disapproval of smoking and in the perceived risk attached to smoking (Johnston, Backman, & O'Malley, 1979). Some surveys have suggested that boys who smoke are usually less convinced of the danger of smoking than non-smokers, and the more heavily they smoke, the less they seem to be deterred by the fear that they might get lung cancer. Smoking and non-smoking teenagers can be discriminated between in terms of four variables: number of friends who smoke; anticipation of adulthood; parents' permissiveness; and whether they are discouraged from smoking by the danger of lung cancer. Young smokers appear to go around in groups largely composed of other smokers, whereas nonsmokers go around in groups largely composed of other nonsmokers. Dobbs and Marsh (1983) provide a brief review of British survey findings on the sociopsychological context of smoking among young people. Findings such as these are relevant social–psychological studies of persuasive communications, such as boomerang effects (Penrod, 1983), latitudes of acceptance (McGuire, 1968), and presentation orders (Hollander, 1981), as well as to those of pressures to conform in small groups.

Derivation of aims and hypotheses

The aim of the following exercises is to produce a self-administered questionnaire that could be used to collect data to test a variety of hypotheses concerning why, for example, teenagers and/or children start, continue, or stop smoking. You, and students in your class, should be able to create several sensible hypotheses. Some survey results suggest that smokers are seen as tough, educationally unsuccessful, and precocious; that all boys tend to value toughness and educational success but that only smokers tend to value precocity. What is the female equivalent of "tough" in this context? Since female smoking habits have been changing and have now come more into line with male smoking patterns, in terms of overall consumption, you

might derive a variety of hypotheses concerning sex differences in reasons
for starting smoking or wanting to give it up.

Exercise 1. Composing the questionnaire

Step 1. (15 minutes). Your instructor will divide the class into groups
and will delegate the roles of chairperson, secretary and/or spokesperson,
if thought necessary. Your instructor will (1) explain that most of the
exercise will be group work (2) mention random sampling and (3) state that
the exercise is to construct a self-administered questionnaire concerning
one of the following topics (it is impossible to cover all three in one 3-hour
session:

- Why do teenage girls (and/or boys) start smoking?
- Why do teenage girls (and/or boys) continue smoking?
- Why do teenage girls (and/or boys) stop smoking?

You are going to use yourself and your fellow students as the target
population for the survey. Your group must decide which topic you want
to work on. Be prepared to justify your decision.

Step 2. (15 minutes). Once your group has decided on a topic, this
information should be fed back to the rest of the class via the instructor.

Step 3. (15 minutes). Your instructor will lead the whole class in obtaining a consensus on which survey topic to work on. This consensus should
be achieved on a *rational* basis. For example, in a group of older teenagers
many may have been smoking for some time, so data on why they continue
smoking, or why they have stopped, might be more reliable than data on
why they started. If very few in the class have ever smoked, you might be
flexible and have as the topic why some teenagers do *not* take up smoking.
The decision as to whether to focus on males or females (or both) should
largely rest on the composition of the class. The general intention is that
this discussion should help you to realize that choice of topic and of target
population have wide practical ramifications and that some choices are
very impractical.

Step 4. (15 minutes). Your group should produce a list of broad areas of
information that they consider relevant to the chosen topic. By "broad
areas" is meant such possible aspects as smoking behavior of possible
models; biographical information; attitudes toward school; attitudes
toward being a teenager; perceptions of smokers and of nonsmokers; ideal
and real self-image; knowledge about smoking and health; evaluation of
knowledge about smoking and health; needs satisfied by smoking; and

advantages and disadvantages of smoking. In a later session your group will take responsibility for elaborating one or more of these major areas that the questionnaire is to cover.

Step 5. (15 minutes). Your instructor (and the class) should obtain feedback from the group spokespersons about the areas considered relevant, and an attempt should be made to integrate these into conceptually clear and distinct groupings. If this proves very difficult, the instructor might try to impose the areas mentioned in step 4, since these have been used in previous surveys. (Again, not all of those areas are relevant to each of the three topics: A study of why people *start* smoking is less likely to benefit from questions concerning the needs satisfied by the *continuation* of smoking.) In this session you must rank the areas to be covered in the survey in order of their importance to the topic.

Step 6. (15 minutes). Your group will be assigned to work on one of the major areas decided upon in the previous session. Your group should then proceed to determine what are the "facets" of the area it is considering. For example, "smoking behavior of possible models" may have facets related to close relatives, teachers, friends, pop stars, television personalities, and athletes. "Attitudes toward school" may be subdivided into attitudes concerning teachers, schoolwork, subjects, discipline, and the extent to which schoolwork is seen to interfere with other interests. "Knowledge about smoking and health" may be subdivided into knowledge about cancer, about heart disease, about shortness of breath, about the effect of smoking on unborn babies, and so on.

Step 7. (15 minutes). The instructor will obtain feedback from your group and the other groups about the facets that each group has produced. It is important in this session that you feel you have a clear idea of what kind of information the major areas and their facets cover, so that you have some notion of how the survey hangs together as a whole, even though you are working on only part of it in your group.

Step 8. (15 minutes). Your instructor will ask your group to examine a set of facets produced by another group. Your group should now attempt to produce written questions pertinent to the survey topic concerning those facets. Before doing this, however, you should familiarize yourself with common format options by inspecting copies of the sample material that your instructor will provide (Sudman & Bradburn, 1982, should be most useful in this respect). The final questionnaire should contain as few open-ended questions as possible to facilitate data coding and analysis in a later exercise that you may be asked to do. If your group wants to use some two-way or multiple choice questions, you may need to get classmates to respond to open-ended questions or to sentence completion material. You can then make a content analysis of their responses, which you can use to determine the range of answers available for your multiple choice questions. The later exercise will enable you to do this, to a limited extent.

Step 9. (15 minutes). If your group wants to pose open-ended questions (for example, "why did you start smoking?") or sentence completion material ("In my opinion, the typical smoker is the sort of person who . . ."), you will be given the chance to state these questions to the class, and the class will act as your subjects. The answers should be passed back to the appropriate groups (written on separate sheets for each question, so that an individual group member can analyze the responses to one question at a time).

Step 10. (15 minutes). If your group is involved in content analysis of open-ended material, you should continue with this, aiming to produce the desired multiple choice answer format for each question. If your group has already formulated questions and their response formats, you should now consider, first, the sequencing of those questions in relation to each other and, second, where the chosen sequence should occur in the questionnaire in relation to other areas being covered.

Step 11. (15 minutes). Your group should now (1) write a 30-word introduction to your series of questions, and (2) check to be sure that each question or series of questions has clear instructions on *how* it is to be answered, where this is necessary.

Final step. (15 minutes). Your group should now produce (1) a neatly written copy of each question; (2) written introductions to your series of questions; and (3) written instructions for particular questions, all in the appropriate positions. You should then staple them together in the sequence agreed upon and hand them in to your instructor.

Administering the questionnaire

Once the material from the first exercise has been collated, the instructor organizes the questionnaire into a coherent form and gives copies to the students to administer between exercises. Each student should endeavor to collect 10 completed questionnaires, as directed by the instructor.

Exercise 2. Revising the questionnaire and analyzing the data

Step 1. (15 minutes). By now you should have about 10 questionnaires to edit. If there are no open-ended answers to be coded at this stage, the editing will be mostly a matter of making sure that a code number is assigned to each answer (for example, "Yes," code 1; "No," code 2; "Don't know," code 3), as well as codes for omitted answers, ambiguous answers, and refusal/can't do responses.

Step 2. (15 minutes). You should now collate the material from your 10 questionnaires onto one master (spare and unused) questionnaire; that is, you should summarize the frequency with which each answer is occurring for each question.

Step 3. (15 minutes) Using your own master schedule, your group should collate the data onto a group master schedule and feed these data back to your instructor.

Step 4. (15 minutes). You should now make a note of the collated data for the class on your own master schedule and, working together, your group should produce descriptive comments on the findings. The emphasis here should be on the implications that the descriptive findings have for revising the questionnaire (i.e., improving both the questions and the response formats). Are there many "don't know" responses, instructions not followed, undiscriminating questions, unanswered questions, questions answered that should not have been? Your group's comments should be fed back to the rest of the class.

Step 5. (15 minutes). Your group should now discuss which relationships between which variables (taken two at a time) should be analyzed and should have a spokesperson ready to explain its decisions to the rest of the class.

Step 6. (15 minutes). Your group will be given a chance to explain its "priority for initial analyses" to the rest of the class.

Step 7. (15 minutes) You will need to retrieve any 10 questionnaires and be prepared to place each one in one of four piles, according to which particular analysis is being done first. This will produce the data for a 2×2 contingency table.

Step 8. (15 minutes). Your group should perform a chi-square calculation, using the electronic calculators provided. Ideally you will arrive at
the same value for chi-square as the other groups, and this value can be
examined for statistical significance, using the tables provided. Your group
should formulate a comment on the result and a hypothesis for "explaining" it.

Step 9. (15 minutes). A second, similar analysis should be made. You
should retrieve any 10 questionnaires and then place them in piles according to the analysis being performed.

Step 10. (15 minutes). This should follow the pattern established for
step 8.

Step 11. (15 minutes). Again, re-sort questionnaires according to the next
analysis being done.

Step 12. (15 minutes). Again, follow the pattern for step 8.

However, more complex analyses of the data (for example, discriminant
functions analyses to find the best way to discriminate between smokers
and nonsmokers) need to be made, using a computer and software such as
SPSS-X, the Statistical Package for the Social Sciences (SPSS Inc., 1983).
Depending on the central aim of the survey, the frequencies analysis
itself should provide some answers to such basic questions as "Why do
teenagers start smoking?", "Why do they continue smoking?", and "Why
do they stop smoking?"

Data presentation

The data from the second exercise that are of the frequency-count type can
probably be best presented in one of two forms. For relatively continuous
variables (such as age at which the first cigarette was smoked), a frequency
curve can be drawn. For classificatory or discontinuous variables (such as
whether the respondent has ever smoked or reasons for starting smoking),
bar charts and/or pi diagrams are more appropriate.

Discussion

The limitations of any conclusions drawn from survey analyses will reflect,
on the whole, the limitations of the questionnaire, the genuineness of the
data, and the nature of the sample from which the data were collected. In

these exercises there will not have been enough time to do a real pilot study; in fact, the data collected for the second exercise should really be regarded more as that required for reformulating the questionnaire before it *is* used in an actual survey.

Conclusion

In doing these exercises you will have learned that producing a questionnaire to act as a scientific data collection instrument is no easy matter and requires preliminary data collection (through pretests and pilot studies) and analyses before the final draft. You also will have learned that it is inappropriate to collect certain sorts of data through questionnaires; that obtaining a satisfactory response rate is vital; and that the response rate is affected by the nature of the survey and the ease (or difficulty) with which respondents are able to follow (and answer) the questions asked. More specifically, you will have become more aware that questions are formulations of words and that words have different meanings for different people. Thus not only should the formulation of clear, specific, and understandable questions be recognized as a major task in constructing a questionnaire, but also, as much thought must be given to developing clear and mutually exclusive coding categories for respondents' answers.

By doing the first exercise, you will also have developed some insight into the way in which group discussions can be used at an early, qualitative stage in survey research. You will have become familiar with the range of ways in which data can be collected by using a self-administered questionnaire and will have gained some understanding of how numerical coding systems are utilized prior to data analysis. By collecting data, you will have experienced at first hand some of the inherent problems of this method of acquiring data and some of the problems in the nature of the questionnaire itself. By carrying out, in the second exercise, a simple analysis of the data, you will have increased your understanding of the necessity for adequate coding schemes and the limitations of the questionnaire and will see the need for further, more sophisticated statistical analyses of this form of data.

References

Arkin, R.M., Roemhild, H.F., Johnson, C.A., Luepker, R.V., & Murray, D.M. (1981). The Minnesota smoking prevention program: a seventh-grade health curriculum supplement. *Journal of School Health*, November, 611–16.

Booth, C. (ed.). (1904). *Life and Labor of the People in London*. New York: AMS Press.

Botvin, G.J., & Eng, A. (1982). The efficacy of a multicomponent approach to the prevention of smoking. *Preventive Medicine, 11*, 199–211.

Bowley, A.L., & Burnett-Hurst, A.R. (1915). *Livelihood and Poverty: A Study in the Economic Conditions of Working Class Households in Northampton, Warrington, Stanley and Reading*. New York: Garland.

Dobbs, J., & Marsh, A. (1983). *Smoking among Secondary School Children*. London: HMSO.

Evans, R.I., Rozelle, R.M., Maxwell, S.E., Rains, B.E., Dill, C.A., Guthrie, T.J., Henderson, A.H., & Hill, P.C. (1981). Social modeling films to deter smoking in adolescents: results of a three-year field investigation. *Journal of Applied Psychology, 66* (4), 399–414.

Green, E. (1979). *Teenage Smoking: Immediate and Long Term Patterns*. Washington, D.C.: U.S. Government Printing Office.

Hoineville, G., Jowell, R., & Associates (1977). *Survey Research Practice*. New York: Heinemann Educational.

Hollander, E.P. (1981). *Principles and Methods of Social Psychology*. New York: Oxford University Press.

Johnston, L.D., Backman, J.G., & O'Malley, P.M. (1979). *Drugs and the Nation's High School Students: Five Year National Trends, 1979 Highlights*. Rockville, Md.: National Institute on Drug Abuse.

Kransnegor, N.A., (1979). *The Behavioral Aspects of Smoking*. Washington, D.C.: U.S. Government Printing Office.

Maxwell, J. (1969). Intelligence, education and fertility: a comparison between the 1932 and 1947 Scottish surveys. *Journal of Biological Science, 1*, 247–71.

McGuire, N.J. (1968). The nature of attitudes and attitude change. In G. Lindzey & E. Aronson (eds.), *The Handbook of Social Psychology*. Reading, Mass.: Addison-Wesley.

Oppenheim, A.N. (1966). *Questionnaire Design and Attitude Measurement*. New York: Basic Books.

Penrod, S. (1983). *Social Psychology*. Englewood Cliffs, N.J.: Prentice-Hall.

SPSS Inc. (1983). *SPSS-X User's Guide*. New York: McGraw-Hill.

Sudman, S., & Bradburn, N.M. (1982). *Asking Questions: A Practical Guide to Questionnaire Design*. San Francisco: Jossey-Bass.

U.S. Department of Health and Human Services (1980). *Directory: On-going Research in Smoking and Health*. Washington, D.C.: U.S. Government Printing Office.

Warwick, D.P., & Lininger, C.A. (1975). *The Sample Survey: Theory and Practice*. New York: McGraw-Hill.

Appendix. A selection of example questions

For more general material on designing questions and questionnaires see Sudman and Bradburn (1982); Oppenheim (1966); Warwick & Lininger (1975); and Hoineville, Jowell and Associates (1977).

				FOR OFFICE USE ONLY	
				CODE	COL
	month	day	year		1–4
1. What is your birthday?					
2. Sex. (Circle the appropriate number)		FEMALE MALE	1 2		5
3. Does your father smoke cigarettes?		YES NO	1 2		6
4. How many of your *good* friends smoke cigarettes?		NONE SOME	1 2		7
5. Does your homeroom teacher smoke cigarettes?		YES NO DON'T KNOW	1 2 3		8

6. Here are some sentences about what you feel about smoking and quitting. Circle the number that is appropriate for *you*. There are no "right" or "wrong" answers. Put down what you really feel.

	True	False		
I like handling a cigarette.	1	2		10
Even now that I've quit, I get a strong urge to smoke sometimes.	1	2		11

15

			FOR OFFICE USE ONLY	
			CODE	COL
When I quit smoking, I found I had less energy.	1	2		12
Quitting smoking was a challenge to me.	1	2		13
Quitting smoking will help me live longer.	1	2		14
Smoking cigarettes used to perk me up.	1	2		15
My smoking was a dirty, messy habit.	1	2		16
If I hadn't stopped smoking, I would be more likely to have heart problems.	1	2		17
When I smoked, having a cigarette helped me to feel more comfortable talking with others.	1	2		18
Since I quit smoking, I have become more physically healthy.	1	2		19

Here are some sentences about what you think *in general*. These questions are NOT about smoking. Circle the number that describes what you think. There are no right or wrong answers.

	Yes	I think maybe	I don't really know	I don't really think so	No		
7. Doing what my friends want me to is important to me.	1	2	3	4	5		21
8. Being able to run and do athletics is important to me.	1	2	3	4	5		22
9. Keeping my friends is important to me.	1	2	3	4	5		23
10. Looking grown-up is important to me.	1	2	3	4	5		24

COL 20

11. I want to do what people who are important to me think I should do.   1   2   3   4   5   25

12. Looking cool is important to me.   1   2   3   4   5   26

On each of the following scales, circle the number that describes what you think smoking is. There are no right or wrong answers. Just say what you believe.

13. <u>SMOKING IS:</u>

beautiful	a little bit beautiful	neither beautiful nor ugly	a little bit ugly	very ugly	
1	2	3	4	5	27

very bad	a little bit bad	neither bad nor good	a little bit good	very good	
1	2	3	4	5	28

very dirty	a little bit dirty	neither dirty not clean	a little bit clean	very clean	
1	2	3	4	5	29

17

For the following sentences, circle the number that describes what *you* believe or think. There are no right or wrong answers.

	Yes	I think maybe	I don't really know	I don't really think so	No	CODE	COL
14. Smoking affects the health of people my age.	1	2	3	4	5		31
15. Smoking can make people my age look more grown-up.	1	2	3	4	5		32
16. Smoking cigarettes causes dizziness.	1	2	3	4	5		33
17. Some people lose friends because they don't smoke.	1	2	3	4	5		34
18. Smoking could cause *me* to look bad (smelly clothes, yellow teeth, red eyes).	1	2	3	4	5		35
19. People my age who smoke can run and do athletics as well as people who don't smoke.	1	2	3	4	5		36
20. Smoking causes the lungs to become slowly blocked.	2	2	3	4	5		37
21. What do you think is the *main* reason people start to smoke cigarettes?							38

_____ 39

_____ 40

_____ 41

18

22. What do you think is the *worst* thing about people your age smoking?

_____ 42

_____ 43

_____ 44

_____ 45

23. Which of the following best describes how often you usually smoke cigarettes? (Circle the one appropriate letter.)

A. I have never smoked any cigarettes.
B. I have tried cigarettes a few times (even if just once).
C. I smoke a few cigarettes a month.
D. I smoke a few cigarettes a week.
E. I smoke about 1 cigarette a day.
F. I smoke between 2 and 9 cigarettes a day.
G. I smoke 10 or more cigarettes a day.
H. I used to smoke regularly but quit.

46

24. If you smoke cigarettes now, how often do you inhale? (That means pulling the smoke into your lungs, rather than holding it in your mouth).

A. I never smoke cigarettes.
B. I *never inhale* when I smoke.
C. I *sometimes inhale* when I smoke.
D. I *usually inhale* when I smoke.
E. I *always inhale* when I smoke cigarettes.

47

48

19

25. How much does your older brother smoke cigarettes? If you have more than one older brother, answer for the one you feel closest to.

A. Never smoked.
B. Smoked, but quit.
C. Smokes very little.
D. I don't have an older brother.
E. Smokes occasionally.
F. Smokes a lot.
G. Don't know if he smokes.

49

26. How much does your best friend (the same sex as you) smoke cigarettes?

A. Never smoked.
B. Smoked, but quit.
C. Smokes very little.
D. I don't have a best friend.
E. Smokes occasionally.
F. Smokes a lot.
G. Don't know if he/she smokes.

50

27. What grades do you usually get in school?

A. A's mostly
B. A's and B's equally
C. B's mostly
D. B's and C's equally
E. C's mostly
F. D's and F's

51
52

28. Some students believe that marijuana smoke is safer than tobacco (cigarette) smoke. Scientists say that this belief is: (Circle as many letters as appropriate)

A. False. Both kinds of smoke are harmful because they both contain some of the same poisonous chemicals.
B. True. Marijuana smoke is safer because it does not contain nicotine.
C. True. Marijuana smoke is safer because it does not contain carbon monoxide.
D. True. Adults always try to make up scary stories about marijuana.
E. I don't know.

53
54
55
56

20

21

29. Researchers believe that teenagers who have the easiest time not starting to smoke are those who: (Circle as many letters as appropriate)

   A. Have fewest family problems.
   B. Have parents and friends who don't smoke.
   C. Are the youngest child in the family.
   D. Attend a school that has a good health education program about smoking.
   E. I don't know.

30. Researchers have found that some students are easily influenced to start smoking cigarettes because they: (Circle as many letters as appropriate)

   A. Think it makes them look more sophisticated.
   B. Want to become popular.
   C. Do not have really strong reasons not to smoke.
   D. Want to look more mature.
   E. I don't know.

INSTRUCTIONS: There are no right or wrong answers to the following questions – just give your honest opinion by circling the one appropriate letter.

Smoking cigarettes would make me (if I started smoking) or makes me (if I already smoke):

31. A. Much more popular in my class.
   B. A little more popular in my class.
   C. Makes no difference.
   D. A little less popular in my class.
   E. Much less popular in my class.

32. A. Look much less mature.
   B. Look a little less mature.
   C. Makes no difference.
   D. Look a little more mature.
   E. Look much more mature.

How important are the following things to you?

33. Staying out of trouble
   A. Extremely important
   B. Pretty important
   C. Fairly important
   D. Slight important
   E. Not very important
   F. Not important at all

34. Look mature
   A. Extremely important
   B. Pretty important
   C. Fairly important
   D. Slight important
   E. Not very important
   F. Not important at all

35. Being popular in your class
   A. Extremely important
   B. Pretty important
   C. Fairly important
   D. Slight important
   E. Not very important
   F. Not important at all

22

2 Personnel interviewing: a mini–training program

Mike Smith

Introduction

This chapter describes a sequence of four exercises designed to improve students' skills in personnel interviewing. Many laboratory classes in psychology give students practice in problem definition, investigation design, or data analysis. In contrast, this program focuses upon the acquisition of another important professional skill: the ability to conduct an effective personnel interview. The complete sequence of four exercises will take only about 3-hours, whereas a personnel-management course in interviewing skills would last a minimum of 2 days, so clearly the exercises can only start to develop interviewing skills. Considerable repetition of the final exercise, plus variations in role-play would be needed to produce a really proficient interviewer.

The interviewing exercises are based upon research and theory on interviewing, which is briefly summarized in the next section; they can also be related to industrial training. (The exercises themselves are a condensed training course, in which the task is first analyzed and then explained to the trainees using the Cumulative Part Method and the role-play learning method: See Toye, 1977.) The exercises can also be related to the social psychology of person perception, especially attribution theory. Furthermore, the skills of personnel interviewing are partly transferable to other types of interviews, such as appraisal interviews, counseling interviews, and exit interviews.

Theoretical background

The function of interviews in a systematic selection process

Job interviews must be seen within the context of systematic selection, which starts with the *analysis of the job* (see Landy, 1985). On the basis of

23

the job analysis and of exit interviews, a *draft job description* is prepared. The job is then considered, to see if it needs to be altered in some way; could it be abolished or merged with some other job? Could it be changed to make it more interesting and satisfying? When the modifications have been decided, a final job description is produced.

The final job description is used to prepare the second important document in the selection process, *the personnel specification*, which attempts to describe the ideal applicant. The format of the personnel specification can vary. One of the most widely used is Rodger's Seven-Point Plan (1968). It categorizes worker characteristics under seven headings:

1. Physique: health, appearance, speech
2. Attainments: education, work qualifications, experience
3. General intelligence: How much is there? How much is normally used?
4. Special aptitudes: mechanical, spatial, verbal
5. Interests: outdoor, scientific, computational, etc.
6. Disposition and temperament: extroverted, neurotic, independent?
7. Circumstances: dependent relatives, family working in same job?

It is also common practice to subdivide worker characteristics further into *essential* and *desirable* characteristics. These are indicated in the shortened sample personnel specification given in appendix 1.

The *personnel specification* is used to draw up a job advertisement. The most promising applicants are *interviewed* and/or given other tests, and the personnel specification is again used in the final stage of "arriving at a decision." From this very brief outline, you can see that the personnel interview is only *one* stage of the selection process and that the interview is easier to conduct if the preceding stages have been done competently.

Research on interviews: the reliability problem

Probably the most serious criticism of personnel interviews concerns their unreliability. As Hollingworth pointed out as long ago as 1929, a candidate interviewed by one experienced manager can do very well, whereas in an interview with another experienced manager, the same candidate is an abysmal failure. Hakel and Dunnette (1970) point out that "periodic reviews of research studies on the employment interview (Wagner, 1949; Mayfield, 1964; Ulrich & Trumbo, 1965) agree in concluding that most personnel interviews are conducted in such a way as to be quite unreliable and usually non-valid" (p. 1). These conclusions have not been overturned by more recent reviews conducted by Webster (1982) and Arvey and Campion (1982). Such damning criticism may be a little unfair, since many critics adopt simplistic and faulty methods themselves; still, the reliability of the typical selection interview remains very suspect.

Sources of error leading to unreliability can be collected together under five headings. *First*, different interviewers use the interview to look for *different traits*. For example, in selecting for the police force, one interviewer may look for a person who is pleasant and physically strong, whereas another interviewer may look for the intellect of Sherlock Holmes. It is not surprising that the interviewers arrive at different evaluations of candidates' qualifications.

The *second* source of error leading to unreliability concerns the setting of the interview. The *physical setting* of the interview can influence the performance of the interviewee: He or she must be able to hear the interviewer and feel that the surroundings are private, free from distraction, and favorable to an exchange of information. The *psychological setting* is probably more important.

The interviewees must not be overwhelmed by the interviewer's status symbols. The psychological climate of a businesslike, sympathetic, problem-solving exchange must be established. Lewis (1980) draws attention to the need to establish an explicit contract in which the interviewer agrees to treat the interviewee fairly if the candidate agrees to provide valid data. Since much of an interviewee's behavior is fakable, Lewis argues that to obtain reliable and valid data the interviewer must adopt a thoughtful, trusting style, more like that of a counselor, in the hope that the interviewee will adopt a complementary role. The opening phase of an interview is probably the most crucial time in establishing a rapport of this kind.

The *third* source of interview error is that most interviewers fail to *structure the interview*. Even when interviewers agree upon a common set of traits, or when a single interviewer is dealing with the candidates, the questioning is often radically different. For example, during the first interview of the day, an applicant may be questioned about all aspects of his or her life. Toward the end of the day an applicant may be asked a few brief questions about qualifications and work experience, whereas home life, personal interests, and ambitions are given little attention. The same applicant can give very different impressions under the two very different situations. Structuring an interview, therefore, almost certainly reduces error and thereby increases reliability. In 1969, Schwab and Henman found that unstructured interviews produced a reliability coefficient of .36, whereas a totally structured interview (i.e., a list of predetermined questions) produced a reliability coefficient of .79. Unfortunately, the totally structured interviews were inflexible, artificial, and made it difficult to establish rapport. The semistructured interview, which specifies the subject areas to be questioned, seems to offer a good compromise. Schwab and Henman found that interviews that were semistructured produced a reliability coefficient of .43. Other research has shown that interviewers rarely cover all the relevant aspects of a candidate's background. In the light of these and other research findings, interviewers are advised to adopt an interview plan. The plan used in the following set of exercises is one example of the many plans available. It has a number of advantages: It is simple and easy to follow; it starts with the most relevant aspects; and the progression from factual to less structured information helps build rapport.

Even when interviewers have agreed upon the traits required, have produced the right psychological climate, and have carefully followed a plan, the results of an interview can still be unreliable because of the *fourth* source of reliability error: the *interactive nature of interviews*. Verplanck (1955) was one of the first investigators to research this subject. He instructed interviewers to react in a specified way whenever candidates stated their opinions: Agreement with the candidates increased the number of opinions they expressed; silence produced a small decrease; whereas disagreement produced a large decrease in the opinions given by the candidates. In a similar vein Davis and Sloan (1974) manipulated the number of self-disclosures (self-revelations) that interviewers made to candidates, and independent judges listened to audiotapes of the interviews.

Their results suggest that "disclosing" interviewers produced more disclosures from the interviewee, but the interviewer had to keep disclosing in order to keep the interviewee disclosing. Keenan (1976) conducted a similar experiment by manipulating the nonverbal approval or disapproval of interviewers and asking judges to rate videotapes that showed only the performance of the interviewees. Interviewers who gave approving nonverbal cues tended to produce interviewees who were friendly, relaxed, and successful in creating a good impression. The amount of the verbal communication done by the interviewer also influences a candidate's behavior. Daniels and Otis (1950) reported that interviewers talked for 57% of the time, candidates talked for 30% of the time, whereas the remaining 13% was spent in silence. With the interviewer claiming the lion's share of interview time, candidates have a poorer chance of revealing their abilities. In order to get the candidate to give extended answers, the interviewer needs to pose open-ended rather than closed questions. The importance of the social and situational determinants of interview decisions is discussed in detail by Arvey (1979).

If the interviewer has avoided the previous four sources of error, there is a good chance that at the end of the interview accurate and relevant information about the candidate will have been obtained. However, the *fifth* possible source of reliability error remains. The interviewer must *use the information* to arrive at a judgment of the candidate's suitability. The first problem involved here is one of human fallibility. Research suggests that by the time the interview is concluded, an interviewer has forgotten half of the information given by the candidate. Consequently, notes of key points are essential. Another common failure of interviewers is that they often make up their minds too early in the interview, which is called the *primacy effect*. Springbett (1958) suggests that interviewers often make up their minds within the first 4 minutes of an interview and that the rest of the time is spent looking for evidence that will support their early decision. Other interviewers make a broad evaluation of a candidate, and the halo surrounding the broad judgment cancels any contrary evaluations of the individual traits contained in the personnel specification. Finally, there are the problems of how the interviewer interprets and weights the information obtained from the candidate. The phenomena of attribution theory and person perception are relevant here (see, for example, Gergen and Gergen, 1981, pp. 57–70). When candidates describe incidents in their lives, the interviewer has to attribute the cause of the incident either to the candidate's "personality" or to the situation in which the candidate was placed. A wrong attribution can lead to erroneous conclusions, and it has been suggested (Herriot & Rothwell, 1981) that interviewers may have a tendency wrongly to attribute causes to the person rather than the circumstances. To add to the difficulty, the various attributions must be weighted before a final decision is reached. Bolsher and Springbett (1961) suggest that interviewers pay too much attention to negative attributions, but more recent work has suggested that *any* unexpected and unusual information about the candidate is given too much emphasis.

This catalogue of the five sources of interview error highlights two points. First, the interviewer is faced with a highly complex task and, second, the reliability of the interview is very closely related to validity. Indeed, in many senses the issues surrounding the interview decision could be regarded as issues of validity.

Hunter and Hunter (1984) used a procedure called *meta-analysis* to combine the results of several studies of the validity of interviews. Results from their combined sample of 2,694 subjects suggests that the validity of the typical interview is only .14.

This program deliberately focuses upon the reliability of interviewing, because reliability is so important in obtaining accurate results. However, the importance of fairness in interviewing must continually be kept in mind. It is both morally and legally wrong to discriminate against candidates on the basis of color, sex, sexual orientation, or age. Furthermore, in many cases it is unfair to discriminate on the basis of physical or mental disability. The guiding principle of fairness is that those who are equally likely to be successful at the job should have an equal probability of being selected. More detailed guidance on avoiding bias can be obtained from standard texts, such as Smith and Robertson (1986), and Landy (1985). Reilly and Chao (1982) assessed the fairness of interviews and other methods of employment selection and, reviewing studies of racial bias, they concluded that interviews are no less subject to bias than tests. The evidence concerning the sex bias of interviews is clearer. As a generalization, males tended to be given half a grade more on a 5-point rating scale. The exact degree of unfairness depends upon other factors such as physical attractiveness and the type of position applied for. Detailed guidance on fairness is given in *Uniform Guidelines on Employee Selection Federal Register* (1978) and Arvey's (1979) paper.

Method

The objectives of the sequence of exercises are to reinforce the research findings concerning interviews and to give students an opportunity to develop skills as interviewers and interviewees.

The exact organization of the program will depend upon the number of students in your class and the available facilities. However, it will generally proceed in five phases.

Preparation

At least 1 day before the exercise, photocopy and complete the application form given in appendix 2. Imagine that

- You are 20 years old.
- You graduated from a technical high school and completed courses in English, mathematics, metal work, engineering, drafting, and woodworking.
- After graduating from high school, you started on an associate degree at a nearby community college but gave it up after 18 months because a friend's father made you an offer of a lucrative job taking bets in a bookmaker's office.
- You accepted the offer, but after about 2 years in the job you are concerned at the lack of career prospects, so you have applied for a job on the police force.

You may invent any other details, provided they are sensible and realistic.

Exercise 1. Openings and closings

Your instructor will explain the importance of having good openings and closings for your personnel interviews and will go over the instructions in appendix 3.

Then the class members will be divided into groups of three; one individual in each group will play the role of the interviewee, and two will play the role of joint interviewers. Interviewers will have about 5 minutes to prepare and decide who is going to cover which topic. They are given the following instructions:

The objective of this exercise is to develop your *skills in starting* an interview, *finishing* an interview, and in *explaining the job*. Please go through these stages of an interview with this candidate. Do not bother about other stages of the interview. Try to take under 4 minutes. If you go over your time, I will give you this signal to stop (demonstrate), and you should finish quickly. You are *not* allowed to consult the instructions during the interview.

One of the groups will be videotaped, and when all the groups have finished, class members will watch the videotape and use the checklist in appendix 4 to assess whether or not the interviewers covered the main points.

Exercise 2. Covering the major points

Your instructor will explain the importance of covering the major points and will discuss the interview plan given in appendix 5. Again, the class will be divided into groups of three (one interviewee, two interviewers), and the interviewers will have about 5 minutes to decide who is going to cover which topics. The objectives of the exercise are explained as follows:

The objectives of this exercise are to give practice in openings, job explanation, and closings. However, the main purpose is to see how well you *obtain the relevant information*. You should open the interview, explain the job, question the candidate, and then close the interveiw. It should take about 15 minutes. If you run out of time, I will give you the signal to stop. Try to be systematic and to cover everything.

One of the groups will be videotaped. Watch the videotape, and use appendix 6 to determine whether the interviewers covered the main points.

Exercise 3. Making them talk

After the instructor has explained the material in appendix 7, role-play a full interview. You will have 5 minutes of preparation time.

Your objectives are to

- Open the interview
- Systematically cover the ground

- *Get the candidate talking*
- Close the interview

When you have finished, watch the videotape of the interview selected to be recorded, and use the checklist in appendix 8 to determine whether the main points were covered.

Exercise 4. Revision, and making a decision

After the instructor has explained the material in appendix 9, role-play a full interview, and decide whether you would hire the applicant.

To make sure that you have learned the skills of personnel interviewing, your instructor may ask you to participate in further role-plays or in a discussion of personnel interviewing as a selection method, and its advantages and disadvantages compared to other methods such as tests.

Reports and data analysis

This session does not require a traditional report. However, if the session has been used with a large group that has been subdivided into many subgroups, the checklists used at the end of each role-play could be collated and analyzed to give an index of the frequency with which interviewers omit various points of good interview technique. The best way of achieving this objective is for the person in charge of the session to make overhead transparencies of the three checklists. Starting with the first checklist, the groups can then call out those points that were missed in their particular role-plays. These can be entered on the transparencies with water based pens (so that the transparencies can be cleaned and reused).

Unless very large groups are available, only a simple analysis can be performed. Instructors can, however, keep a cumulative record of the results, and then the results can be compared with the results from previous times.

It might also be sensible to ask participants to write a report on the last person they interviewed. It should try to simulate the reports that interviewers might make to employers. Here is one format that could be used.

1. Background Data
   - Name of job involved in the application
   - Name of interviewee
   - Age of interviewee
   - Date of interview
   - Name of interviewer
2. Factual Record of the Interview. This is a factual record of the main points of

the interview. It should be about 150 to 200 words long and should not contain any interpretation of the facts.
3. Assessment of the Candidate's Strengths
4. Assessment of the Candidate's Weaknesses
5. Recommendation for Employment

In some cases a further discussion could be organized to compare these reports and to discuss the psychological assumptions that underlie them.

References

Arvey, R. (1979). Unfair discrimination in the employment interview: legal and psychological aspects. *Psychological Bulletin*, 86, 736–65.

Arvey, R., & Campion, J.E. (1982). The employment interview: a summary and review of recent literature. *Personnel Psychology*, 35, 281–327.

Bolsher, B.T., & Springbett B.M. (1961). The reaction of interviews to favorable and unfavorable information. *Journal of Applied Psychology*, 45, 95–103.

Daniels, A.W., & Otis, J.L. (1950). A method for analysing employment interviews. *Personnel Psychology*, 3, 425–44.

Davis, J.D., & Sloan, M.L. (1974). The basis of interviewee matching of interviewer self-disclosure. *British Journal of Social and Clinical Psychology*, 13, 359–67.

Gergen, K.J., & Gergen, M.M. (1981). *Social Psychology*. New York: Harcourt-Brace.

Hakel, D.M., & Dunnette, M.D. (1970). *Checklists for Describing Job Applicants*. Minneapolis: Industrial Relations Center, University of Minnesota.

Herriot, P., & Rothwell, C. (1981). *The selection interview: a theoretical account and some data*. Paper presented to B.P.S. Occupational Psychology Conference, York, U.K.

Hollingworth, H.L. (1929). *Vocational Psychology and Character Analysis*. New York: Appleton-Century-Crofts.

Hunter, J.E., & Hunter, R.F. (1984). Validity and utility of alternative predictors of job performance. *Psychological Bulletin*, 96, 1, 72–98.

Keenan, A. (1976). Effects of non-verbal behaviour of interviewers on candidates' performances. *Journal of Occupational Psychology*, 49, 171–6.

Landy, F.J. (1985). *Psychology of Work Behavior* (3rd ed.). Homewood, Ill.: Dorsey Press.

Lewis, C. (1980). Investigating the employment interview: a consideration of counselling skills. *Journal of Occupational Psychology*, 53, 111–16.

Mayfield, E.L. (1964). The selection interview – a re-evaluation of published research. *Personnel Psychology*, 17, 239–60.

Reilly, R.R., & Chao, G. (1982). Validity and fairness of some alternative employee selection procedures. *Personnel Psychology*, 35, 1–62.

Rodger, A. (1968). *The Seven-Point Plan*. Windsor, U.K.: National Foundation for Educational Research.

Schwab, D.P., & Henman, H.G. (1969). Relationship between interviewer structure and inter-interviewer reliability in an employment situation. *Journal of Applied Psychology*, 53, 214–17.

Schmitt, N. (1976). Social and situational determinants of interview decisions: implications for the employment interview. *Personnel Psychology*, 29, 79–101.

Smith, M.J., & Robertson, I.T. (1986). *The Theory and Practice of Systematic Staff Selection*. London: Macmillan.

Springbett, B.M. (1958). Factors affecting the final decision in an employment interview. *Canadian Journal of Psychology*, 12, 13–22.

Toye, M. (1977). *CRAMP: A User's Guide to Training Decisions*. Cambridge: Industrial Training Research Unit.

Uniform Guidelines on Employee Selection Procedures. (1978). *Federal Register*, 43, No. 166 38290–38309.

Ulrich, L., & Trumbo, D. (1965). The selection interview since 1949. *Psychological Bulletin*, 63, 100–16.

Verplanck, W.S. (1955). The control of the content of conversation: reinforcement of statements of opinion. *Journal of Abnormal and Social Psychology*, 51, 668–75.

Wagner, R. (1949). The employment interview – a critical summary. *Personnel Psychology*, 2, 17–46.

Webster, E.C. (1982). *The Employment Interview: A Social Judgement Process*. Schomberg, Ontario, Canada: SFP Publications.

Appendix 1. Police personnel specification

Note: this abbreviated specification is intended for illustration only.

1. PHYSICAL	*Essential:*	Good eyesight and hearing, clear speech, adequate height (5'4", women and men)
	Desirable:	Good grooming
2. EDUCATION	*Essential:*	At least a high school diploma or equivalent
	Desirable:	Ability to drive
3. INTELLIGENCE	*Essential:*	In top third of population
4. SPECIAL APTITUDES	*Essential:*	Good writing skills
	Desirable:	Organized approach to words and dealing with problems Ability to follow instructions
5. INTERESTS	*Desirable:*	Persuasive, clerical, social welfare interests
6. CHARACTER AND TEMPERAMENT	*Essential:*	Self-confident, prudent, even-tempered, able to use initiative, realistic
7. HOME LIFE	*Essential:*	Circumstances that do not prevent shift work and long hours of work

CONTRAINDICATIONS: criminal record, excessive impulsiveness

Appendix 2. Job application form

APPLICATION
FORM

Please return this form to _____

Not later than _____

1. POSITION APPLIED FOR
2. PERSONAL DETAILS
   Last name _____   First name _____
   Address _____   Telephone Number _____
                                      Date of Birth _____
                                      Marital Status _____
                                      Ages of children (if any)
                                      _____yrs_____yrs_____yrs
                                      _____yrs_____yrs_____yrs

Name and address of closest living
relative or individual to be cont-
acted in case of emergency

_____

_____ Telephone: _____

Names of friends or relatives in this company/position

3. WORK HISTORY
   Name and address of your present (or last) employer

_____

   Date and job title on starting
   Title of present job
   Brief indication of type of work

_____

   Reason for leaving

_____

   Salary of present (or last) job
   If you have already left your last job, give the date of leaving
                            (continued)

3. WORK HISTORY (continued)
Names and Addresses of
other previous
employers   <u>Job Title</u>   <u>Date</u>   <u>Reason for leaving</u>

4. EDUCATION AND TRAINING
<u>Names and Type of High School or College</u>   <u>Dates</u>
Please list any other degrees you have
received or training that you have completed

5. MEDICAL HISTORY
Have your ever suffered from
Back trouble   Yes/No   When?
Nervous trouble   Yes/No   When?
Alcoholism   Yes/No   When?
Would you be willing to have a medical examination?   Yes/No

6. GENERAL
What are your hobbies and pastimes?

7. REFERENCES
Please give the names and addresses of TWO people who know your
work.

Appendix 3. Instructions for exercise 1

Introduction

A typical interview has four phases: the opening; questioning the candidate; explaining the job; and the closing. Interviewers need to prepare the openings and closings very carefully, since a good opening sets the right tone for the interview, and a good closing sends the candidate away with a good impression. In these stages, events are very predictable, and interviewers are able to build up a standard "line" of response. The physical setting for an interview is important. It should be private, free from interruptions and distractions, suitably furnished, and supplied with a clock.

Openings

- *Greet candidate by name.* This checks that you have the right candidate and establishes a friendly but formal tone.
- *Introduce yourself clearly.* Give your name(s) and job title(s).
- *Indicate where candidate should sit.*
- *Talk about something nonthreatening* but job-related, so that the candidate is put at ease and becomes used to the sound of his or her voice.

Thank the candidate for his or her application and explain the purpose of interview.

Job explanation

- Study the job description and work out an introduction. You may not like the sound of the job, but do not run it down. (Beware of qualifiers such as "just" or "only.")
- Prepare answers for standard questions on pay, promotion, hours, and reason why the vacancy arose.
- Do not make rash promises. Do not tell lies.
- Mention the positive aspects of the job.

Closings

- Say how helpful you have found the visit.
- Except with a talkative candidate, ask if there are any other questions.
- Explain that you have had a wonderful response to the advertisement and that you must see several other candidates.
- Ask what other applications the candidate has made. Tell the candidate *when* and *how* he or she will hear the result of the interview.
- Thank him or her again for her applying.

Appendix 4. Checklist for Exercise 1

Explanation

Watch the videotape carefully. To what extent did the *interviewer* cover all the main points? Check them off on the following list as they occur.

Opening

Was the candidate greeted by name?   ———
Did the interviewer introduce himself/herself clearly?   ———
Did the interviewer give his/her own job title?   ———
Did the interviewer indicate where the candidate should sit? ———
Did the interviewer put the candidate at ease?   ———
Did the interviewer thank the candidate for his/her application? ———
Did the interviewer explain the purpose of the interview?   ———
Was the opening stage kept under 2 minutes?   ———

Closing

Did the interviewer say something positive but noncommittal
about the interview (e.g., "It has been a useful talk")?   ———
Did the interviewer say that there have been other candidates? ———
Did the interviewer tell the candidate when and how he/she
will hear the result of the interview?   ———
Did the interviewer ask the candidate about his/her other
applications?   ———
Did the interviewer thank the candidate for his/her interest? ———

Physical setting

In this exercise, the physical setting was not under the control of the interviewer. But, nevertheless, how did the physical setting match up to requirements?
Was it free from interruptions?   ———
Was it private? Could others see? Could others hear?   ———
Could the interviewer see a clock without it being obvious? ———
Was the furniture suitably arranged?   ———
Was the room located near a suitable waiting area?   ———

General impression

Did the interviewer give the impression that he/she was a fair
and sympathetic person?   _____
Did the interviewer give the impression that the job was
important and worthwhile?   _____
Did the interviewer give the impression that he/she was
efficient and friendly?   _____

Appendix 5. Instructions for Exercise 2

Research has repeatedly shown that interviews are much more reliable if they are properly structured. A number of plans exist, but one of the least complicated is outlined below.

Job background

- Ask candidate to describe his/her present job: establish exact nature of duties.
- Ask why he/she has left, or wants to leave, his/her job. Discuss in detail employment during the last 5 years.
- Without direct questions, verify the details given in the application blank. Probe any unexplained gaps.
- Ask what he/she wants from his/her job.
- Ask what he/she thinks he/she will be doing in a few years.
- Ask why he/she wants this job.
- Ask direct questions about qualifications, licenses, and essential trianing.

Interests

- What are the candidate's interests and hobbies?
- How deep is the interest, and what standard has been reached?

Job skills

- Ask about specific skills that would be helpful in the job as policeman/ woman.
- Ask how the candidate would attempt to deal with some specific practical policing situations, such as
  A motorist traveling 5 mph over the speed limit in an urban area
  Youths vandalizing property
  A student demonstration
  Parents reporting their 12-year-old daughter missing
  A housewife who has locked herself out of her home
  Dealing with a neighbor's complaint of a noisy party
- If necessary, explain to the applicant that you will play devil's advocate and that you will respond as a problem citizen might (but do not be overenthusiastic or unrealistic in your own role-play).

Appendix 6. Checklist for Exercise 2

This exercise is concerned with the middle section of the interview, where the interviewer is trying to get relevant information from the candidate. To what extent does the interviewer systematically cover all the major points? Check off the points as they occur.

Job background

Did the interviewer discuss the last 5 years' job history thoroughly?   _____
Were any employment history gaps adequately probed?   _____
Has the interviewer established exactly what the candidate's duties were in each of his/her jobs?   _____
Has the interviewer established how well the candidate performed his/her duties?   _____
Has the interviewer established *why* the candidate left each of his/her jobs?   _____
Has the interviewer established why the candidate has applied for this job?   _____
Has the interviewer established what the candidate wants from the jobs he/she does?   _____
Has the interviewer established the candidate's qualifications, the licenses, and training?   _____

Interests and hobbies

Has the interviewer established the candidate's spare-time activities?   _____
Has the interviewer established the depth of the candidate's interest in his/her hobbies and his/her competence at them?   _____

Job skills

Did the interviewer ask about specific skills?   _____
Did the interviewer probe the way the applicant would deal with specific situations?   _____
Did the interviewer play an adequate role of devil's advocate?   _____

Fairness

Did the interviewer avoid questions, comments, and actions that placed women or minority groups in an unfavorable light?   _____

Appendix 7. Instructions for Exercise 3

An interviewer tries to get information by getting candidates to talk freely and openly. Interviews are very interactive processes, and the interviewer can exert a strong influence upon the willingness of the candidates to reveal information about themselves. The following "eight commandments" should be obeyed.

1. *Don't talk too much yourself.* Generally, interviewers talk too much (about 57% of the interview time). It is impossible for candidates to give information if the interviewer talks all the time.
2. *Don't use stress tactics* (except in exceptional circumstances, such as the CIA selecting foreign agents). Stress tactics force people into a defensive role where they refuse to reveal unfavorable information.
3. *Do not emphasize status differentials.* We normally confide in people of our own level. We are usually reminded of our status by our possessions and physical setting. Therefore, interviewers should not play status games. Do not place candidates on a lower, obviously inferior chair.
4. *Vary your voice, and use gestures.* Avoid giving candidates the impression that they are boring you. Vary the pitch of your voice and the speed of talking. Use facial expressions such as raised eyebrows or half smiles.
5. *Use comments.* In most social situations, comments are more effective in stimulating conversation. For example, "That sounds interesting" is much more effective than the question "What else interested you?" To keep the candidate talking, make liberal use of approving comments such as "You don't say" and "really."
6. *Use open-ended questions:* These are questions that cannot be answered by a one-word answer such as yes or no. The main purpose of open-ended questions is to get expression of opinion, feelings, and attitudes. The majority of questions in an interview should be open-ended.
7. *Use summaries and transitions.* At the end of each section of the interview, summarize the ground you have covered. It lets candidates know you have been paying attention, and it allows them to correct any misunderstandings. Announce to the candidate when you are moving on to another main category.
8. *Take notes*, but do not make an immediate note when the candidate says something against him/herself. Wait until the conversation has moved to a different topic. Do not try to hide your note taking from the candidate. Inform him/her that you will be jotting down some brief notes in order to help you remember what was said.

Appendix 8. Checklist for Exercise 3

This exercise is also concerned with the middle section of the interview, where the interviewer is trying to get relevant information from the candidate. For the purpose of this exercise, assume that the interviewer systematically covers all the major points. Instead, concentrate on how well the interviewer gets the candidate talking. Check off the points as they occur.

Key aspects

Does the interviewer avoid undue stress?   ———
Does the interviewer avoid showing his/her own personal
reactions to the candidate?   ———
Does the interviewer avoid status games?   ———
Does the interviewer avoid being openly critical of the
candidate?   ———
Does the interviewer talk for less than 25% of the time?   ———

Other aspects

Does the interviewer vary the speed and pitch of his/her voice?   ———
Does the interviewer use any gestures?   ———
Does the interviewer use comments for added explanation?   ———
Does the interviewer use mostly open-ended questions?   ———
Does the interviewer summarize the candidate's answers?   ———
Does the interviewer seem to have kept an open mind until
the end of the interview?   ———
Does the interviewer dogmatically state his/her own opinions?   ———
Does the interviewer make smooth transitions between
topics and announce them to the candidate?   ———
Does the interviewer avoid arguing directly with the candidate?   ———

Appendix 9. Instructions for Exercise 4

The final stage of interpretation is probably the most difficult stage. Skill in the interpretation of interviews takes years to acquire. Interpret the interview, along with information in the application blank, without delay, because research has shown that interviewers quickly forget information about specific candidates.

Some ways of avoiding standard interviewer faults:

1. *Avoid making a decision too early.* Many interviewers come to a conclusion during the first 4 minutes of an interview and are taken in by the "smart aleck" who gives a good impression but is useless except for talking. They also run the risk of overlooking an excellent candidate who takes a little time to settle down.
2. *Beware of the halo effect.* Do not allow your judgments to be swamped by one outstanding characteristic.
3. *Weigh information carefully.* Be particularly careful not to give too much weight to negative information or unexpected information.
4. *Make due allowance for the candidate's circumstances.* Do not automatically attribute failures to the candidate's personality. Often, the circumstances surrounding a candidate are the most important factors in determining success.
5. Make due allowance for the "social" aspects of interviews.

3　Attitude measurement

Bram Oppenheim

Summary

This exercise is designed to introduce students to attitudes and their measurement and to give them an understanding of the practical and theoretical issues involved by constructing a Thurstone Attitude Scale. After discussion, students select a suitable topic for the scale and write a series of attitude statements related to the topic, preferably after interviewing other people. This item pool is then edited, and the remaining items are judged by class members in terms of the position, on a *favorable/ unfavorable* dimension, of someone who agrees with each item. Item analysis and item selection follow, to eliminate items on which there is too much disagreement among judges. Finally, a scale is constructed of items at equal-appearing intervals from each others. The problems involved in constructing this and other attitude scales are brought out, as well as the issues connected with the use of such scales.

Aim

The aim of this exercise is to give students some familiarity with attitudes and their measurements by attempting to construct a Thurstone Attitude Scale. The intention, then, is to give a practical understanding of the nature of attitudes, as well as some understanding of the theoretical issues involved.

Most people probably have some vague ideas about attitudes, values, and opinions and may often assume that they can be measured by means of single questions in large-scale surveys, such as public opinion polls. This exercise introduces some of the broader aspects of attitude theory in social psychology; the difficulties and subtleties of conceptualization that arise when we try to measure attitudes about which relatively little is known; and the unreliability of single-question measurement, which has led to the development of classical scaling techniques.

44

At the practical level, students will begin to acquire scale-building skills and will discover how much care is needed during interviewing and item writing when dealing with attitudes. Students will also become aware of the problems of conceptualizing components of a given attitude; problems of language and the expression of feelings; and the risk of unintentional bias.

By going through the exercise of building a simple attitude scale, students should also acquire a much more critical understanding of the theories involved. It is not crucial for the exercise that the building of the scale itself is completely successful; what *is* important is that students begin to understand and to question some of the assumptions – both about attitudes and about the nature of scaling – upon which the procedure depends. Does it make sense to think of attitudes as straight lines? Are interval scales appropriate? How "deep" can attitude statements go? Do attitudes overlap with each other? How can any item pool do justice to the variety of attitudes held by different people about a given topic? Can the meaning of items be accurately judged by item judges, and how can we choose the best items? How can we evaluate any form of measurement, and, in particular, an attitude scale? How should we choose between different methods available? What are some of the practical applications of attitude scales? These and many other issues can be raised, and partly answered, by the following exercise.

Introduction

Why do scaling?

It may be useful at the beginning to distinguish between factual and attitudinal topics or questions in survey research. Such a distinction cannot be maintained precisely because the two areas overlap and because in most cases even "factual" questions contain many attitudinal and subjective components that will influence the answers, but loosely speaking, a factual question is one for which there is, or could be, a "true" or "correct" answer: For example, "When did you last go to the dentist?" This is a much simpler problem than trying to find out someone's attitudes toward civil liberty issues, immigrants, or a political party; the exploration of these topics may require more and different questions, using a variety of methods or approaches.

Put in measurement terms, we usually find that it is possible to obtain reliable answers from single questions where the topics are factual, but not when the topics are affective or attitudinal. A single-attitude question, such as "How do you feel about people who drink and drive?" or "What are your views on the teaching of sex education in the schools?" can be asked and can be quantified, after a fashion, by means of coding frames, but often such questions do not produce measurements that are sufficiently reliable or do justice to the problem. This is because the issues are complex and often sensitive and emotional, and because the answers are likely to be influenced by various underlying components or dimensions, such as the respondent's feelings about alcohol, about set, about schools, and so on. We find, therefore, that factual topics are generally dealt with by means of single questions, whereas in the case of attitudinal topics this does not work.

The dilemma has, from the early twenties onward, produced a number of different solutions in the form of attitude *scaling* methods. (It has also led to the development or adaptation of a number of projective techniques for attitude measurement and to still other methods, such as the Semantic Differential). It is the purpose of the present exercise to introduce the student both to some aspects of attitude *theory* and to some methods of attitude *measurement* by having you attempt to produce an attitude scale.

Let us first ask ourselves what an attitude is and how it works or what it does, and then go on to see what can be done to measure it reliably and – we hope – validly by means of a group of items that together form a scale.

What is an attitude?

There have been many attempts to define attitudes. One way is to think of them as "states of readiness," as predispositions to notice, to perceive, to select, to feel, to remember, and to react to a particular issue or topic (in reality, or in abstract verbal form) in a particular way whenever it arises. Thus attitudes affect most of our cognitive processes as well as our emotional ones; they dominate important aspects of our social life such as religion, marriage, politics, work and leisure; and they tend to be long-lasting and difficult to change.

An attitude is a construct, an abstraction that cannot be directly grasped. It is an inner component of mental life that expresses itself, directly or indirectly, through more obvious processes such as stereotypes and beliefs, verbal statements or reactions, ideas and opinions, selective recall, anger or satisfaction, or some other emotion – and in various overt aspects of behavior; however, the links between underlying attitudes and, say, the expression of hostility toward an ethnic minority are subtle and complex, so we must never assume that attitudes can directly predict behavior (nor, for that matter, can we reliably infer attitudes from observations of behavior).

It may help us to conceptualize attitudes in terms of "levels." If attitudes can be said to "underlie" more "superficial" expressions such as beliefs and opinions, then underlying the attitudes, in turn, are still deeper and more lasting constructs such as values, philosophies of life, and, ultimately, some aspects of personality. The deeper we go, the broader, more pervasive, and influential will be the constructs we encounter, and the more long-lasting and change-resistant they become. Thus, a male chauvinist may, at a superficial level, seem to treat women as equals and may admire a clever woman for her achievements, but deeper down his orientation will remain sexist, and this may be linked to a somewhat authoritarian and inflexible value system and to a certain rigidity of personality throughout life.

This example, tracing some of the linkages of male chauvinism, also serves to illustrate another important aspect of attitudes, namely that they are not isolated "boxes" but are linked and interwined in many ways – upward and downward and across – to other attitude domains. Attitudes form patterns, and in each of us such patterns create our own unique outlook on life. Yet in the formation of such patterns there are also common elements, so that, in a given society or subculture, we frequently find certain patterns that repeat themselves in many people. For example, it would not surprise us if our male chauvinist also expressed himself in favor of strong political leadership, was against abortion on demand, against random breath testing of drivers for blood alcohol level, against legalized pot, in favor of hunting, and not convinced that "Small is beautiful." We come to recognize such patterns intuitively; we sometimes give them labels (such as "left-wing" or "bourgeois" or "progressive"); and we are also aware that, over the years, issues that make up such a pattern may gradually change and will differ from culture to culture.

We note also that these patterns are not logical: They are irrational "psycho-logical." There are no *logical* reasons why someone who favors abortion on demand should also be unconcerned about homosexuality, or why someone who is hostile to immigrants should also want a return to capital punishment: Such patterns come to exist because there is an underlying web of attitudinal strands that have more to do with emotions and with personality needs than with logical or scientific thinking. In any case, most of the attitudes we hold are not the results of our own analysis or experience; they are more likely to have been adopted or taken over from significant others as part of our culture and socialization.

If you try to think about your own attitude to almost any topic, you will probably experience this as something subtle and complex, of uncertain shape, and colored by various emotions; to try to approach it by means of some kind of linear scaling system would hardly seem likely to do it justice. This is probably because the art of attitude measurement is still in an early and relatively crude state. We can hope to deal with the more common attitude patterns that exist in large numbers of people, but not with the detailed subtlety of private attitudes, and the measures we can generate will, at best, be able to produce crude correlations or to divide large samples into five or six subgroups on some attitude continuum with a fair degree of reliability, but they should not be used for individual cases nor for the prediction of behavior.

Let us now *sum up* what we have learned that may be relevant to our problem of attitude measurement.

First, an attitude is a construct, an organizing principle behind a pattern of feelings and expressions. We cannot hope to pinpoint it by means of a single item or question; it will need a multiple-item approach, using the attitudinal surface expressions (beliefs and opinions) to map out the components beneath, by means of a series of triangulations.

Second, we cannot be sure what we will find. Neither logic nor dictionary definitions will be a sure guide to the complex ways in which people think and apprehend their world. We must be ready for a mapping exercise, taking nothing for granted and following the paths through our data to see where they lead and what pattern will eventually emerge. Thus we may think that "cleanliness of mind and body" is a single attitude, but it may turn out to be two, or none, or to be but two small parts of a much wider attitude domain.

Third, we must not overestimate what we can do. By applying a linear scaling model to such a complex, amorphous construct we can only hope to extract a relatively crude measure, effective only with large numbers. Attempts to go into finer detail tend to lose themselves in a maze of unreliabilities.

Problems of attitude measurement

Among the better-known methods of attitude measurement is the Thurstone scaling procedure. This, like other scaling procedures, tries to fulfill the requirements of the linear scaling model, as far as possible. The linear scaling model has been widely used in the fields of cognitive testing, personality testing, aptitude testing, and so forth. Basically the model has the following requirements:

1. Unidimensionality (the measure should be "about one thing at a time"
2. Reliability (consistency)
3. Validity (the scale must measure "what it is supposed to measure")
4. Equal (or equal-appearing) intervals and scoring norms.

(Note that we are not dealing here with ordinal or nominal forms of measurement).

The notion of *unidimensionality* is not difficult to understand when we are dealing with qualities such as length, weight, or temperature; it becomes more difficult when we have to deal with something like neuroticism, and even more difficult when we try to measure attitudes. There is no evidence that an attitude such as vegetarianism, dislike of animals, or love of country can be conceptualized as a straight line or as a single measure that is "about one thing at a time." Exploratory interviews with people about, say, their attitude toward the police will probably show many components: links with their own fathers, with teachers and school authority, with traffic violations, with childhood fear of monsters, with uniforms and armed services, with traffic control, with burglary and crime generally, with helping the young or the sick, with motorcycles, television fiction, and so on. If we were in the process of creating a scale of Attitudes toward the Police, we would have to take all these subdomains into account and see if we could justifiably merge them into one conglomerate on which people can be given one score each, to represent their position on a single pro–con dimension.

The notion of a scale's *reliability* concerns its capacity to measure something consistently, so that we get approximately the same score if we repeat the measurement process over and over again. There will always be human and instrumental errors of measurement, even under the most stable conditions, but we must try to minimize these. When we repeatedly administer verbal or pictorial scales to human beings, we experience additional problems because the respondents may remember some of the items and will either try to be consistent with what they said before or try to say something new, and if we wait a while before repeating the scale, some genuine changes may meanwhile occur in the respondents, leading to inconsistencies. Several methods have been developed to overcome these problems, such as the "split-half" measure of reliability and the use of parallel scales. A scale's reliability is usually represented by a single correlation coefficient, such as Cronbach's alpha.

Reliability needs to be stressed as a most important requirement for without it there can be no validity: We will never be able to measure length accurately if we use an elastic tapemeasure.

A scale's *validity* is likewise expressed in the form of a correlation coefficient (note that a scale can have more than one validity coefficient, depending on its various applications). A scale has high validity if it measures what we want it to measure and very little else. However, this statement avoids a further question, for how do we know what the scale really measures? It is not enough to go by the scale's label or by the word of its creator (*face validity*), nor can we rely on the scale's manifest contents when we read some of the items (*content validity*), for further research often shows that such assumptions are incorrect. Sometimes we can get a little farther in the process of validation by comparing our scale with some earlier scale or with some other measure that we believe to be valid (*criterion validity*), or by seeing if behavior forecasts made with the aid of the scale actually come true (*predictive validity*). Another approach to validation is through *construct validity*, where we have strong theoretical reasons for expecting our scale to form a particular pattern with other neighboring measures.

However, in the field of attitude research, attempts at validation are often unsatisfactory, mainly because there are so few ways of obtaining an outside criterion measure of the attitude in question that is itself valid and reliable. Some researchers have tried to find *behavioral* criteria – but just what could be regarded as a valid and reliable behavioral measure of say, people's attitude toward the police? Membership in certain groups or associations might be indicators, for extreme cases, but clearly people join associations for many different reasons that may, or may not, reflect their attitudes directly. Other researchers have tried to use *construct* validity: Presumably they would argue that respondents who score high on the F scale should also score favorably on our Attitude to the Police Scale – but this is hardly conclusive evidence of the scale's validity. Indeed this whole problem highlights the fact that we do not yet have much well-established knowledge of the attitude systems in people's minds, nor do we know in detail how such attitudes contribute to the explanation of overt behavior.

It is important to realize that validity and reliability *interact*: Validity will inevitably be poor when reliability is too low, but if reliability is high (say, .80 or above), then there is at least the possibility of making the scale valid. We need to make sure, therefore, that at the very least our scale is sufficiently reliable.

Ideally, we would also like our scale to have equal (or equal-appearing) *intervals*, so that we can give numerical scores to each respondent and relate these to *norms* from which we can tell, by comparison with other groups, whether our respondents are particularly favorable or unfavorable in their attitude to the topic of the scale.

When we review these scale requirements, we may feel that this approach can never hope to do justice to the complexity, subtlety, and emotionality of individual attitudes. Hence many researchers have preferred to use projective or other nonscaled methods of attitude study and have sought to obtain evidence of reliability and validity in different ways. Yet it is not surprising, given the many advantages of the linear scaling approach, that other research workers have persisted in trying to apply it to attitude measurement, for both theoretical and practical studies. The results of their efforts have produced several rather different scaling methods based on the work of Guttman, Bogardus, Likert, and Thurstone, each of which fulfills some, but not all, of the scaling requirements we have listed.

In any piece of research, our choice of scaling method will be guided by its *appropriateness* – that is, we will want to choose the method of scaling that is right for what we need in our particular study. For example, the Thurstone scaling method can often produce two parallel scales (two scales that use different items yet produce comparable scale scores); it follows that this would be the method of choice when we do a "before-and-after" study of, say, the impact of a short film or a television presentation on our subjects. Each scaling method has its own strengths and weaknesses, and none of them fulfills all our scaling requirements.

Method

Subjects

The exercise is suitable for a class of 10 or more students. Additional subjects are not necessary, since class members can generate items for analysis by interviewing each other. Otherwise students can, if they wish, interview people outside the class.

Resources

The exercise requires a classroom with desks or table tops on which to work, and a blackboard. Also required are writing materials, paper, rulers, some envelopes, a set of ogive graphs (see appendix 1), and a set of percentage tables or a calculator.

Procedure

Basically this exercise goes through the steps of creating an attitude scale according to the Thurstone scaling method. Thurstone and his colleagues developed this method in the early 1930s, and it has found very wide application since then. His main concern was with the problem of obtaining equal (or rather, equal-appearing) intervals along a linear continuum. To do this, he first designed a considerable number of attitude statements, all dealing with the topic of the scale but in varied and different ways (the item pool). After that, he submitted each of these statements to a number of "judges" – that is, to ordinary people who were similar to those for whom the final scale was intended, and who were asked to "judge" each state-ment according to its meaning: Did the statement indicate a positive attitude, a strongly negative attitude, a mildly negative attitude, a neutral attitude, and so on. Usually, several dozen judges were used, to give stability to the findings. He then assembled all the judgments for each statement and used these to choose the best items from the pool for use in the final scale.

To look at the exercise procedure in more detail, it consists of three sessions: an introductory session and two laboratory sessions.

Introductory session

Instructors will probably start with some background discussion of the issues involved in attitude scaling. Instructors may also have available some examples of other attitude scales for the class to look at.

One of the main functions of this session is to choose a suitable scale topic – for example, attitudes toward smoking, toward alcohol drinking, toward civil liberty issues, or toward college football. It is best to choose a relatively clear-cut and well-known topic, and to avoid new or vague or hypothetical topics on which there may not be many clearly formed attitudes.

The other important task that should be completed before the first laboratory session is the creation of an item pool. This is perhaps the most important step in the attitude scaling process: All subsequent stages amount to little more than item analysis and item selection from among the items in the pool, and no amount of clever scaling or statistical manipula-tion can produce a good scale from a poor item pool. A full attempt at scaling would be preceded by a review of any existing scales and relevant background literature. After that, researchers would conduct several dozens of long, freestyle or in-depth interviews (recorded on tape), to give the necessary insight into the ways in which other people think and feel about the selected topic, what subtopics there are, and what the probable links would be with neighboring attitudes; this would enable researchers to *conceptualize* the nature of the topic being measured. The importance of this early, sensitive, and intuitive stage cannot be overstated. In addition, the interview tapes would yield natural and expressive phrases that could readily be turned into attitude statements – and most, if not all of the statements in the pool should come from the interviews.

In theory the item pool will consist of a number of attitude statements (some 60 or 70 or more) that each try to "get at" the topic of the scale in a different way, much as different items on an arithmetic test are designed to measure the child's arithmetic achievement in different ways. Each attitude is likely to have a number of subdomains, and these should all be represented, more or less systematically, to produce a varied item pool with good coverage of every aspect. Throughout we should bear in mind the assumption that each item can be placed on a linear continuum running from a positive extreme (i.e., in favor of the topic of the scale), through a neutral area, to a negative extreme (i.e., hostile to the topic of the scale). It helps therefore, to try to "translate" every statement into the form "I like X" or "I hate X." When editing an item pool, there should be a rough, approximate balance between the number of positive and negative items.

Writing good attitude statements requires a special knack. Some help can be given to beginners by suggesting errors that should be avoided. For example, statements should be brief, should not use proverbs or common sayings, should use simple, direct language, should not be too "intellectualized," and should not be "double-barreled." Thus, the statement "I like a man to be strong, silent, and a hard worker" is virtually useless, because it is multibarreled, for how would a respondent answer if he or she agreed with "strong" and "silent" but not with "hard worker" – that is, agreed with only part of a complex statement?

A typical error made by many students is to produce a great many descriptive statements, of the kind "Policemen wear uniforms" or "Some policemen stop people on suspicion." The trouble with descriptive statements is that they do not unambiguously express an attitude; they require us to make an inference (which may, or may not, be warranted). Thus, agreement with this statement "Policemen wear uniforms" may suggest a favorable attitude to the police *only* if we can be sure that the respondent thinks that uniforms are something admirable or good. Likewise, if some respondents agree that some policemen stop people on suspicion, what does this tell us about their attitudes to the police? Very little, unless we can be quite sure that stopping people on suspicion is something that the respondents disapprove or approve of, so that agreement with the statement would indicate an unfavorable (or favorable) attitude to the police. (It stands to reason, of course, that in some descriptive statements the intended inference is obvious – for example, "I think the police are wonderful.")

Perhaps a useful test for the inclusion or revision of any statement is to see if it can readily be translated to mean either "I like/approve of X" or its opposite. Even so, it is best to avoid descriptive and cognitive-belief kinds of statements because, after all, they are not *attitude* statements, in that they are not warm, personal, perhaps emotional expressions of feelings. It also helps to avoid generalizations, by making statements more personal. Here are some examples of attitude statements about police:

> "I always feel better when I see a policeman."
> "I think the police throw their weight around far too much these days."
> "If I had a son who wanted to join the police force, I would be very proud."
> "I sleep more safely at night because our police are the best in the world."

And so on.

Ideally, after agreement has been reached about the central topic for the attitude scale, the class should conduct a series of individual interviews with randomly selected respondents in order to generate attitude statements that come "from the horse's mouth." For students this may not be practicable, and so – contrary to what has just been said – members of the class will be asked to interview each other or their friends, or sometimes just to examine their own feelings about the topic, in order to produce attitude statements. By whatever means, they should each write, and hand in anonymously, some half dozen attitude statements by a given date, to be included in the item pool.

If possible, members of the class should first look at some books or articles that contain examples of attitude scales or collections of attitude scales (see References).

First laboratory session: item judging and the generation of item statistics

In the first part of this session, students will be asked to make a judgment on every item in the item pool that has been collected by the instructor. At the start of the class the instructor will give each student an envelope containing numbered slips of paper on which the different attitude items are written. A straight line will be drawn on the blackboard to represent the attitude continuum. This line will be divided into 11 intervals, and the class should agree with the instructor which end of the continuum is to be regarded as *favorable*, and which end is *unfavorable*. Category 6, in the middle, will represent the *neutral* category.

Class members now have to act as item judges, ignoring their own attitudes. They should first read through all, or most, of the attitude statements and then take each item slip in turn, read the item, and decide whether a subject's agreement with the statement would indicate a favorable or an unfavorable attitude, and to what degree. In effect, students should ask themselves: If someone agrees with this item, where does that person stand on the attitude continuum – in a favorable very favorable, very unfavorable, or a neutral position, or where? They should then place the item in the category that reflects this position – that is, in category 3, 10, 5, or whatever. Students must feel free to use all 11 categories, as well as number 6, the neutral category, but there is no need to have the same number of statements in each category; each item should be placed where it seems to belong. As more judgments are made, students may change their original judgments and place the items in different categories, until they are entirely satisfied. When all the items have been judged, students should write in the right-hand margin, and as clearly as possible, the category number in which each item has been placed. When this has been done, the item slips should be put back into their original order, according to the item numbers on the left-hand side.

The next stage of the procedure involves using the students' judgments to choose the best items for the scale. We need to be able to place each item precisely where it belongs on the *favorable–unfavorable* continuum, but not all the judgments will coincide for every item; in fact, for some items there may well be quite a lot of disagreement, or "spread," among the judges. Obviously, items that cause a lot of disagreement are not very useful for measuring people's attitudes, and so they have to be eliminated. The easiest way to do this is to draw a frequency distribution curve for each item, using all the judgments. Some items will have tall, thin curves – these are useful items on which the judges mostly agreed with one another; other items will have low, wide curves – such items have to be left out because there is too much spread or disagreement among the judges. The measure of spread that will be used in this case is the semi-interquartile range.

In Thurstone's original procedure, he used an additional criterion of "irrelevance" to select final items from the pool; items were rejected if subjects who agreed with them also agreed with others that had significantly different scale values. However, to adopt this measure would make the exercise unnecessarily cumbersome, since it would require additional groups of subjects and judges, and the exercise runs very well without it. If students are particularly interested in pursuing this point, they will find details in Thurstone and Chave's book *The Measurement of Attitudes* (Chicago: University of Chicago Press, 1929.)

Once items with too much judge disagreement have been eliminated, it is then necessary to look for items that are at equal-appearing intervals from each other; to do this we need a measure of *central tendency* for each item, that is, a kind of average (in this case the median). With such a measure we can locate items on our scale continuum and select items with equal intervals between them. If our purpose is to build a set of 11 items, one for each point on the scale, then we select the items with medians nearest to each scale point – something like 1.1; 1.9; 3.0; 4.2; 5.1; etc.

In the second part of this session, then, instructors should give each student a small number of items and ask them to work out the item statistics just described – that is, the median and the semi-interquartile range (SIQ) for each item. This means that once students have been assigned items they should be sure to collect from other class members all the judgment slips for the items for which they are responsible. It is a good idea to check that there are as many slips as there are student judges for each item before beginning the calculation. (*Note*: It sometimes happens that item slips get lost, are illegible, or have no judgment recorded on them; to save delay and complications, enter such missing category values in the modal or most common category.)

Medians and SIQs can be calculated as follows:

First, for each item, produce a frequency distribution from 1 to 11 of all the judgments. (Total frequency must correspond to the number of student judges.) Then convert these frequencies into percentages, either by using a calculator or by reading off from a percentage table that the instructor has placed on the blackboard. After that, convert the percentages into *cumulative* percentages.

An example for a hypothetical item no. 23, and assuming a class of 15 judges, is given in Table 3.1. The cumulative percentage figures are next transferred to the ogive graph (see appendix 1). It is sufficient to do this in a rough-and-ready way, by eye, and the entry marks can then be connected to produce the *S*-shaped ogive curve. A long, low-angle ogive curve suggests a poor item with a big spread; we are looking for items with a steep curve, suggesting little disagreement among the judges.

To find the *median*, students should drop a prependicular line to the baseline from the point at which the ogive curve crosses the 50% line drawn across the graph. For the example given in Table 3.1, the median would be approximately 8.4.

To find the *quartile* values, students should drop perpendicular lines from the points at which the ogive curve crosses the 25% and 75% lines on the graph. These baseline values should be read off by eye, and the difference between them calculated; half this difference is the SIQ value. Typically, for poor items such values will exceed 1.5 and 2.0. For the example in Table 3.1, the quartile values are approximately 8.9 and 7.8. The difference between them (the interquartile range) is 1.1, and the semi-interquartile range will be 0.55.

Class members should calculate medians and SIQs for each item they have been assigned to work on. Meanwhile the instructor should have put on the blackboard a table showing the item numbers down the side (run-

Table 3.1. *Item 23*

Category	F	%	Cumulative %
1	0	0	0
2	0	0	0
3	0	0	0
4	0	0	0
5	0	0	0
6	1	7	7
7	1	7	14
8	2	13	27
9	8	53	80
10	3	20	100
11	0	0	100
	15	100	

ning from 1 to 60, 70, or whatever) and two headings across the top: "Median" and "Semi-interquartile Range" (SIQ). When all these values have been calculated, students should enter them in the appropriate place in the table.

Finally, students should receive from the instructor a booklet containing all the items in the item pool and should copy from the blackboard the table of item statistics. Both the booklet and the table should be brought along to the second laboratory session.

Second laboratory session: construction of the final scale

At this point it becomes possible to construct a Thurstone scale, though perhaps not a complete one. Under the guidance of the instructor the class should look at the item statistics, reading out the text of items that did well or poorly, and with each member noting the location (medians) of the items they had written themselves. The scaling process can then begin with the setting of some fairly arbitrary upper limit for SIQs, depending on the item statistics available: For example, one might proceed by ignoring all items with SIQs above 1.7. After that the class needs to decide how many items there will be in the scale: 11, at unit intervals? Twenty-two, at half-unit intervals? Or is, perhaps, some fine discrimination required on a particular sector of the scale, say in half units between 6 and 8, and in whole units above and below these values? And do they want to make up a parallel scale too? Having made these decisions, class members and the instructor can list, for each point on the intended scale, the medians of the items with values nearest to that point; say, for 4.4, items with medians of 4.2, 3.9, 4.1, and so forth. From among these, they should choose each time the items with the lowest SIQ, but with a small item pool and an inexperienced group of item writers this often becomes a trade-off problem: it may happen, for example, that the item with the lowest SIQ is also the item with a median that is farthest away from the desired scale point, or else that an item with a median right on the scale point has an unacceptably high SIQ.

By proceeding in this way and assuming fairly adequate item statistics, eventually a scale of, say, 11 items will emerge. These should be listed together with their medians or scale values and critically examined. It should be noted at this point that in some research projects, if the results are not satisfactory, some items have to be revised and improved, new items have to be written, and the whole judgment procedure has to be repeated before the best possible scale items are obtained. It should also be noted that if the scale were being used in an actual research project, then the text would have to be reproduced and a scoring procedure developed, as follows.

If we assume that the exercise has yielded a set of, say, 11 items finally chosen to make up the scale, for each of these items we would have a median, which is the scale value of the item. However, it is obvious that when we give the scale to groups of respondents, these scale values would be omitted. The chosen items would be reproduced in random order, along with two columns headed "agree" and "disagree" (*not* a 5-point Likert format), and respondents would be asked to read each item and then mark the appropriate column.

The score for each respondent will be the median of the scale values of all the items marked "agree" (usually not more than two or three items, each with its scale value that is not known to the respondent). Items not marked, or marked "disagree," are ignored. The rationale for this procedure is that if the scale is well constructed and if the respondents are consistent, they would agree only with the few items that most nearly represent their own positions on the attitude continuum and would disagree with all the items that are too extreme or that express the opposite point of view.

Results and discussion

Summary of findings

The main yield of the exercise will be the creation of a Thurstone scale, that is, a set of attitude statements chosen from a specially constructed item pool, judged accurately to represent points at regular intervals along an attitude continuum, and that can be scored for each respondent to indicate a position on that continuum, from *most favorable* to *least favorable* to the topic of the scale.

The effort that has gone into making the scale is meant to ensure that such a scale is, in important ways, superior both to a single-attitude question in an interview or questionnaire and to a miscellaneous collection of attitude statements that have not been through the scaling procedure. The scale is expected to be superior for three reasons:

1. It is based on an item pool that itself has been carefully assembled to cover all, or most, of the relevant aspects of the attitude in question.
2. A scale, as opposed to qualitative or arbitrary devices, has characteristics that should ensure that it is more reliable and potentially more valid, as well as reflecting more accurately the views of the respondents.
3. The scale can yield a quantitative score, making reliable group comparisons possible.

However, not everyone agrees that attitudes are best represented by straight lines or that a respondent's personal attitude to a given issue can be adequately represented by a point on such a line. Nor is the Thurstone method the only, or necessarily the best, method of attitude scaling. As so often in science, theory and method interact: Different attitude theories and problems require different types of measurement, and improved measurement techniques will elaborate, change, or falsify attitude theories. The student-researcher is therefore faced with a choice: Since no single method of attitude measurement combines all the virtues, our selection must be based on the *appropriateness* of the measuring technique to our problem and our theoretical orientation.

In this exercise students will have had firsthand experience in constructing an attitude scale. They should now consider how such a scale can be evaluated and what kinds of research questions it may help to answer.

Scale evaluation

Taking first the purely measurement point of view, the criteria for scale evaluation will be (as was described in the introduction)

1. Unidimensionality
2. Reliability
3. Validity
4. Scores and norms

The class should note (1) that in Thurstone scaling the choice of dimension is based on pilot interviews but is essentially subjective; (2) that its linearity is assumed; and (3) that its division into 11 equal categories symmetrically located around a neutral point is arbitrary – but convenient. Unless the exercise is extended, the class will not be able to compute a *reliability coefficient* (Thurstone reliability coefficients tend to be around .80 or better), but different methods of calculating reliability can be discussed, as well as the possibility of developing two parallel scales from the same item pool. Likewise, the class will not be in a position to calculate any *validity coefficient* (see the introduction), but problems of validation should be discussed in relation to different types of validity (Thurstone scales, initially, have only *face validity*, until they can be related to other measures). The scoring procedure should also be discussed – for example, the loss of information by not scoring the "disagree" responses. These issues should be discussed in class with the instructor, who will also be able to explain the points raised in the next section.

Limitations of design and procedures

The procedure described in this chapter, because it is primarily a student exercise, has certain limitations: lack of sufficient open-ended and exploratory interview material; inadequate conceptualization of the attitude domain; inexperienced item writers; too few item judges, possibly not of the same background as the respondents for whom the scale is intended; item analysis based on inadequate numbers; no opportunity to improve the items and rescale them; no applications that would yield estimates of reliability, validity, and sample norms; no evidence of unidimensionality.

In addition, the procedure is limited by various aspects of attitude scaling generally, as well as by the disadvantages of this particular scaling method. Specifically, the class might discuss the obviousness of any measurement method using language; the culture-bound nature of attitude statements; the many possible sources of bias in the judges; the questionableness of the assumptions about linearity and equal-appearing intervals; and the lack of subtlety in dealing with such emotional and complex human attributes.

Finally, the whole exercise is affected by the current state of attitude theory. For example, if we knew more about the way in which attitudes somehow combine knowledge, beliefs, feelings, reasoning, and emotions, we would be in a better position to design suitable measures. For the same reason, we need to know more about the way in which many attitudes form patterns (value orientations or philosophies of life) within each person. We also know too little about less obvious, inadmissible, and subconscious attitudes, which may require quite different measurement methods. The relatively unformed attitudes of children are another important problem.

Last but not least, too little is known as yet about the many complex and indirect ways in which attitudes relate to behavior.

Possible applications

The class can now consider what kinds of psychological questions this type of scaling procedure could answer.

Studying group differences. Scaling comes into its own not as a form of individual measurement (such as an IQ test) but for the study of group differences. With the aid of attitude scales, we can compare different kinds of people: older and younger; women and men; well-educated and poorly educated; people from different countries or regions, and so on. Or, using the opposite approach, we can give the scale to a large population and then compare and contrast groups who score high, medium, and low on our scale. Or again we may be studying particular groups (for example, certain political parties, minority groups, parents versus teachers) and want to obtain measures of their attitudes. In most such applications there will be considerable overlap among the group distributions, and our interest will focus on the significance of mean differences. For example, on the average are young people more hostile to authority figures than older people? Are teachers in favor of streaming or tracking? Do people with strong hostility to aircraft noise also score high on a neuroticism scale?

Sometimes we study such group differences for *practical* reasons, for example, why do some people not apply for the welfare benefits they are entitled to? Sometimes we study group differences for more *theoretical* reasons, for example, are theories of anomie correct in postulating a cluster of interrelated attitudes of powerlessness and normlessness?

Measuring attitude change. The Thurstone scaling procedure is particularly useful in situations where we need to measure attitude change. Thus, if we are conducting a group experiment or an effects study with a before-and-after design, then we will want to measure the attitudes of the same respondents twice – before and after the manipulation. If we were to administer the same attitude scale twice, we might get some distortions, because respondents will recognize the items and may try to be consistent with their previous responses or perhaps will try to react differently the second time. However, the Thurstone scale can, under favorable circumstances, yield two parallel scales – that is, two sets of different items that still measure the same dimension. In before-and-after designs, the Thurstone method therefore seems particularly appropriate.

Measuring attitude patterns.   Scaling procedures are useful in attitude research – that is, in situations where we want to examine the composition, ramifications, and patterning of certain attitudes, for theoretical reasons. We might, for example, be studying such broad attitude complexes as authoritarianism or political conservatism, perhaps as these express themselves in different countries. Or we may be studying parental attitudes or "modernism" in developing countries. We might be involved in testing certain theories about such attitude patterns or in trying to establish construct validity. Factor analysis is often used to find the underlying components of a set of scales or items. For example, in a study of self-esteem, are self-love and self-hate each other's opposites, or are they independent, so that each respondent should have a score on both, perhaps with an "ambivalence index" as well? Factor analysis can guide us here.

Studying links between attitudes and internal variables.   Attitude scales can be used to study links with personality and other internal variables such as emotions, perceptions, and thought processes. For example, we might wish to study the links between the tough–tender aspect of political attitudes and neuroticism. Or we may be exploring the connections between religious attitudes and internal–external locus of control. In children, we might study the development of certain attitudes in relation to cognitive complexity.

Studying links between attitudes and behavior.   Finally, attitude scales can help us when we try to study the complex links between attitudes and behavior. We may be seeking an explanation for observed behavior – for example, a consumer decision, or a political act – or we may try to predict a certain kind of behavior – for example, the rejection of members of an out-group or the use of contraception. Fishbein's (1967) work has shown some of the steps that are necessary to build effective models of such processes, with the aid of attitude scales.

Discussion questions

Students should now be able to discuss the following questions:
  1. Why scale at all? Why not just use single-attitude questions?
  The answers here have to do with the differences in subtlety and complexity between factual questions and attitudinal ones that involve beliefs, knowledge, feelings, and values. The use of language in single-attitude questions tends to lead to a great deal of unreliability and lack of validity; when properly applied, scaling techniques usually have good reliability and yield quantitative measures that can be validated. However,

they are relatively crude measures and are based on some questionable assumptions.

2. Is the particular scale we have built any good?

The answers must lie in its relevance or appropriateness to the research problem and in the technical qualities of the scale – that is, its calculated reliability, validity, unidimensionality, and scoring procedures.

3. How does Thurstone scaling compare to other scaling procedures, such as Likert scales, factor-analytic scales, Guttman scales, multidimensional scaling, and projective techniques?

Likert scales and the Guttman scales offer better assurances of "purity" – that is, of unidimensionality, especially when factor analysis is applied to Likert scales. Likert scales also make it possible to include some more speculative, less "obvious" items and do not require a judging procedure. On the other hand, these scales do not produce equal-appearing intervals, and they do require substantial pilot samples, as well as a more complex statistical analysis. Projective techniques and multidimensional scaling usually deal with covert (concealed) or inadmissible topics, whereas Thurstone scales are overet (not concealed): It is obvious what they are getting at. Unless special steps are taken, only Thurstone scales can yield two parallel scales from the same item pool.

To oversimplify, we can say that Likert scales (with the aid of factor analysis) are most useful in exploratory studies and where comparatively large pilot samples can be obtained. Thurstone scales come into their own in well-known attitude domains; if no computer is available; if equal-interval scoring is important; and where parallel scales are needed – for example, in effects studies.

4. How can we use it? What do we get out of it?

Some of these answers have been given in the section entitled "Possible Applications."

5. When should we not use scales?

(1) When there is much doubt about the dimension, its linearity, or its constituents; (2) when the only judges available differ markedly from the groups to which the scale is to be applied – for example, university students acting as judges for a scale to be used with factory workers; (3) when respondents may have language or literacy problems; (4) when measures are needed of covert or inadmissible topics; (5) when we are dealing with topics about which only a few people have attitudes.

Conclusions

What are some of the lessons that students can learn from this exercise?

1. The advantages of scaling procedures over single-question attitude items, in terms of reliability, purity, or unidimensionality, potential validity, and meaningful quantitative scoring.
2. The need for self-critical application of scaling techniques, since each procedure has weaknesses as well as strengths. All of them are relatively crude and may not do justice to the more covert or subtle aspects of attitudes.
3. That choice of scaling technique is a matter not of overall superiority but of appropriateness to the research problem.
4. The need to continue to question the various assumptions underlying both attitude theory and attitude scaling procedures.
5. The fact that many attitude scales reach adequate standards of reliability and other evaluation criteria and are widely used in large-scale studies, as well as in laboratory research.
6. Insight into the current state of attitude theory in social psychology and into the links between attitudes and various kinds of group membership, between attitudes and personality attributes, and between attitudes and behavior.

References

Fishbein, M. (1967). *Readings in Attitude Theory and Measurement*. New York: Wiley.

Lemon, N. (1973). *Attitudes and Their Measurement*. New York: Wiley.

Oppenheim, A. N. (1966). *Questionnaire Design and Attitude Measurement*. New York: Basic Books.

Rokeach, M. (1968). *Beliefs, Attitudes and Values*. San Francisco: Jossey-Bass.

Shaw, M. E., & Wright, J. M. (1967). *Scales for the Measurement of Attitudes*. New York: McGraw-Hill.

Summers, G. F. (1970). *Attitude Measurement*. Chicago: Rand McNally.

Appendix 1. Cumulative frequency graph

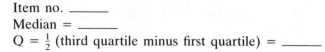

Item no. _____
Median = _____
$Q = \frac{1}{2}$ (third quartile minus first quartile) = _____

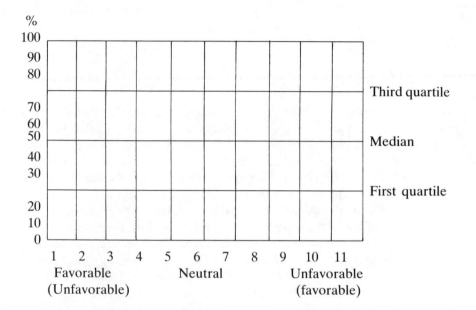

4   Social interaction: an observational analysis

Hugh Foot

Summary

A simplified version of Bales' Interaction Process Analysis forms the basis of this exercise. A group of four discussants are selected from the class and engage in a series of discussion problems. The remaining members of the class all act as observers and code the utterances and other social acts of the discussants, using a modified 8-category scheme derived from Bales' 12-category system. The first discussion problem is tape-recorded: It serves as a warm-up for the discussants and provides training to the observers in the definitions and use of the categories. This is followed by a practice problem and by two "test" problems for which data from the class are collected and entered into matrices on the blackboard. The class is given a set of predictions about group process derived from characteristic findings made by Bales in working with a wide variety of groups. Types of data analysis are suggested, and guidelines for report writing are provided.

Introduction

Studies of groups and of individuals within groups are numerous. This is hardly surprising, in view of the difficulties of capturing all the essential facets of group life within the bounds of a single study or series of studies. The wide variations in the methods and levels of analyses adopted, therefore, reflect the richness of the data available.

One of the first analytical attempts to create a general-purpose descriptive and diagnostic tool designed to produce theoretically important measures for all kinds of small groups was the technique of Interaction Process Analysis (IPA), developed by Robert Bales in the late 1940s and 1950s (Bales, 1950a, 1950b, 1958; Bales & Strodtbeck, 1951). From a historical perspective, IPA was grounded in the group-dynamic tradition, with emphasis upon the functional and structural properties of small face-to-face, problem-solving groups. Its special application to problem-solving groups was based upon their dynamic, task-orientated nature in which

66

"phase patterns" can be differentiated as the groups proceed from problems of orientation to problems of solution. Thus the technique is particularly suitable for plotting changes in the quality of the group's activities as it progresses through time toward solving a problem.

Initially Bales used his system of analysis for studying the activities of Alcoholics Anonymous groups, but IPA can be applied to many types of groups (Bales, 1950b). They include: (1) groups concerned primarily with problems external to their own process, such as planning groups, policy-forming groups, boards, panels, seminars, and classroom groups; (2) groups concerned with their own procedures or with their own interaction and interpersonal relations, such as training groups in human-relations skills, family groups, social and recreational clubs, children's play groups, and adolescent gangs; and (3) groups concerned with the personal situation or experience of their individual members, such as therapy or counseling groups. Although specifically designed for on-the-spot recording of group situations, IPA can be applied to a video or sound recording or to a written transcript of the proceedings. Inevitably the lack of visual cues will to some extent diminish the accuracy of the system. The size of group to which IPA can be applied may vary between 2 and about 20, but it is important that they are groups where the attention of members tends to focus in turn upon individual speakers, rather than groups where more than one person may be talking at once.

Despite the length of time that IPA has been in use as a tool for analyzing group process, it has aged comparatively well: It is still of value in relation to more recent theories of social structure, social differentiation, and attribution, and it is still being used practically and commercially as a training device in management and human relations. It has, for example, been used to train how groups "should" go about solving problems successfully. It is also used as a vehicle for giving feedback to individual group members concerning their effectiveness, or lack or it, in promoting the group's objectives. Some modification of the technique has occurred over the years (see Bales, 1970), and it formed the basis for other more expanded systems (see Borgatta, 1963; Borgatta & Crowther, 1965). Methods of scoring and analysis have, of course, developed greatly since the technique was first devised. Bales and Cohen's (1979) Systematic Multiple Level Observation of Groups (SYMLOG) represents a package of methods for the processing and analysis of data, including computer programs.

Specific background to the exercise

IPA is a method of observing and recording the specific actions of a group of people that go to make up the flow of interaction. "The heart of the method is a way of classifying behavior act-by-act, as it occurs in small face-to-face groups, and a series of ways of analyzing the data to obtain indices descriptive of group process and derivatively, of factors influencing that process" (Bales, 1950b, p. 258). Essentially then, IPA is a structured observational approach that provides a preestablished system of categories to be used to classify every interaction that occurs in the group. Bales developed 12 categories that seemed to encompass most of the kinds of social acts that are likely to be emitted in problem-solving groups. Each item of behavior, whether a verbal comment or merely a sigh, a shrug, or a laugh, is classified in one of these 12 categories. For each such item or "act," the person initiating it and the person (or persons or group as a whole) to whom it is directed are recorded. Bales' original category system (see Bales, 1950a) has been reproduced and is easily found in many social psychology texts (for example, McDavid & Harari, 1968). Twenty years later (1970), Bales modified the labels attached to several of the categories to encourage wider use of them. For example, his rather extreme categories of "showing solidarity" (category 1) and "showing antagonism" (category 12) became "seems friendly" and "seems unfriendly," respectively, to allow for milder expressions of positive and negative social feeling. This modified version of the scale is given in Table 4.1 and is also found in many social psychology texts (such as Hollander & Hunt, 1971; Secord & Backman, 1974). Bales also developed a method for gathering data concerning the interpersonal perceptions of group members.

The question of what constitutes a single codable act is, of course, crucial. Bales does not really describe the rules to use in dividing the acts; he sees it as a purely pragmatic problem. The amount of verbal or nonverbal behavior necessary is that which permits the observer to make a classification. In his own words, he defines the basic unit of observation as "the smallest discriminable segment of verbal or nonverbal behavior to which the observer, using the present set of categories after proper training, can assign a classification under conditions of continuous serial scoring" (Bales, 1950a). In practice, a string of sentences all aimed at asking a question may constitute a single act, and a brief exclamation or raised eyebrow might also do so: In terms of the analysis of the interaction, they would carry equal weight.

It is clear that much depends upon the interpretation of acts by the observer: A comment or gesture in one context, or made in a certain way, may be considered meaningless and therefore ignored; in another context, or made in another way, it might be considered highly significant and might be assigned to a category that attributes the perceived intention of the initiator. Bales tried to minimize subjective inferences by instructing the observer to interpret each act in terms of the act that immediately preceded

Table 4.1. *Bales' 12-category system and the modified 8-category system used in the exercise*

	Bales' 1970 categories	Function	Modified categories
Positive social-emotional area	1. Seems friendly	Integration +	} 1. Acts warmly
	2. Dramatizes (jokes)	Tension +	
	3. Agrees	Decision +	2. agrees
	4. Gives suggestion	Control	3. Gives suggestion
Task area (neutral)	5. Gives opinion	Evaluation	} 4. Gives direction
	6. Gives orientation	Communication	
	7. Asks for orientation	Communication	} 5. Asks for direction
	8. Asks for opinion	Evaluation	
	9. Asks for suggestion	Control	6. Asks for suggestion
Negative social-emotional area	10. Disagrees	Decision −	7. Disagrees
	11. Shows tension	Tension −	} 8. Acts coldly
	12. Seems unfriendly	Integration −	

it, but this may still lead to some subjective bias. It is also possible that a single act may be classified in more than one way: An act of agreement may also be an act that reduces tension, or giving an opinion may also be an act of rejection. It is hardly surprising that Bales suggests a month or more as the time necessary for thorough training in using the method. Through training, quite high reliability coefficients are typically reported, about .90 for categories that occur with high frequency, reducing to .60 for categories with lower frequency.

The 12 categories fall within two main classes of behaviors: those concerned with social-emotional activities of the group members, and those concerned with task-related activities. The social-emotional behavior itself divides into positive acts – being friendly, dramatizing (joking), agreeing – or into parallel negative acts – being unfriendly, showing tension, or disagreeing (see Table 4.1). Basically these reactions are associated with the organization of the group, involving the maintenance or destruction of harmony, the management of personal tension, and group integration or disintegration. Task-related activities divide into questions and attempted answers, with differentiation between asking/offering suggestions, asking/offering opinions, and asking/offering information. These activities are emotionally neutral and are geared toward pursuing task goals: defining the task situation, developing shared value systems, attempts at control, and progress toward solutions.

The categorization of social acts may have a structural coherence but is of little functional use unless consistencies in the patterns of activity can be related to dimensions of group process or social evaluations. The main value of IPA for predicting social acts involves the stages in the problem-solving sequence and the dimensions of group interaction. The typical sequence of activities in problem-solving groups starts with an initial stage, the *information-assertion* stage, where the emphasis is on problems of orientation, defining the task, stating the objectives, and sharing information. The second stage, the *evaluation* stage, involves a concern with attitudes and opinions: What attitudes should be taken toward the situation, and what values are to be accepted? This is the in-group formation stage, and it may be characterized by higher initial amounts of disagreement, followed (if the group task is to be successfully completed) by higher amounts of agreement. The third stage, the *solution* stage, emphasizes problems of control: deciding what action should be taken.

The other main line of research has focused upon the dimensions of social evaluation, with particular reference to the emergence of leadership. Three such dimensions of evaluation have been identified: *power*, *likability*, and *contribution to the task*. "Power" refers to the degree of perceived dominance or prominence that a person has over the other group members. "Likability" refers to the degree of pleasant or unpleasant feeling aroused by that person, and "contribution to the task" concerns the leader's task-related activities. These three dimensions are taken to be the primary dimensions by which people judge one another. They should be thought of as unrelated to each other; thus, knowing someone's position on one dimension does not predict that person's position on the other two. Put into concrete terms, the group member who is emotionally supportive and popular does not necessarily help the group in completing its tasks. This itself has led to interesting speculation about the composition of groups and the characteristics of leaders. In theory, the concept of a "great leader" is of one who achieves high ratings on all of these three social dimensions. Such men and women are comparatively rare; in practice there is a greater likelihood that people highly rated on task-oriented leadership are poor in terms of the emotional support they give the group, and vice versa. It can be argued that the success of many long-term "traditioned" groups lies in the balance of leadership roles within those groups; one member, the task specialist, takes the lead in relation to group activities and another, the social-emotional specialist, constantly bolsters morale and cements interpersonal relations.

The exercise

The purpose of the exercise is to explore some of the properties of a problem-solving group as identified by Bales and to examine the behavior of individuals within the group, using a simplified coding system in which Bales' 12 categories are collapsed into 8, as presented in Table 4.1.

Summary of procedure

Session 1

1. The instructor gives general introduction to the analysis of interactions, and to the Bales technique in particular.
2. The class is divided into discussants and observers, and the seating is rearranged.
3. Discussants engage in their first "training" discussion problem (appendix 1), which is tape-recorded (or video-recorded).
4. Training response forms (see appendix 2) are distributed to the class; categories of interaction to be recorded are explained by the instructor, while an assistant (graduate or undergraduate student) copies the first part of the taped discussion onto the blackboard or an overhead slide.
5. The recording is played back to the class, act by act. Class members classify each act independently, until a sequence of exchanges has been completed.
6. The sequence is then played back again to the class, and class members reveal the way they classified each act. Differences of opinion are revealed and ironed out.
7. A second sequence of acts is similarly classified, first independently by class members and then, after replay, a consensus is taken. This training procedure may be repeated several times.
8. Discussants are then sent out of the classroom briefly; practice and test problems are distributed to observers, with the appropriate response forms (appendix 3). Observers are instructed in the use of the response forms before being assigned to observe a particular discussant.
9. Discussants are then recalled back to the classroom and given the practice problem. Any further classification problems are then gone into, while the discussants briefly withdraw from the classroom a second time.
10. Discussants return and then do test problems 1 and 2 (appendix 4), with observers recording the interactions.

Session 2

11. Observers pool their data by averaging the frequency of emission of each category of social act.
12. Group data are entered into matrices on the blackboard.
13. The instructor provides a thorough explanation of Bales' 12-category system, the modified 8-category system used in the exercise, and the functions of the social acts.
14. The instructor suggests the forms of analysis to be done, on the basis of the hypotheses or questions generated.

Session 1

A brief account of the background to the exercise is given by the instructor, and the purpose of the exercise is explained in terms of training students in observation, recording, and analysis of group discussion.

The instructor then assigns four class members to act as discussants. The discussants are seated around a table in the center of the room; their positions are marked by large free-standing labels, *A*, *B*, *C*, and *D*. The other class members are designated as observers, and they take up any position around the edge of the room.

With no further instruction, discussants are given their training problem, which is a soluble arithmetic problem (see appendix 1). Each discussant is presented with a card that contains one piece of information. The information from all the cards has to be shared before a solution can be worked out. To facilitate oral exchange, discussants are instructed to keep their information card in front of them, not to write anything down, and not to share or pool cards. The question card is placed in the middle of the table for all to see. Once discussants have their respective information cards and know the question, they are asked to start the discussion, speaking as clearly as possible and not addressing anyone outside the discussion group.

After discussion of the training problem has ended, the class is given training response forms (see appendix 2) that relate to the simplified 8-category system used in this exercise.

The instructor takes the class through the categories and attempts to define them in turn, and gives examples. Since the definitions are not entirely self-explanatory, students should keep in mind the following points:

- It is necessary, for coding purposes, to decide what constitutes a single unit of interaction (*act*): It may typically be a sentence or part of a sentence, but in practice, several sentences spoken in sequence by the same interactant could constitute a single unit, if they are all directed toward the same purpose, such as giving a piece of information or asking a question.
- An act does not have to be a meaningful verbal utterance: It could be an exclamation, a sigh, a laugh, a gesture, or any form of significant non-verbal response. For the purposes of training, only the auditory information provided by the tape-recording can be used, but for test problems 1 and 2 nonverbal cues may also be worthwhile recording.
- Categories of acts are not necessarily mutually exclusive. A single act may be recorded in two categories simultaneously. Thus, in *giving a suggestion*, a discussant may also be *disagreeing* with what has just been said.

While the instructor is discussing the categories of acts with the class, the assistant takes the tape recorder into a nearby room, replays the tape, and makes a transcript. Fifteen minutes should be allowed for this, and at least the first 20 to 30 units of interaction need to be transcribed. The transcript should then be written on the blackboard or an overhead slide. The speaker's identification is irrelevant at this stage.

Once observers have had the interaction categories explained to them, the recording is played back act by act, and the class follows the transcript on the blackboard. After the first act has been played, class members make independent judgments about how it should be classified and check the appropriate row under column 1 on the training response form. The instructor plays the second act on the tape, and the class members again make their independent judgments, checking the appropriate row in column 2. This sequence continues for the first 10 acts, so that there is at least one checkmark in each column.

The tape is rewound, and the interaction is then played back again; this time class members indicate by a show of hands how they coded each act. Differences of opinions are discussed, and an attempt is made to reach a consensus on each act.

This procedure is repeated with the next set of 10 acts, class members first making independent judgments and then, on replay, voting publicly. By this time class members should have a clearer idea of how the category system is to be used and should be agreeing much more of the time. A third sequence of 10 acts (if they have been transcribed) can be presented in the same way, if time permits.

Once the instructor feels that the observers are learning to use the categories with some confidence, the four discussants are briefly sent out of the classroom. A similar number of observers are then specifically assigned to each discussant – A, B, C, or D – and positioned so that they will have a clear view of their target person when the discussants return to the classroom. The instructor distributes the response forms (appendix 2) and draws attention to the way in which observers are to tabulate their recordings. The response forms require observers to identify the discussant to whom acts are directed by the discussant they are observing. For simplicity, the observer puts a checkmark by the category of act emitted, in the column for the discussant to whom it is directed. If the interaction is directed to several of the discussants or to the group as a whole, then the checkmark is put in the column for the group. The emission of each type of act is thus represented by a series of checkmarks. The column under each discussant is divided into first and second halves. These refer to the first and second halves of the discussion period. If a 12-minute discussion time is permitted for each problem, then the instructor quietly announces when 6 minutes have elapsed, and observers simply switch coding from the first-half column to the second-half column. The reason for collecting first- and second-half data separately is to permit subsequent examination of whether the social acts change as discussion proceeds.

The discussants are then recalled to the classroom and given the practice problem, which can be any kind of open-ended discussion task. One particularly suitable kind of problem, for example, is a design problem: The group is instructed to discuss the planning of a new shopping center, a new traffic system, the layout of an exhibition, and so on. Group members may be supplied with different pieces of information or with the same piece of background information. The discussion may last up to 10 or 12 minutes.

This practice problem is optional but desirable: It provides an opportunity for observers to become experienced in using the categories and response form. Any further difficulties in categorizing interactions or using the response forms are finally discussed, after the discussants have briefly withdrawn from the classroom for a second time.

Discussants are then given instructions for starting the two test problems. Test problem 1 (see appendix 4, pt. a). depicts a discussion situation in which the discussants are to role-play probation officers and social workers reaching agreement about how to advise a juvenile offender. Test problem 2 (see appendix 4, pt. b) requires discussants to role-play the members of a family who, in the circumstances described, have competing interests. The time allotted for each discussion is between 12 and 20 minutes. Session 1 ends after the completion of the two test problems.

Session 2

Assuming that all the data have been collected, the session starts with the instructor directing observers to gather into groups in the classroom, according to which discussant they observed in Session 1. To pool their data, class members should simply add up and then average the frequency with which each category was recorded as having been used by the discussant in interaction with each other discussant and with the group as a whole. Thus, for each test problem the observers of discussant A, for example, generate an average number of "asks for suggestion" acts directed at B, C, and D in turn, and at the group; and so on for each of the other categories of acts. Separate frequencies are generated for first and second halves of each discussion period. For the purpose of analysis the average frequencies, based on the pooling of individual observers' scores, form the basic data. Despite the lack of precision in requiring that averages be rounded to the nearest whole number, they do take account of differences in observer group sizes. There is no point in collecting group data for the practice problem.

The averaged data from groups are then collected by the instructor (or assistant) and written, in matrix form, on the blackboard (see appendix 5), using a different symbol for each type of act (for example, A+, agree; A−, disagree). There is a separate *interaction matrix* for each of the two test problems, and first- and second-half frequencies are entered in separate cells in the matrix. The matrix permits the display of the number of acts initiated by each discussant toward each other discussant and toward the group.

Before proceeding with a discussion of the data analysis, the instructor describes Bales' 12-category system and explains how the 8-category system used in the exercise was derived. Attention is drawn to the functions that different types of social acts serve during discussion. Problems associated with the exercise in particular, and with the classification of speech and nonverbal behavior in general, can be raised and discussed briefly.

Data analysis and discussion

There should be enough data for a variety of detailed analyses of individual categories of social acts. The main analyses are outlined later in this section. From the interaction matrices, the total number of acts addressed by each discussant to each other discussant and to the group as a whole should be calculated. These subtotals can be added to yield an overall total for each row of the matrix, which represents the total number of acts initiated by each discussant. Similarly, column totals represent the number of acts each receives from others. The "total participation" of each discussant is represented by the total number of acts initiated plus the total number received.

With these data a number of questions and hypotheses can be examined, based mainly upon the repeated findings of Bales' own research.

First, the overall amount of participation of each discussant remains the same for each problem. This is particularly interesting to explore in the light of the differences in the type of problems, one essentially nondivisive and the other essentially divisive.

Second, the amount of interaction initiated by one discussant toward a specific other discussant tends to be as large or small as the amount the second discussant addresses to him or her. More accurately, the lower of the two participators addresses a little more to the higher participator than the higher participator addresses to him or her. If discussants are rank ordered in terms of the number of acts they initiate and the number they receive, there is generally a high correlation between these rank orders.

Third, the higher participators tend to address proportionately more of their initiated acts to the group as a whole than to specific individuals. Indeed, in many groups the amount the highest participator addresses to the group as a whole exceeds the total that that person addresses to all the individual discussants put together. On the other hand, the amount that the lowest participator addresses to the group as a whole tends to fall short of the amount that that person addresses to any individual discussant.

Fourth, upward and downward mobility within the group can also be detected, according to Bales: If lower participators address more of their acts to the group than to the other individual members, they are assumed to be trying to move upward; if higher participators address more of their acts to other individual members than to the group, then they are assumed to be attempting to move downward.

Analysis of these questions rests upon looking at *overall* rates of participation. A more interesting topic is the analysis of types of acts engaged in, which involves determining what task-related and social-emotional contributions individual discussants make to the group process. At a fairly holistic level it may be possible to tell if the two complementary types of group leader that Bales has identified (task specialists and social-emotional specialists) actually emerge in the two discussion groups by examining the patterns of acts.

Fifth, from the interaction matrices it is possible to get a rough idea of the power position of each person by counting the number of agreements they receive, compared to the number of disagreements. This may not give the full picture, of course, because many statements or directives may be made by powerful members that meet unspoken, and therefore unrecorded, agreement.

Sixth, power can also be measured in terms of types of acts initiated: High contributors attempt more solutions and provide more information; low contributors ask more questions and provide less information.

Seventh, task specialists typically play aggressive, unsentimental, idea-orientated roles; social-emotional specialists (usually the best-liked members of groups) play more passive roles and concentrate on reducing tension and giving rewards. Such individuals may be identifiable from the interaction matrix.

In addition to representing the data numerically in the interaction matrix, the contributions of discussants can be plotted graphically in an *interaction profile*, which is an array of the rates of activity in each category. This can be plotted for the group as a whole or for individual members, and it is based upon the percentage of the total acts initiated that fall into each category. Profiles can also be plotted for acts received. This is a particularly useful way of making comparisons of group activity between problems, and comparisons within problems of group activity from the first half of the discussion period to the second half. It is also another means of comparing individual contributions to the group.

Eighth, on the basis of the types of discussion problem chosen, more negative social-emotional acts (disagreement, tension) should be generated in test problem 2 than in test problem 1.

Ninth, if the group is close to a decision on either or both problems, then the first half of the discussion period should be characterized by information asking and giving, and by disagreement; the second half should be characterized by directives, agreement, and tension release.

The sophistication of the statistical analyses to be employed may vary according to the progress of the students. Simple descriptive statistics in terms of averages, totals, or percentages are an obvious first step.

The final observation to be made concerns the collection of subjective data. Bales has laid great emphasis upon the various dimensions of social evaluation mentioned in the introduction to this exercise, and he has devised methods for collecting evaluative data on group members' likes and dislikes for each other, their opinion about who had the best ideas and who showed the most leadership. There is no reason why the instructor should not seek to obtain subjective reports from the discussants, in particular about their perception of their roles and the roles of the other interactants. Such data could usefully be matched up with the quantitative data derived from the observers.

This discussion may have given the impression that the amount of total participation by individual members is in some real sense a measure of their group effectiveness. Clearly this is not necessarily so, because quantity of acts does not imply quality. Very talkative group members may well be overrepresented on all the quantitative measures. There is not space to go into this question here, except to mention it as justification for collecting subjective data, but students should not overlook it. A concise discussion of this issue is to be found in Bales (1958).

Guidelines for student report

The report to be produced by the student should follow relatively conventional lines. The introduction provides a clear outline of the main features of IPA and its applications. The "Aims" of the exercise must be clearly stated, both in terms of specific hypotheses about group process and in terms of training students in observational skills. The "Method" section should contain all the relevant information relating to location, resources, and materials used; class division; and the procedure step-by-step, from the initial training problem to the final test problem. The level of analysis, for inclusion in the "Results" section, is dependent upon the stage of the course that students have reached. The group-data matrix permits, on the one hand, a purely descriptive account of group processes by manipulating frequency scores. On the other hand, various tests can be employed to yield a more inferential approach. Students should be guided by their instructors concerning which particular questions about group process they should attempt to answer; the data should be sufficiently rich to enable other questions to be tackled that are not specifically mentioned in this text. In addition to a full discussion of the results, the "Discussion" section should include a careful appraisal of the categories of interaction used, their operational difficulty, and their appropriateness for the problems presented to discussants in the exercise.

Conclusions

As mentioned earlier, IPA represents a structured observational approach, and its strength as an exercise lies in teaching students some of the problems associated with classifying social interaction and interpreting the meaning and function of various social acts within the group. The exercise can, of course, be taken out of the classroom and into the field, where students can gain valuable insights into the proceedings of real decision-making groups. Students might have an opportunity to do this through clubs and societies to which they belong within their own schools or colleges: They could sit in on committee meetings, discussion groups, and so on. Also, at a local government level, there may be public meetings of bodies concerned, for example, with education, housing, environmental health, social services, or transportation and highways that would provide opportunities for some kind of interactional analyses. In groups that have highly formal and stylized structures (making formal reports and permitting little open discussion) IPA would not be appropriate, but where open discussion is permitted it is an excellent means of exploring group processes and differentiation within the group.

References

Bales, R. F. (1950a). *Interaction Process Analysis: A Method for the Study of Small Groups*. Reading, Mass.: Addison-Wesley.

Bales, R. F. (1950b). A set of categories for the analysis of small group interaction. *American Sociological Review*, 15, 257–63.

Bales, R. F. (1958). Task roles and social roles in problem-solving groups. In E. Maccoby, T. Newcomb, & E. Hartley (eds.), *Readings in Social Psychology* (3rd ed.). New York: Holt, Rinehart & Winston.

Bales, R. F. (1970). *Personality and Social Behavior*. New York: Holt, Rinehart & Winston.

Bales, R. F. & Cohen, S. P. (1979). *SYMLOG: A System for the Multiple Level Observation of Groups*. New York: Collier Macmillan/Free Press.

Bales, R.F., & Strodtbeck, F.L. (1951). Phases in group problem solving. *Journal of Abnormal and Social Psychology*, 46, 485–95.

Borgatta, E.F. (1963). A new systematic observation system: behavior scores system (BSc. system). *Journal of Psychological Studies*, 14, 24–44.

Borgatta, E.F., & Crowther, B. (1965). *A Workbook for the Study of Social Interaction Processes*. Chicago: Rand McNally.

Hollander, E.P., & Hunt, R.G. (1971). *Current Perspectives in Social Psychology* (3rd ed.). New York: Oxford University Press.

Liggert, J., & Cochrane, R. (1968). *Exercises in Social Science*. London: Constable.

McDavid, J.W., & Harari, H. (1968). *Social Psychology: Individuals, Groups, Societies*. New York: Harper & Row.

Secord, P.F., & Backman, C.W. (1974). *Social Psychology* (2nd ed.). New York: McGraw-Hill.

Appendix 1. Training problem: soluble arithmetic task

Information distributed among discussants:
1. Joe is 5'8" tall and is halfway between Peter and Christopher.
2. Christopher's height is exactly halfway between that of John and Peter.
3. Robert is 2 inches shorter than Peter.
4. John is 4 inches taller than Robert.
Question: How tall are John, Robert, Peter, and Christopher?
Answer: John $5'9\frac{1}{2}''$
       Robert $5'5\frac{1}{2}''$
       Peter $5'7\frac{1}{2}''$
       Christopher $5'8\frac{1}{2}''$

Source: J. Liggert & R. Cochrane, *Exercises in Social Science* (London: Constable, 1968), p. 98.

Appendix 2. Training response form

Categories	Acts														
	1	2	3	4	5	6	7	8	9	10	11	12	13	14	15...
1. Acts warmly															
2. Agrees															
3. Gives suggestion															
4. Gives direction															
5. Asks for direction															
6. Asks for suggestion															
7. Disagrees															
8. Acts coldly															

Note: For each act the observer places a checkmark (or checkmarks) in the appropriate row/column(s).

Appendix 3. Response form for the practice problem and for test problems 1 and 2. Discussant observed _____

Categories	A 1st half	A 2nd half	B 1st half	B 2nd half	C 1st half	C 2nd half	D 1st half	D 2nd half	Group 1st half	Group 2nd half
1. Acts warmly										
2. Agrees										
3. Gives suggestion										
4. Gives direction										
5. Asks for direction										
6. Asks for suggestion										
7. Disagrees										
8. Acts coldly										

Note: For each act initiated by the discussant under observation, a checkmark is entered in the column corresponding to the discussant addressed and in the row corresponding to the perceived act.

Appendix 4. Test problems

a. Test problem 1

Information items

1. John is 21 years old; he works as an apprentice toolmaker in a factory; he has held this job for 3 weeks. Since he left high school he has spent 6 month on unemployment insurance; he likes his work and is anxious to keep his present job.
2. John is the youngest of three brothers; his two brothers (22 and 24) have both been in trouble with the police; his oldest brother was jailed for 2 years, at the age of 19, for assault and causing grievous bodily harm; both brothers are unmarried and live at home, rarely holding down a job for more than a few weeks at a time.
3. John lives at home with his mother, who never exercised any control over her three sons; his father was a drunkard, who, when the children were younger, used to beat up his wife frequently; since John was 10, his father has lived away from home, and his mother had to bring up the boys on her own and manage on what little earnings they brought into the house.
4. John has never been in trouble with the police before; except for taking part in a few wild exploits at school, he was never in serious trouble with the school authorities; he was by no means a bright pupil but took his school work seriously and is ambitious.

Problem

John has been caught red-handed helping his brothers in a warehouse robbery; since it is his first offense he had been put on probation for 2 years. You are probation officers and social workers and are considering what advice should be given to the boy and his mother after he leaves the custody of the court. Come to some agreement about the advice you would give.

b. Test problem 2

Information items

1. You are Dad: You are 48 years old and the owner and manager of a small hardware store in the suburbs of a large city; you like mixing with other people, enjoy baseball and drinking, and never go to the country except for occasional picnics and vacations; you don't much like the country and only go at all to keep your wife happy.
2. You are Mom: You are 45 years old. You were brought up on a farm in a rural area and love the country; since you married and moved into town to raise a family you never had much opportunity to go to the country except occasionally during vacations or for picnics; now that the children have grown up and can fend for themselves, you would dearly love to move to the country again.
3. You are Roger: You are 18 years old and living at home; you are about to graduate from high school and have applied to an agricultural college; you take after your mother and love the land and farming; you have spent all your school vacations down on your grandparents' farm helping out, and your ambition is to own a farm of your own.
4. You are Sally: You are 19 years old, also living at home and helping your parents in the store; you are engaged to a local boy; your interests are mainly social – you like dancing and going to the pictures or theater – and you don't really know the country.

Problem

Dad's uncle has just died, leaving to Dad and his family a large country house (in good condition) standing in about 10 acres of rough, rocky ground on a stretch of rugged coastline about 200 miles from where they live. The house passes to the family on the condition that they keep it in the family for at least 40 years. The family is gathered together just after they have heard the will read in order to decide what they are going to do with the property.

Appendix 5. Interaction matrix for collection of group data

Test problem _____

	Person addressed									
	A		B		C		D		Group	
Initiated by	1st half	2nd half	1st half	2nd half	1st half	2nd half	1st half	2nd half	1st half	2nd half
A										
B										
C										
D										

Note: Average the number of each type of act initiated by each discussant to each other discussant. A simple code system can be devised to denote each type of act: for example, 5A+ might mean 5 "agrees"; 2S− might mean 2 "asks for suggestions," and so on.

5   Ethogenic methods: an empirical psychology of action

Rom Harré

Summary

This chapter introduces the principles of the "ethogenic" method. It contains four exercises that can be used to explore how social action is rule governed and how these rules can be ascertained and interpreted through the collection and negotiation of the accounts actors give of their actions.

Introduction

There are two ways of defining psychology. Recent tradition has assumed that human actions are the effects of causes and that psychology is the science devoted to discovering the mechanism by which such causes operate. According to this view, human beings as persons are assumed to be essentially passive. Advances in psychological theory have drawn attention to an alternative conception of psychology. According to this view, people are thought of as active beings, concerned with fulfilling their plans and intentions and with thinking out what to do. The methods outlined in this chapter are intended as an introduction to some of the techniques that are needed to study human actions according to the second of these conceptions of psychology.

To grasp the significance of adopting the "ethogenic" methods of investigation, a student needs to have some understanding of the controversies concerning the nature of psychology that have led to their development. Shotter's book (1975) is an excellent introduction to the main theories of psychology that are involved in the controversy. For more detailed discussions, see Harré and Secord (1973) or Hollis (1977).

In studying human action, there are two kinds of things we might want to find out. We could ask what someone must know in order to be able to carry on some well-defined activity: for example, for someone to be able

I am grateful to David Pendleton, Andrew Ockwell, and Marga Kreckel for the use of material from their researches that forms the documents printed in the appendixes.

86

to play chess well, a person must know the rules governing the moves of each of the pieces. But just having these resources does not make someone a competent chess player. Players must know how to use their knowledge on particular occasions when they are actually required to make a move. In ethogenic psychology, we treat two problems: the problem of discovering and presenting what someone must know (his or her *resources* for action), and, separately, the problem of discovering how the person uses those resources to act (his or her procedures or *performances*). Different methods are required to discover a person's resources for social action from those needed to uncover the ways performances are actually done successfully.

A scientific investigation begins with the realization that there are patterns in the phenomena. Crystals have regular shapes; the forms of family quarrels repeat themselves. The patterns may not be immediately obvious to those who have not been trained to look for them. The identification of patterns depends partly upon having an adequate conceptual system or analytical model that makes them stand out from the background of social action we take for granted. Scientific thinking derives from the perception of patterns and from the curiosity that a person with a feeling for science has about how those patterns came to be. In human social interaction there are many examples of patterned behavior, some that are easily understood through common sense and some that can only be identified through sophisticated analytical models. The methodology described in this chapter is based on the theory that there are at least three sources of patterned behavior in human interaction.

The first source is genetic endowment and biological necessity. There may be cases where there is a direct preprogramming of a pattern of interaction through psychological structures related immediately to some inherited patterns of genes. Direct preprogramming, however, seems to be very rare in human social actions and feelings. The fact that men find women with large pupils more attractive than those with small pupils may be an example (Harper, Wiens, & Metarezzo, 1978). These are exploitations of patterns of behavior that derive indirectly from genetic inheritance through the cultural exploitation of a biological necessity. For example, there is a biological necessity to eat, but, as anthropologists have demonstrated clearly, meals are more than merely taking in nourishment; they are used as ways of displaying social status and hierarchy. They are endowed with meaning (Douglas, 1972).

Other patterns of behavior seem to be the product of habits learned from a person's upbringing, training, and education. Like those rare cases where there is an obvious relationship to physiological preprogramming, such habits are acted upon without conscious attention being paid to the process

of selecting an appropriate action. For example, Collett and Marsh (1974) discovered a pattern of stance and body posture by which people pass each other in the street that is different for men from that displayed by women. This pattern is probably not the result of genetic endowment or biological necessity, though people are not conscious of the regular way in which they adjust their body posture to one another. My guess is that a pattern of this sort is a habit learned early in life, comparable to the ability to ride a bicycle.

These kinds of semiautomatic patterned behavior could be investigated by the naive type of experiment in which an action is simply interpreted as being caused by environmental conditions. For such behavior, breaking down the event into variables and manipulating them against each other seems a reasonable way of proceeding. One cannot, though, conclude that the discovery of a pattern of cause and effect reveals a universal human tendency. For example, the experiments on gaze, so fashionable a few years ago, showed that there were patterns in the ways people looked at each other. But the patterns of gaze are different in different cultures (Harper et al., 1978). Such experiments, if they do not take culture into account, can give the false impression that the results apply universally.

Most human social activity does not have its source in either genetic inheritance or learned habits. The sources of the patterned behavior that dominates most social episodes are the social rules, conventions, demands, exemplars, interpretations, legal requirements, and codes of honor that differentiate one culture from another. Such rules involve a much higher and sophisticated level of cognitive processing than occurs in the case of patterns based on habit. Ethogenic method is concerned with this third and most prevalent kind of social pattern. In most cases, when people are acting in accordance with the requirements of their culture, exhibiting their knowledge by using the "proper" behavior in pursuit of their goals, they are rarely conscious of the process by which that knowledge is transformed into action. However, it is clear from the investigations described later in this chapter that (1) they once were conscious of these intentions, and (2) they can be made conscious of them again at any time.

To summarize: There is a small place – "in the corner," one might say – for the naive experiment, but to investigate the most prominent process by which human beings create social order, a dual methodology must be used. There must be a way of finding out what people know about the rules, conventions, and so on, of their society, and a way of finding out how they utilize these, moment by moment, in performing appropriate actions. In short, we need to investigate people's social resources and the processes by which their social resources are utilized.

How to study resources

Account analysis

The basis of the ethogenic method is the analysis of the accounts that actors give of the actions in which they have taken part. They may also give accounts of actions that have not yet been done. Fortunately, the way social life is actually lived involves a good deal of challenge to, and doubts about, what is going on in the social episodes of daily life. Actors are then ready, if challenged, to provide interpretations and justifications for what they have been doing. These are accounts. Empirical investigation of accounts has shown that they include interpretative schemata for making clear what an action means, as well as indications of the rules and conventions of proper action (Lyman & Scott, 1970). Accounts not only serve to keep social life running smoothly, but they also reveal bits and pieces of an actor's knowledge of how social life *ought* to run.

Account analysis is the first step, then, in the investigation of the knowledge and beliefs that actors bring to their social life. Account analysis yields material that helps us to understand the resources of actors. But actors sometimes do not produce the resource material that was actually involved in the production of a particular action, perhaps because to do so would expose them to criticism. The ethogenic method does not assume that the contents of accounts and the resources employed coincide, moment by moment, in day-to-day social activity – but it does assume that they coincide in the long run. Studying accounts of a mode of social interaction for considerable periods of time, and for as many of the interactors as possible, will yield an adequate representation of their resources. However, even with this reservation it is clear that we should not expect account analysis to give a complete picture of all the rules, conventions, and meanings involved. There will be many fragments of knowledge relevant to the action that an actor may have used without being subject to criticism and without consciously thinking about them. In these circumstances individual actors will not be aware of the principles of their action, since no defense has been requested. Account analysis must be supplemented by further techniques.

Observer attributions

Outsiders, adopting the stance of anthropologists "looking in" at the life of a strange tribe, offer their own accounts of events for which the natives have offered theirs. It is an essential part of the ethogenic method that

actors' interpretations and observers' interpretations are given equal weight initially and negotiated one with the other. Actors can supplement outside observations, often in startling ways. For example, women's rituals among the Trobriand Islanders, mistaken by Malinowski for an economic activity, were seen to be relevant to the preservation of tribal honor when Annette Weiner talked to Trobriand women (Weiner, 1976). Observers as outsiders can supplement actors' understanding by suggesting theories about the functions of certain kinds of social events. Actors are, of course, the best authorities on the question of local meanings and the structure of interaction rituals, but observers may have a viewpoint that allows them to inform actors about such matters as unintended consequences of actions, knowledge that could actually affect the survival of a culture.

Analytical models

However, if they are to be scientific, observers' outsider attributions require explicit analytical models to use in identifying the main features of the action and in classifying these features. Naive empiricist methodology worked on the mistaken assumption that there was some "real" behavior that would be the foundation of all observations. The absurdity of this idea has been demonstrated in theoretical discussions of epistemology in recent years (Walsh, 1972), so we do not need to comment on that old error. Just as Robert Boyle formulated a conceptual system for analyzing the behavior of gases, explicitly on the basis of an analogy with the behavior of springs, so social psychologists who want to be scientific ought to be as careful as Boyle in laying out their analytical models. Ethogenic work has emphasized four models, and no doubt there will be many more. These are

- *The dramaturgical model:* treats episodes as if they were stage performances; involves concepts like "role," "script," "setting," "costume," etc.
- *The liturgical model:* treats social events as if they were rituals; involves concepts like "action," "conventional upshot," and so forth
- *The game model:* treats social events as if they were games – that is, rule-bound competitions with conventionally defined wins and losses; involves concepts such as "social strategy" and "social tactics," "social success," and "social failure"
- *The work model:* treats social events as if they were the production of social products; involves such concepts as the "production of the means of production of social events," "symbolic capital," and so on

Each of these models casts an oblique light on different aspects of a complex reality. If we are to follow the natural sciences in their triumphant unraveling of the secrets of nature, we must resist any attempt at setting up

a descriptive vocabulary for analyzing social episodes that is not specifically rooted in a well-organized set of analytical models.

Coordinating account analyses with observer attributions

The results of these model-controlled analyses must then be coordinated with the results of account analysis. Ideally, the analytical models employed by an outside observer ought to emerge as the very models that the actors used to create the social event in question and that were reflected in their accounts. Then we would have a fully coordinated system. If there is a lack of coordination, and unless there is positive evidence to the contrary, we have to assume that a discrepancy between observers' analyses and actors' accounts shows that the reality with which we are dealing is complex. In no circumstances can we say that the account analyses are false or defective, since they are authoritative as to the moment-by-moment interpretations that actors put upon events in face-to-face interaction; therefore, if the actor intends to insult someone and that person interprets the actor's actions as insulting, no outsider's reinterpretation can take away the fact that a public insult has occurred.

Example: "Football aggro"

The work of Peter Marsh (Marsh, Rosser, & Harré, 1978) in investigating the social psychological factors and processes involved in the violence that breaks out among fans at soccer games in Europe is a good example of the ethogenic method at work. Such violence involves rival supporters attacking and insulting each other and the police, disrupting the game, and has met with widespread public condemnation. The ethogenic study does not pretend to explain how particular soccer fans on particular occasions use their knowledge to put on performances of hooliganism but instead reveals the kind of knowledge, the kind of interpretations of meaning, beliefs, and so on, that the fans share as competent members of their group.

Accounts appear on two different kinds of occasions. When the fans themselves are discussing "aggro" within their own scheme, their accounts include very distinct rules for regulating action, for defining what is proper within the conventions of their micro-society. Those who break the rules, including the rules governing the interpretation of an action, are told the rules and then punished for breaking them. By investigating these accounts, Marsh was able to provide a systematic representation of members' knowledge, up to a certain point. Accounts were also produced in a second way, when Marsh himself asked fans to give their version of events.

Typically, these accounts gave a version different from that which had appeared in the national press. Marsh's own "outsider's analysis of 'aggro'" depended on the employment of the model of social ritual, and of a career structure within the microsociety that was ordered by the outcomes of the ritual events that the fans construed as "fights." Marsh's interactions with the fans took the form of a negotiation between himself, as outsider, proposing analytical models, and the fans, as insiders, dialectically relating their accounts to his. It turned out that accounts by other outsiders – particularly the descriptions of events in newspapers – were something yet again. They were best seen as social actions that themselves needed interpretation, forming a further and more complex framework in which the fans' actions were treated as part of a wider social activity in which other citizens, the police, and little old ladies were engaged.

But the knowledge that was obviously being used by the fans in categorizing members of their own and other groups into different social classes, relative to the aggro events that were the center of the whole business, showed that some further investigative technique was required. To understand the way in which costumes were read as symbolic representations of social status, Marsh constructed a Kelly Repertory Grid to explore the code of interpreting different items of clothing at soccer games. This revealed a very specific symbolic system that had perhaps never been explicitly formulated by any fan but was clearly operating as a kind of language throughout their activities. Stages in their careers were marked by the addition of scarfs, boots, rosettes, and so on; symbolic accessories that, as their personal fame grew, were quietly dropped.

Two models were at work in the organization of this investigation. A general dramaturgical model controlled the way in which events were analyzed on the larger scale: drawing our attention to specific settings for action, to the existence of a "script," and to categories of persons who see to it that the script is realized in the proper fashion, and to the use of distinctive costume to identify particular social categories of actors. A liturgical model drew attention to the ritualistic aspects of much of the activity. The interpretative procedure by which fans themselves talk of these events as "fights" is a device that is shared with the newspaper reporters, who use a similar language. But use of the liturgical model suggests a closer look at what constitutes a fight, bringing to the observer's attention the symbolic nature of much of the action.

The final story of football aggro is, then, essentially complex. The yield from the kind of ethogenic investigation that Marsh made is a description of the ideal resources required by a fan perfectly competent in football aggro.

Systems of knowledge

How, then, should the yield from such an investigation be structured? Other work has suggested that such systems of knowledge ought to be organized in the following way.

- The most general distinction is that between socially differentiated situations. For example, a soccer fan can recognize a distinction between a confrontation with the members of another club and the stories that are told about it in the pub after the game. Each distinctive social situation has a distinctive system of conventions that controls the interpretation of propriety of action in these situations (Argyle, Furnham, & Graham, 1981).
- Each situation also has its authorities on proper action; these are usually distinctive people, whose reactions are noticed by the others and used as a guide to correct behavior.
- Studies by Rosser (1977) and others have shown that part of the resources needed by a competent social actor is a knowledge of the forms of self-presentation appropriate to particular situations. Should one appear shy, retiring, soft-spoken, and eager to please, or hard, abrasive, touchy, and difficult? Each kind of situation calls for a distinctive personal display, and part of the resources of a competent social actor is a knowledge of the conventions governing such display.

How to study performance

Before we turn to detailed examples of methodologies for studying performances, let us review the basic theory of how actions are produced. An individual actor (say a child squabbling with another child over possession of toys) sets – or is set – a goal, conceived within the demands of the social situation as seen by the child. The child then thinks of a *means* of achieving that *end*, or goals. But these means generally involve intermediate ends, each with its own means. This creates a means–end hierarchy that could diagrammed as in Figure 5.1.

In some cases, the relationship between the ultimate end and the intermediate ends will be isomorphic with (parallel or similar in meaning to) the distinction between the act (or acts) achieved in a social interaction and the actions by which they are performed. Each action can be seen as an accomplishment (or end) for which there are appropriate movements (means). So the means–end hierarchy lets us analyze the conduct of the persons engaged in the action in terms of a threefold distinction: movement, action, act. In general, this theory takes on a cybernetic cast, because the means–end hierarchy is further structured by the existence of feed-back and feed-forward loops, so that goal setting can be continuously revised.

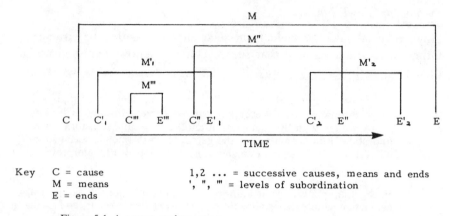

Key   C = cause   1,2 ... = successive causes, means and ends
      M = means   ', ", ''' = levels of subordination
      E = ends

Figure 5.1 A means–end structure.

It is natural to interpret the nesting of the means–end structure as representing two different relationships between ends and intermediate ends.
One relationship is that (already mentioned) between acts, actions, and
movements, which may have no relation to any layout of "thoughts" in real
time and could be of classificatory significance only. On the other hand,
there are many incidents and activities in which the intermediate ends do
temporally precede the ultimate end, and a graph of the hierarchy could
also be thought of as representing the time span controlled by particular
goals, so that a long-term end can be linked to the terminology current in
phenomenological psychology. I shall call the representation of long-term
ends *projects*, and the representation of short-term ends *intentions*. Means
for realizing both projects and intentions may be very varied, and may be
represented by items as different as rules, conventions, habits, manuals,
prayer books, exhortations of shamans, and so on.

How one devises a method for studying the way in which means–end
hierarchies are formed and the role they play in the production of action as
a real process depends upon this distinction between projects and intentions. *Projects* are relatively permanent features of a person's life. To find
out about them, we would do an investigation very similar to the ones using account analysis and observer's attributions that have been described
earlier. Projects somewhat resemble the permanent resource structure of
social knowledge that an actor draws upon in performances. The most
powerful method that has been devised so far for studying projects is the
de Waele assisted autobiography, in which, by a systematic analysis and
augmentation of an individual's recollections, the investigator and his or
her team are able to discover various themes that are present in a particular

life course. Some of these themes – those that are clearly enough directed toward goals – can serve as the representation of projects. To become a competent violinist, or be a graduate, or to be an accepted member of the upper middle class, would all be projects in this sense.

It is more difficult to study means and ends in relation to short-term goals and intentions, because of people's tendency to concentrate so hard on the end that they forget the means. We need a method for studying intention/rule-of-realization pairs that are actually in use *at a particular moment in real time*. It should be quite obvious that the use of account analysis cannot assist in the study of performance and its mode of production. There is no particular reason to think that a person in normal circumstances would be able to give a moment-by-moment description of how he or she set intermediate goals, ran over his or her knowledge of appropriate means, chose from various alternatives that which was most suitable for the occasion in question and then followed it. It would be very surprising if a person in normal circumstances consciously paid attention to such processes. In fact, if one were to do so, action would be paralyzed.

Fortunately, a psychological phenomenon known as the *hesitation phenomenon* has enabled us to develop a method to use in studying the production of action in real time. Linguists and others have observed that when the system (whatever it may be) that an individual is using to produce a speech or some other kind of public performance is about to break down, there is a hesitation in the smooth flow of the action. At these points research has shown that the individual actor has become momentarily conscious of the means–end hierarchy, or some portion of it in use at that time. Perhaps this is an adaptive psychological device by which breakdown is dealt with and smooth action restored. By taking an actor back over a recording of a performance to those moments where there are marked hesitations in the action, the momentary conscious representation in the intention-rule pair in play at that moment can be made available for report.

Two distinct methods have been developed from this phenomenon.

- By examining a number of parallel cases and looking for different points of breakdown in similar kinds of action, production, recording, and playing back for the actor, it is possible (at least theoretically) to cover a considerable amount of the production process, since the random distribution of accidents allows one to investigate the process from beginning to end. But one can hardly rely on accidents to achieve total coverage. Indeed, there is some evidence that there are certain nodal points around which accidents tend to cluster. However, it is still worth the attempt, and the work of Hacker (1982) has demonstrated that, at least for certain short action sequences, the recording, playback, and investigation of hesitation phenomena do pay off, in that the actor can report having paid attention to a fragment of the means–end hierarchy.

- But conscious representation of means–end hierarchies would be a far
  more powerful method if the breakdown could be controlled. Considerable success has been achieved by Von Cranach and his team in setting up
  relatively realistic social events in which there is a continuous breakdown,
  achieved by subtle choice of task and actor (Von Cranach & Harré, 1982).

Von Cranach's most successful attempt at contriving continuous breakdown depended upon choosing actors to work together on projects that
were already known to involve disagreements as to how to proceed. In
these circumstances he was able to demonstrate that there was practically
continuous breakdown of automatic, smooth-working means–end hierarchies. In some cases, almost every step was queried, and each means–
end element negotiated. The task was complex. A married couple were
asked to wrap a baby carriage in paper and string. Various kinds of material were available, including strong but ugly paper, rope, and ribbon,
as well as fragile but decorative wrapping material. In some cases the
husband-and-wife team shared a very large proportion of the goals and
intermediate goals that were involved in the process. In those cases there
was very little breakdown and little access to consciously represented
means–end structures. But in some cases the goals were different enough,
from the start, to produce continuous breakdown. For instance, in some
cases the husband wished to wrap the carriage securely, without particular
attention to how it would look, whereas the wife was less interested in
security and more in appearance. In those cases every step was negotiated,
and every move queried. Von Cranach was able to record these negotiation processes and to discover a large part of the means–end hierarchy.

This method is comparatively new. It has been used in eastern Europe
for the study of industrial processes and has yielded much the same kind of
result (Hacker, 1982). It is clear that the production of action does involve
means–end hierarchies and that a good deal of the goal setting is available
to conscious representation if difficulties occur.

However, not all means–end hierarchies involve conscious or uncon-
scious cognitive goal setting and a search of our resources of knowledge for
the appropriate means of reaching the goal. We have already noticed that
there are times when the actions performed by human beings in coordina-
tive episodes are more like habits, and even sometimes preprogrammed
routines. In such cases one can use experiments of the traditional kind,
identifying dependent and independent variables and testing for relationships by manipulation. But this simple method can work only if we are
justified in presuming that each habit or routine is independent of other
parts of the action; that is, that the action sequence is not structurally
integrated in such a way that the meaning that each element has depends

upon its location in the structure. It is clear that relative to the act-action-movement distinction reflected in the structure of means–end hierarchies, the level at which experimental manipulation will work is that of the lowest subroutines, since they can be shifted from episode to episode as wholes. A kiss is an osculation, whether given by Judas Iscariot or the president of France. It is only when we rise to the level of action and act that the structural limitation on experiments becomes crucial. Since all our categorizations must be "top down" – that is, we must use acts to identify actions, and actions to identify relevant movements – the simple experiment can find a place in empirical social psychology and indeed in various other branches of psychology (industrial, developmental, and so on) only as the very last stage of an empirical investigation. It is called for only when we think we have analyzed a means–end hierarchy so finely that we have reached the subroutines that are common to a very large number of different structures.

However, this kind of investigation also requires developmental studies attempting to identify the origins of subroutines, in order to distinguish between those subroutines that are physiologically based and depend more or less directly from genetic endowment, and those that are the product of social phenomena like training and education. Bruner (1973) has shown that in many cases it is a combination of these conditions – genetic pre-programming and socially determined educational practices – that builds up a complex routine out of subroutines. Shotter (1975) has described this as the acquisition of personal powers on the basis of natural powers.

How to test hypotheses

The methodology of the natural sciences suggest that one should check an analysis by recreating the original entity – that is, that an experiment recreates a real-life situation. What would be an analogue of this traditional test procedure in the analysis of the psychological phenomena that generate social activity? We already have an institution, found in almost every society, in which syntheses of social reality are routinely performed – namely, drama. The playwright and the actor, working with a producer, are concerned to reproduce a slice of life. Of course, there are all kinds of different projects involved in the performance of drama, ranging from mere entertainment to religious ritual and symbolic representations of universal truths. For our purposes, we will focus on only one feature of drama, namely that aspect in which the events that are the staged simulations of social episodes are like or unlike, convincing or unconvincing representations, of naturalistic episodes of social life (Ginsburg, 1979).

It turns out that there are two distinct ways in which the relative naturalism of a performance being deliberately staged is tested. Some systematic work on this has been done by Coppieters (1977) and Mixon (1972). In their investigations they each demonstrated a different way in which the realism of a drama is testable. Coppieters studied audience reactions very closely. At different times after a performance he compared an audience's expectations, moment-by-moment experiences, and remembered reactions. He was able to demonstrate that people have strong intuitions as to the social and psychological authenticity of the staged performance.

It is not really surprising that audiences have strong intuitive judgments as to whether or not a simulated social event is a believable representation of real life. Even more interesting is the result that Mixon first demonstrated and that has since been amply confirmed (also by Coppieters). Actors themselves become emotionally involved in the action as if the events were real (Zimbardo, 1973). Mixon's classical study of the Milgram experiment involved hypotheses as to the rule systems and means–end structures that were involved in the various reactions to Milgram's instructions to deliver dangerous electric shocks. By asking the actors – in this case ordinary people recruited as actors – to take part in several short plays, whose scenarios were various versions of the rules, interpretations, and means–end hierarchies thought to be involved in the original Milgram experiments, Mixon was able to demonstrate that even though the actors were fully aware that what was occurring was just a simulation of the real events, they nevertheless experienced genuine emotions and strong intuitions as to the believableness of the reconstruction. In this way, by using the results of the two methods outlined earlier, the intuitions of the people can be used as a direct test of the plausibility of the proposed rules and interpretations. This parallels exactly the use of native speakers' grammatical intuitions to test the correctness of grammar by using them to construct trial sentences.

The exercises

The method outlined in this chapter does not lend itself to short, simple, experimental studies. Ethogenic investigations are intended to uncover the social knowledge and skill required for some fairly complex forms of social life, such as the intimate culture of a family, the modes of adaptation to life in a monastery, soccer violence, and so on. For the purposes of this manual, three documents have been chosen, representing typical social episodes drawn from specific ways of life. (These particular exemplars are all episodes involving natives of Great Britain.) Only certain limited aspects of the actual events that took place are recorded in the documents. Appendix 1 is a transcript of a commonplace episode with which most people are familiar at firsthand – a medical consultation. But more is going on here than the exchange of symptoms and cure. The second document (appendix 2) records an accounting session concerning episodes that take place offstage, so to speak, and of which we, as analysts, have no direct record. In the third exercise (appendix 3) a record of an episode and of an account of this episode are both presented. The fourth exercise uses documents prepared by the researchers themselves.

In each case the exercise involves the analysis of written records of the speech and other social performances that formed part of a social episode. Written records or documents are interesting in their own right. For instance, one can ask how they are created out of the material available and how the selection and presentation of material is related to the interests of the person who wrote the document. It is well established that grammatical form may be a poor guide to the social force of the speech: For instance, the sentence "Why don't we have supper now?" is not really a question. The documents presented here could be quite misleading as to the social processes of the structured interactions they are supposed to represent if we only took account of their obvious linguistic features. To overcome such difficulties involves a highly skilled technique, which it is possible to test out in Exercise 3.

A tentative analysis of each document is expected from each participant in the exercise. A useful method for coding one's results is the Social Cognitive Matrix, in which the social knowledge of each participant involved in the episode, described and manifested in his or her speech and action, can be recorded systematically (Table 5.1). Empirical studies have shown that individual people know a great many such systems of rules and interpretations, sometimes as many as 13 or 14. The cognitive resources of each person involved in an episode should be coded in this form.

This matrix representation allows for the systematic analysis of episodes that consist of more than one phase of social interaction, where the situation may be redefined and the rules and personality display thereby changed. It also allows for the possibility that each interactant may see the social forces and meaning of the episode differently, so that each actor may yield a different matrix.

Discussions among analysts, after they have prepared an analysis of participants' social knowledge, can serve not only to sharpen their analytical skills but may also help to open up the idea that any social episode may be in reality a complex and multifaceted entity, which is capable of

Table 5.1. *Social cognitive matrix*

Knowledge unit	Social situation as defined	Rule system assumed to be operative	Personality displayed	Arbiter of social propriety
1 [Example]	Informal: morning coffee as friendship ritual in suburban home	Guest served first, milk + sugar, offered, cookies etc. Topic for talk rules, etc. Arrival and departure rules, etc.	Solicitous; in-formal; symbols: tidiness in appearance.	Imagined presence of spouse or local minister

several complementary analyses, each of which is true. It is not at all un-usual for several different social events to be going on at once, all within the same episode.

Ideally, exercises like this should use material created by the analysts themselves, using video and audio recording and supplemented with their own observations. Only in a multimedia approach are the ways people create and manage everyday life likely to be shown in a reasonably com-prehensive way.

All four exercises are aimed at discovering social resources; that is, the *knowledge* of rules and interpretations that competent actors require. Real-time performance studies are more difficult. Techniques for studying the use people make of means–end hierarchies in bringing their resources to bear on their conduct can be found in Von Cranach and Harré (1982).

Exercise 1

This exercise involves analyzing a document representing a social episode to detect the social meaning of the actions performed – for instance, whether what someone says is a plea, a request, a reprimand, and so on – and the means by which the occasion is used as a platform or stage on which to show to others the kind of person one wants to be seen as. By answering the following questions, students should begin to get a feel for the kind of analysis involved.

- What was the ostensible or official goal of the interaction?
- By what speech forms (for example, questions and answers) was it carried forward? What vocabulary did it employ: for example, everyday, technical, or typically male?
- What was the actual goal of the participants in interacting the way they

did? If different from the official goal, by what signs are alternative goals manifested?

- By what speech and action was the project to achieve an unofficial goal carried forward?
- Describe the personalities of the various interactants. Identify any specific speech forms in which those personalities were particularly clearly presented.
- Who directs what happens?

Findings should be set out as three sets of "rules":

- Rules for defining the meaning of the events that took place. For example, how is reassurance achieved?
- Rules for controlling the development of the episode. For example, how are diversions cut off?
- Conventions for the display of personality and social role. For example, the use of "we" rather than "I" by those in authority.

For a discussion of more detailed analyses of the social meaning of pronouns, see Kroger (in press).

Exercise 2

A common task for account analysts is to identify a complex hierarchy of definitions with which a certain category of actions is being managed in talk that is being used to justify some action of the speakers. For instance, by studying apologies one might be able to build a classification of insults. One might start by differentiating verbal insults from insulting gestures. Were insults based on physical defects treated differently from those based on character defects? Are any categories of insults so deadly that no apology would possibly repair the social damage they inflict?

In appendix 2 an English schoolboy gives an account of what bullying means to him. The account is also a social action in itself. It must be seen as a production for the ears of the investigator, aimed at displaying what the speaker conceives to be an appropriate personality. This document should first be used to set up a hierarchical classification scheme for acts of bullying and then to relate the justifications for bullying, implicit in the account, to that scheme. Remember that the classification schemes are a reflection of the document. It was produced for a complex of social purposes. The second stage of analysis involves identifying some of those purposes. Can any of the features of any of the definitions of bullying that are offered be related to those purposes? In a full-scale study of bullying, this definitional study would be related to studies of episodes defined as bullying that are actually occurring in a school playground and to the moment-by-moment commentary on those sequences provided by victim and aggressor.

There is no special reason for using the particular document printed in appendix 2 as the material for this exercise. It may be profitable to create your own documents representing occasions on which someone provided a commentary on a social event. *Under no circumstances* should this way of creating documents be called "data collection." The document is the datum, not that which it purports to describe. The document is a text, for which the analyst must provide an interpretation.

Exercise 3

A social episode is created by the interactions of two or more actors. In the course of an episode, various social effects are brought about, such as change of an actor's status. Sometimes the actors have similar projects, and sometimes they have dissimilar ones. To understand an episode we have to try to find out what projects the actors might have, so that our study can be directed to the way actors go about realizing their aims and plans. This is what Goffman (1969) has called the "strategic" aspect of an interaction.

But to work all this out one must first be able to identify the social force of what the actors have done or said, and what they have said about what they have done, are doing, or are about to do. This involves assigning meanings to the events that make up the episode. For practical reasons, the exercises in this chapter have to be confined to unraveling the meaning of a reported conversation. Real life involves much more. But even to read a conversation, you must be able to "hear" it. To facilitate this, we ask analysts to practice the skill of reading for social meaning by running through appendix 3 and underlining the words that they think would have been stressed by the speaker. This should be followed by a second reading in which stress is placed on different words. Analysts should test their intuition by asking themselves and their fellow students whether this new stress pattern alters the interpretation of the social force of what the actors are saying.

Stress markings should be checked against those suggested by Kreckel in the second part of appendix 3: Her stress markings are derived from a discussion with the family among whom the conversation took place as to the social force of the speeches and the means by which this force was indicated and understood (Kreckel, 1982). They represent the actors' account of how they conducted a family discussion.

Using one of the stress-marked versions of this conversation, specific social interpretations of speech incidents should be identified, using commonsense categories such as plea, complaint, and so on. These interpretations are hypotheses that can be tested by following the conversation through to pick up later speech incidents that seem to be dependent on particular interpretations of earlier remarks. At this stage, the structure of the episode can be described in terms of the categories that have been tested in interpreting the social force of the speeches recorded. Regularities, say between complaints and countercomplaints, can be expressed as rules.

Two hypothetical conversational fragments could now be constructed, using commonsense categories such as those used to analyze the example above. One fragment should preserve the overall social force of the conversation, and one should change it. These abstract structures can be fleshed out in imagined speech. Thus, if Complaint–Remedy appears as a regularity, it could be fleshed out as "Why don't you pay any attention to what I say?" "Sorry, I was thinking of something else." The technique of creating a dialogue from speech-act categories is a useful technique. It is used to construct scenarios to test the intuitive reasonableness of the structures one has built up on the basis of hypotheses about the rules followed explicitly or implicitly by the actors (for more details, see Harré, 1979, Chapter 3).

The imagined conversations should be tested on other people for naturalness. In this way intuitions of social propriety can be used to test hypotheses about the expressive techniques used by speakers to convey social force.

Exercise 4

Among the items of social knowledge a competent social actor must have access to are the rituals by which social relations are transformed from one stage to another. We are all familiar with formal rituals such as marriage and graduation ceremonies. But there are also informal rituals. For example, Douglas has suggested (1972) that different forms of hospitality can be used to mark successive stages in a relationship. Since the events in question are usually spread out over a considerable period of time, participants in this exercise are asked to keep a "friendship diary" for 2 or 3 months. In this diary they should record the sequences of invitation to coffee, meals, and so forth, through which a relationship was built up and ritualistically ratified. There has been some controversy about how far such rituals permeate the whole of society. Results from this exercise can be compared with the sequences described by Douglas in her article "Deciphering a Meal" (1972).

Strengths and limitations of ethogenic analysis

The method of studying the way people talk about and justify their actions to one another, coupled with the use of analytical models such as the dramaturgical analogy, is meant to be used to investigate a whole form of life. The actors are conceived as knowing what is required of them, though that knowledge may be divided among the members of a group. The basic psychological process involved in social action is taken to be expressed in the cybernetic model, here called a means–end hierarchy. In practice this will often be experienced by an actor as following a rule or convention to realize some intention or other. What is intended is thought of as part of what is required to carry out some project, such as acquiring a hoped-for social status.

The method is not addressed to the study of those smaller-scale units of human behavior that have been referred to here as "routines." The study of how someone puts together a complex sequence of movements into a handshake, or a deferential retreat, or something of that sort would require very different methods. There are also limitations on how far one can generalize from the way reasoning presents itself to someone as he or she is consciously working something out, the process assessed by the methods of Von Cranach, to the structure of nonconscious "information" processing. In the former case, the conventions and mode of organization of a person's native language play a central part, but it is not at all clear how to understand the processes involved in the latter.

References

Argyle, M., Furnham, A., & Graham, J. A. (1981). *Social Situations*. Cambridge: Cambridge University Press.

Bruner, J. (1973). Organization of early skilled action. *Child Development* 44, 1–11.

Collett, P., & Marsh, P. (1974). Patterns of public behaviour: collision avoidance on a pedestrian crossing. *Semiotica*, 12, 281–89.

Coppieters, F. (1977). *Theoretical recollections: a psychological study*. Unpublished doctoral dissertation, University of Antwerp.

De Waele, J.-P., & Harré, R. (1979). Autobiography as a psychological method. In G.P. Ginsburg (ed.), *Emerging Strategies in Social Psychological Research*. New York: Wiley.

Douglas, M. (1972). Deciphering a meal. *Daedalus*, Winter.

Ginsburg, G.P. (1979). The effective use of role-playing in social psychological research. In G.P. Ginsburg (ed.), *Emerging Strategies in Social Psychological Research*. New York: Wiley.

Goffman, E. (1969). *Strategic Interaction*. Philadelphia: University of Pennsylvania Press.

Hacker, W. (1982). Objective and subjective organization of working activities. In M. Von Cranach and R. Harré, *The Analysis of Action: Recent Theoretical and Empirical Advances*. Cambridge: Cambridge University Press.

Harper, R.G., Wiens, A.M., & Metarezzo, J.D. (1978). *Non-Verbal Communication: The State of the Art.* New York: Wiley.

Harré, R. (1979). *Social Being.* Oxford: Blackwell.

Harré, R., & Secord, P.F. (1973). *The Explanation of Social Behaviour.* Oxford: Blackwell.

Hollis, M. (1977). *Models of Man.* Cambridge: Cambridge University Press.

Kreckel, M. (1982). *Communicative Acts and Shared Knowledge in Natural Discourse.* New York: Academic Press.

Kroger, R. (in press). Explorations in ethogeny: with special reference to the rules of address. *American Psychologist.*

Lyman, S.M., & Scott, M.B. (1970). *A Sociology of the Absurd.* New York: Appleton-Century-Crofts.

Marsh, P., Rosser, E., & Harré, R. (1978). *The Rules of Disorder.* London: Routledge & Kegan Pual.

Mixon, D. (1972). Instead of deception. *Journal for the Theory of Social Behaviour, 2,* 145–74.

Rosser, E. (1977). New directions in social psychology: the ethogenic approach with special reference to adolescent perceptions of the social world. B. Litt. dissertation, Oxford University.

Shotter, J. (1975). Acquired powers: the transformation of natural into personal powers. In R. Harré (ed.), *Personality.* Oxford: Blackwell.

Von Cranach, M., & R. Harré (1982). *The Analysis of Action: Recent Theoretical and Empirical Advances.* Cambridge: Cambridge University Press.

Walsh, D. (1972). Varieties of positivism. In P. Filmer et al. *New Directions in Sociological Theory.* London: Collier Macmillan.

Weiner, A.B. (1976). *Women of Virtue, Men of Renown.* Austin: University of Texas Press.

Zimbardo, P.G. (1973). The mind is a formidable jailer: a Pirandellian prison. *New York Times*, April 8, 1973.

Appendix 1. Document for Exercise 1

Doctor (DR) seated at desk; knock at the door.

DR: Come in.	Mother (M) and daugher (D) enter.
Mother (M): Morning.	
DR: Morning, hello, sit yourselves down.	Similing, gesturing to chair.
M: (to D) What have you got to say?	Still smiling.
DR: (to D) Hello.	Generally, not looking at anyone.
Daughter (D): Hello.	
DR: Sit yourself down.	
M: I haven't had time to read it yet. I was going to read it on the way down. What does it say? Tell me.	
DR: What?	Still smiling.

Patient starts to read anyway so no reply given. Patient reading while removing daughter's coat. Reads for approximately 9 seconds.

DR: Don't let it worry you.	
M: It needn't worry me?	
DR: No.	
M: Oh all right.	Immediately looks up.
DR: Now what can I do for you?	
M: We've got boils on our backside . . . again.	Immediately looks up. Waves hand.
DR: Again?	
M: (to D) Stand up. Can you stand up?	Looks away at notes. Picking her up.
DR: Let's us have a look.	DR has been sitting back in chair looking at mother up to this point. Now starts looking at daughter.
M: (to D) With your back to Dr. S. That's a good girl. Stand up there and we'll show him your bum. There's a good girl.	

M: (to DR) Now they haven't really cleared up and gone away sufficiently, but I've now got to the stage where I think that something really ought to be done about it.

DR: Uh huh. Are these the same ones that she's had, or do they keep on . . .

M: Oh no . . .

DR: Keep on . . .   Examining bottom.

M: You can see all down her leg look.

DR: Uh huh. See, all right.   Reassurance to daughter whilst stroking affected area with finger. Daughter twisting to look.

M: (to D) Stand up nice and straight.

DR: Yes, they're leaving little lumps aren't they?

M: Yes . . . and on the other side you see. But it's only round . . .

DR: It's only inside the . . .   Strokes relevant area.

M: Yes, but you see she's dry at night now.

DR: She's quite dry . . . yes.   DR moves away, looks at mother again.

M: I mean fair enough she wears a nappy because I don't want her . . . not to wear a nappy until after we've moved in, in case we sort of go back a step and then it will be . . . you know but er . . . she's dry, completely dry at night.

Note that the gaze pattern changes at this point to a regulative question and answer pattern.

DR: Has she had a cold at all?
A runny nose or anything.

M: No.

DR: And she's been all right in herself?

M: Yes apart from a cold she had. Yes all right.

DR: And you saw, well, Dr H. . . .   Looking at notes.

M: Dr H. I think was the last one we saw.

DR: About four months ago wasn't it?

M: Yes, well, maybe. I didn't think it was as long as that but perhaps it would . . . Yes it might be.

DR: Oh.   Continues looking. Keeps mother talking.

M: And, er, we bought some Sizal soap?

DR: Uh huh.

M: And, er, we washed with that but you know it didn't seem to . . .

DR: Uh huh . . . OK. No sort of runny nose or crusting in the nose or anything like that or so on?

M: No.

DR: All right.

                                                       Looks away and changes seating position completely. Moves to leg and feet under the desk. This changes the phase of the consultation? Takes out pen.

I think if it's persisting like this er . . . In fact I saw you before that didn't I?   Looking away reading notes.

M: Yes well, she's had them for I should think about a year now.	
DR: Uh huh.	Still writing.
M: Well I mean, I don't know but ...	
D: Go in Rober.	
M: You're going back in the Rover, yes.	
DR: Uh huh.	Still writing.
M: Show off.	Laughs.
DR: Uh huh. What?	Still writing. Laughs.
Oh yes.	Moves head from side to side, sharing in the joke.

Pause

DR: I'll give you some er ... some penicillin. You should give her one spoonful three times a day, for a week alright? I think you should carry on ...	
	Changes posture/seating position. Looks at mother from this point.
with some antiseptic baths ...	
M: Yes.	
Dr: I mean it is just a superficial er ... sort of skin infection.	
M: I tell you the stuff that cleared it up last time that you gave me was the stuff I put in the bath.	DR looks away. Starts up.
DR: Uh huh.	Still writing.
M: Whatever that was.	
DR: Hibitane.	Still writing.
M: Er ... but that cleared it up.	
DR: Do you remember how big the bottle was?	Reaching for a form.

M: Only a little one. An
    ordinary . . .

> Gestures to show size but DR not
> looking.

ordinary medicine size.   Laughing.
DR: Yes.

> Looks at mother. Laughs.
> Takes book for reference.

M: You sort of know that . . .

> Gestures again to show size. DR
> looking at book.

Long pause while mother looks at child, looks around room. DR consulting book and begins writing prescription.

DR: Er . . . It's a big bottle.   Still busy with papers.
     I had a letter from er . . . I
     can't remember who it was
     now . . .
M: (indistinct)
DR: T.
M: (indistinct) Yes.
DR: Er . . .. They're supplying all   Adjusts seating position to look at
     the . . .   mother.
M: Yes, I've given up . . . I
     mean
DR: Mm.   Looks away.
M: Especially I . . . you know I
     . . . I started my period last
     night. That just about did it.
     Ha. And er . . . I can't really
     . . . Can't be bothered with
     my . . . You know . . . If
     . . . If I knew . . . that I was
     going to . . .

> Gestures.
> Still looking away.
> Looks at doctor.

. . . happen within a year,
then fair enough. Do you
know what I mean?
DR: Mm.
M: Er . . . I don't . . . I've got to   Nod, still looking at her.

the stage where I can't even talk about it.

    Attempts to compose herself. Adjusts seating position. Puts down child. Looks away, fumbles with paper, deep breath, straightens skirt, shakes head, waves hand, stands up.

D: Are you coming?

  M: Er . . . I'd better go.

    Stationary.

DR: Do you want to talk about it? I Mean . . .   Waves hand.

  M: Not really . . .   Standing obliquely to DR.

Not really er . . .   Raises hand to lips (obviously on the point of tears).

Because I feel such an idiot.   Brushes hair with hand, turning even more away from DR.

Er, I don't want to talk about it.   Heading for door, sniffs, takes door handle, stops.

Oh Dear.   Sniffs.

I can't walk out like this, can I? 'Bye.

DR: Do you want to come and talk about it some other time when you're not . . .

  M: No it's hard to get rid of . . .   Laughs.

I won't let go you see.   Laughs.

DR: Laughs.

  M: Cheers anyway. Thanks very much.   Exits.

DR: Alright. 'Bye.   Looks away.

End

Appendix 2. Document for Exercise 2

Paul (P): What do you mean "bully"?

Interviewer (I): Well, that's for you to decide. You tell me what you
think bullying is.

P: What, picking on other kids, or smaller ones or bigger ones?

I: Well, that's for you to say.

P: Depends on what you call bullying. Some people just pick on 'em or
beat 'em, you know, hit them. Some people tease 'em. There's a lot
that goes on around here now.

I: There's a lot of . . .

P: More of a joke really. Most people do it. More of a laugh. Some
people take it serious, some don't.

I: Do you think it's possible that sometimes if you mean it as a joke, it's
not taken as a joke by others?

P: It means you're word powerful. If you say something and they get
offended, but you say it as a joke. They say "Oh teacher, they are
bullying me." Some of them go running to teachers all the time.

I: Who gets bullied?

P: Mainly the Pakis [Pakistani students, minority in Britain]. Mainly.

I: Why's that?

P: Well, for what they are.

I: Why do you think that, then?

P: I don't really like them, but . . . I don't really pick on them.

I: What about the chap outside? [Referring to tall, easy-going Pakistani
kid]

P: Well, he's all right. He's our pal. Get on well with him.

I: Well, he's a Paki, isn't he?

P: He's a Paki, but I still don't like them. I don't like many blacks, but
some are all right. Some aren't.

I: What about F? (Referring to black kid known to be P's closest friend)

P: Well, he's all right. I go around with him. Some blacks get on my
nerves.

I: Don't some whites get on your nerves as well?

P: Oh yes. I mean, if someone causes trouble they can *look* for trouble.
And they don't. Mainly black versus white. What it usually is,
anyway.

I: The thing I don't understand, Paul, is that you say it's mainly black
versus white, but one of your best friends is black. And you just said
it's Pakis that get picked on. And I said "Well, what about the one
outside?," and you said "Oh no, well, he's a good guy."

P: Depends if you know 'em. I mean I know him. We get on all right. But you get some other kid, third or fourth year or something you don't know. You always as they come past say "Paki" or "Greasy git" or something. It's so common. Everyone says it. Even the girls say it.

I: Don't you think some kids might be hurt by that?

P: Some of them are. Some of them go around the corner and call you all sorts of names.

I: Doesn't it matter to you that they are hurt by this?

P: Depends who it is. Some of my friends. Probably yes. I think about it and won't do it again. Someone I don't know when you cross the road and you never seen them before, wouldn't care.

I: What sorts of people would you have as your friends?

P: A lot of people I know. Mainly from this school. I mean D, and other people I never knew them before I came to this school. We have our arguments. But it's all in a joke way. Some take it serious and some don't.

Appendix 3. Document for Exercise 3

Note: the first transcription of the conversation between Marian and Tom is printed in the way it would appear in a play or novel. But to rid ourselves of our normal ways of understanding printed conversations, our usual ways of representing conversation must be eliminated. Comparison between the ordinary (the first) representation and the stress-marked (the second) unpunctuated version of the conversation (following the method used by Kreckel [1982]) should make this clear.

Throughout the episode Marian is eating.

Conventionally printed dialogue

T: Important are they?

M: ... to me they are. To you they probably don't mean a bloody thing, but there you are.

T: Such as?

M: One, for a start, get the main one over with ...

T: Marriage.

M: Yes.

T: Well, what did I tell you what was it, about two ...

M: I know what you told me – you told Mum different.

T: I see ...

M: You told Mum different.

T: I told ... What I told your mum love is only what I told you a few weeks ago.

M: You never told me you'd never marry me, that's what you told Mum.

T: I see ... that's it ... we've had this out with your mum already, love. I didn't say I wouldn't marry you.

M: Nobody bloody includes me.

T: Because I tell you, I said I didn't fancy getting married just at the moment, not just jet.

M: Why not?

T: I want to wait until we've been in the flat right?

M: I don't want to go in the flat again.

T: I just ... hang about ... see, you won't hear me out.

M: Go on then. Go on.

T: I want to wait until we've been in the flat, right.

M: Yes.

T: Been in there a couple of months, got the place all done out, get all the knickknacks in there, right?

M: It don't want much doing to it, and we ain't go many knickknacks.

T: But I mean ... I tell you what ...

M: So that is a poor excuse, I'm afraid, and if you can't come up with something better than that then you know what to do.

T: Well I told you about the 27th of April and that yous made that date up between yous, didn't yous?

M: If it was left up to you to do any arranging at all you'd never bloody get it done.

T: Course I would.

M: Arseholes.

T: Well, I just don't like ... outsiders, people, lot of people interfering.

M: Well bloody do it yourself then, other people wouldn't interfere now, would they? You made a promise to me and you're bloody ...

T: All right, then, all right then, fair enough then. I'll get a place, I'll get a place to my liking, and that, and get married then.

M: Oh to your liking then? Doesn't matter about me.

T: All right, then, our liking then. You can't move in just like that. Can you?

M: We've got most of it anyway.

T: Such as?

M: We've got paper for a start. That's a good start that is.

T: What paper's that?

M: Wallpaper, dear.

T: What – them five rolls what you got down at your Gran's or something? Well, where will they go? What will they cover?

M: I don't know. I mean you could put something on one wall and have a contrast on the others. It don't cost much for a tin of paint. At least that's something done. It don't cost much for a tin of paint, does it?

T: No, it doesn't.

M: Well, there you are, then. We're halfway there already with it decorated.

T: Oh you are.

M: Don't you laugh at me, mate.

T: I'm not. I've always got a smile on my face. You know that.

M: Arseholes.

T: I have.

M: You have not, you have not.

T: I have, I'm always happy.

M: Arseholes. So you're going to name a date then?

T: Yeah. But it won't be in the next two months, though – two or three months.

M: Why not?

T: I don't want to get married in the next two or three months.

M: Why not?

T: I just don't want to.

Stress-marked dialogue

T: *important* are they

M: to *me* they *are*

to *you* they probably don't mean a bloody thing but *there* you are

T: *such* as

M: *one*

for a *start*

get the *main* one over with

T: *marriage*

M: *yes*

T: well what did I *tell* you

what was it *about* two

M: I know what you told *me*

you told Mum different

T: I see

M: *you* told Mum *different*

T: I told

what I told your *mum* love is only what I told you a few *weeks* ago

M: *you* never told me you'd *never* marry me

that's what you told *Mum*

T: I see that's *it*

we've had this out with your mum *already* love

I didn't say I *wouldn't* marry you

M: nobody bloody includes *me*

T: because I *tell* you I said I didn't fancy getting married just at the

moment not just yet

M: why *not*

T: I want to wait until we've *been* in the flat *right*

M: I don't *want* to go in the flat *again*

T: I

just *hang* about

see you won't hear me out

M: *go* on then *go* on

T: I want to wait until we've *been* in the flat *right*

M: yes

T: *been* in there a couple of months
 got the place all done out
 get all the knickknacks in there *right*
M: it *don't* want much doing to it and we ain't got many knickknacks
T: but I mean
 I *tell* you what
M: so that is a *poor* excuse I'm afraid and if you can't come up with
 something better than that then you know what to *do*
T: well I *told* you about the 27th of April and that *yous* made that date
 up *between* yous *didn't* yous
M: if it was *left* up to you to do *any* arranging at all you'd *never* bloody
 get it done
T: *course* I would
M: *arseholes*
T: well I just don't like *outsiders*
 people lot of *people* interfering
M: well bloody do it *yourself* then other people *wouldn't* interfere now
 would they *you* made a promise to me and *you're* bloody
T: *all right* then
 all right then
 fair *enough* then I'll get a place
 I'll get a place to my *liking* and that and get *married* then
M: oh to *your* liking then
 doesn't matter about *me*
T: *all right* then
 our liking then
 you can't move in just like *that*
 can you
M: we've got *most* of it *anyway*
T: *such* as
M: we've got *paper* for a start
 that's a *good* start
 that is
T: what *paper's* that
M: *wallpaper* dear
T: what them *five* rolls what
 you got down at your *Gran's*
 or something
 well where will *they* go
 what will *they* cover

M: *I* don't know
I mean you could put something on *one*
wall and have a *contrast* on the others
it *don't* cost much for a tin of *paint*
at least that's *something* done
it don't cost much for a tin of *paint* does it
T: no it *doesn't*
M: well there you *are* then
we're halfway there *already*
with it decorated
T: oh you *are*
M: don't you *laugh* at me mate
T: I'm not
I've always got a *smile* on my face
you know that
M: arseholes
T: *I* have
M: *you* have not
you have not
T: I *have*
I'm *always* happy
M: *arseholes*
so
you're going to name a *date* then
T: yea but it won't be in the next two months though
two or three months
M: why not
T: I don't want to get married in the next two or three *months*
M: why *not*
T: I just don't *want* to

Part II

Technique applications

6 Speech style and employment selection: the Matched Guise Technique

Peter Ball and Howard Giles

Summary

This exercise demonstrates the Matched Guise Technique, which is a method used to study speech in interpersonal evaluation. The design explores the impact of speech rate and pronunciation upon the ratings of an interviewee for a job, using the criteria of competence, pleasantness, and suitability for various types of work.

Introduction

This exercise illustrates the investigation of the contribution of speech style to employment selection by means of the Matched Guise Technique, originally devised by Lambert, Hodgson, Gardner, and Fillenbaum (1960). As an extra feature, the exercise includes a demonstration of the same social inference process in reverse: the assignment of speech style on the basis of information about a person's success or failure in seeking employment. The following content areas are covered:

- The influence of small social cues on decisions that have profound implications for the courses of people's lives
- Halo effects in social judgment
- Stereotyping of social and ethnic groups
- Social perception as an active process of assimilating new information to existing concepts

The student is introduced to the following methodological aspects of social psychology:

- Manipulation of individual social cues as independent variables in laboratory experiments – in this case, speed of speech and pronunciation – with experimental control over materials
- Use of rating scales and content analysis as alternative measurement devices

121

- Matching of subject groups on possible contaminating factors
- Checking the success of manipulations carried out

Speech style and social relations

Knowledge of the social significance of speech styles in interpersonal and intergroup relations has advanced rapidly in recent years (Shuy & Fasold, 1973; Giles & Powesland, 1975; Giles & St. Clair, 1979; Scherer & Giles, 1979; Ryan & Giles, 1982). The speech styles of dominant ethnic groups have been shown to carry advantages for their speakers in terms of impression formation, particularly as far as impressions of ability are concerned. In bilingual Canada, for example, Lambert (1967) observed that both English- and French-speaking Canadians ascribed greater intelligence, dependability, and ambition to English than to French speakers. Similar differences in favor of speakers of Received Pronunciation (commonly known as "BBC English"), the most prestigious English accent, were reported by Giles (1970, 1971) in Great Britain.

In the United States, it is often argued, accent does not carry such potent social significance as in Britain, yet Ryan and Carranza (1977) reported that speakers with Hispanic accents are assumed to have low ability, and Ryan and Bulik (1982) found German-accented speakers to be judged less positively than speakers with standard American accents by Anglo-American undergraduates on a series of scales, including social class, status, social distance, and intelligibility.

It is certainly true that most American research on the social significance of accent variations has drawn comparisons between standard American accents and the accents of immigrant and other minority group members with first languages other than English, rather than between the accents of Anglo-American groups from different regions or socioeconomic levels. Nevertheless, the presence in New York City of evening classes for adults anxious to shed their Bronx or Brooklyn accents and acquire speech styles more evocative of Middle America attests to the existence of a gap in the American research literature and a likelihood that the social significance of accent among the native English-speaking subculture has been underestimated. The challenge for students wishing to plug this gap in the research lies in identifying which accents are salient in their own local or regional circumstances, taking account of the group composition of the communities concerned (see the remarks on intergroup theory and social identity that follow).

Not all the sociolinguistic advantages turn out to lie with the dominant groups, particularly when listeners are not judging status and ability. It has frequently been found that subordinate groups exhibit loyalty to their own speech varieties, where judgments of social attractiveness, warmth, and generosity are concerned (Lambert, 1967; Strongman & Woosley, 1967; Giles, 1971) and that their views are shared, to some extent, by members of the dominant groups. Similarly, Stewart, Ryan, and Giles (1985), comparing American undergraduates' perceptions of speakers with English Received Pronunciation versus standard American accents, found that the former created impressions of higher status and faster speech, but that the listeners viewed them as harder to understand and felt less solidarity with them than with the American speakers.

Intergroup theory and social identity

Intergroup theory (Tajfel, 1978) suggests that individuals define themselves in terms of comparisons between their in-groups and relevant out-groups, attempting to maximize their distinctiveness by using criteria that favor the in-group. If frustrated in this, they may adopt strategies of "social creativity," devising new dimensions of intergroup comparison or just reversing their evaluation of dimensions yielding unfavorable comparisons with out-groups (for example, "Black is beautiful"). Speech is commonly used as a dimension of intergroup comparison in this way (Giles. Bourhis, & Taylor, 1977), with emphasis on language (Taylor, Bassili, & Aboud, 1973) or accent (Bourhis, Giles, & Tajfel, 1973) as part of minority-group members' identity. Individuals also change their styles of speech, accentuating their distinctiveness from the out-group when their identity is threatened (Bourhis & Giles, 1977; Bourhis, Giles, & Tajfel, 1979), so that when members of a subordinate group are trying to join the dominant group from below and members of the latter are creatively engaged in continual invention of new in-group markers, a "sociolinguistic pursuit race" may result. Ryan (1979) has answered the question of why, given the social disadvantages they present, low-prestige language varieties continue to exist. She argued that their speakers simply do not wish to give them up because these speech styles contribute to their sense of social-group identity. Nevertheless, even if they did relinquish such speech characteristics, they would be likely to find themselves merely speaking a new low-prestige variety as the dominant group changed its speech style to re-establish its distinctiveness.

Speech accommodation

A theory of speech accommodation has been developed to explain strategies of linguistic style shifting in interpersonal encounters (Giles, 1973; Giles & Smith, 1979; Thakerar, Giles, & Cheshire, 1982). Individuals generally modify their speech to make it more like that of the person they are addressing (*convergence*), especially when trying to create a good impression. This may be seen as intuitive application of similarity-attraction theory (Byrne, 1971) and the initiation of a social exchange transaction (Homans, 1961). When people perceive an encounter as hostile or wish to make it so, they are likely to *increase* interpersonal dissimilarities (*divergence*) on one or more linguistic levels (dialect, lexical diversity, etc.), as an intergroup strategy for accentuating distinctiveness. Since language varieties differ in prestige, accommodative shifts may be upward or downward on the status continuum. There is a perceptual side to this as well: the listener interprets convergence or divergence favorably or unfavorably, according to any evidence for a friendly, hostile, or ingratiating motive and according to the presence or absence of external coercion. Thus, Simard, Taylor, and Giles (1976) found that French-Canadian listeners responded more positively to nonconverging English-Canadian speakers who were known to have been forbidden to converge than to those who could have, if they had wished to do so, and likewise more positively to speakers who were shown to have made a convergent choice voluntarily than to those instructed to converge.

People's attitudes to speech varieties have practical consequences, and this has implications, in applied fields such as education and employment, that will be referred to later in this chapter. In second language learning, too, attitudes have been shown to affect motivation and, thereby, proficiency (Gardner & Lambert, 1972; Gardner, 1979). Second language learners have also been observed to feel that their social identity is threatened by increasing competence in their new language, and they may try to reaffirm it by divergently reinstating previously discarded foreign markers in their second language speech. In other words, they may even *retreat* from the proficiency they have attained in their second language, in order to maintain their psychological distinctiveness (cf. Lambert & Tucker, 1972).

Language, sex, and power

In what has been covered so far, the emphasis has been mainly on accent as a speech style type, but that is not necessarily the only speech style that could be considered. Since the early 1970s, there have been studies of male–female differences in speech and interpretations of the findings in terms of intergroup and power relations between the sexes (see Smith, 1985, for extensive coverage of this field). It has been argued that as far as English is concerned, language has been dominated by men and has evolved to suit their interests, rather than those of women. It has also been argued that women have developed a characteristically "powerless" style of speaking, consistent with a traditional social role as members of a subordinate sex. The issues in this area are subject to some dispute, and the actual sex differences in speech themselves are fairly small differences of degree, rather than categorical indicators. Nevertheless, one experimental study in Britain (Hogg, 1985) upheld a hypothesis, derived from intergroup theory and accommodation theory, that female speakers interacting with male speakers would tend to converge toward a masculine speech style when sex groupings were made salient, whereas their male counterparts would diverge toward a more masculine style than they would use when sex groupings were not made salient. Not a great deal of research on listener attitudes toward speech styles differing in masculinity or femininity has yet been reported, but variations on the present exercise, concentrating on sex-linked features of speech in relation to the theoretical principles already introduced, would be possible.

Matched Guise Technique

Some of the most important research leading to these theories has been conducted using Lambert's Matched Guise Technique (MGT) (Lambert et al., 1960). MGT is among a number of methods termed *verbal guise techniques* by Agheyisi and Fishman (1970) when they reviewed research methodology in language attitudes. Verbal guise techniques all involve presenting recorded speech to listeners who are required to estimate the speakers' capabilities, personalities, emotional states, and various other social or linguistic characteristics. In order to control speech content and emotional impact, speakers are normally asked to read a standard piece of prose, but naturalistic dialogues are also sometimes prepared. Stimulus recordings differ from each other in some aspect of speech that is being manipulated as an independent variable – usually the language itself (i.e., French, Spanish, etc., using a translated passage) or accent. The listeners' judgments are analyzed statistically to establish whether the linguistically contrasted "guises" convey significantly different impressions of the speakers.

MGT differs from other verbal guise techniques in that the guises are matched for vocal variables irrelevant to the hypotheses being tested, such as "breathiness" and fundamental voice frequency, since all are recorded by the same speakers, specially chosen for bilingual or bidialectal skills. "Buffer" stimulus recordings made by other speakers in their natural voices are often interspersed among the experimental stimuli, in studies involving repeated measures, to make it less likely that listeners will recognize successive presentations of the same speakers. Because of the tight control it provides, when materials are skillfully produced and thoroughly checked for authenticity MGT is a powerful research tool.

Despite its advantages, MGT has been criticized (Tajfel, 1962). Robinson (1972) suggested that guises merely help listeners identify speakers as members of social groups, to which they then apply the same stereotypes that they would use in responding to group labels (e.g., Katz & Braly's 1933 procedure). However, differences between stereotypes obtained with MGT and with mere labels have been found (Ball, 1983), so the former may be specifically sociolinguistic in nature. Lee (1971) raised three objections to MGT: false interguise contrasts, resulting from stimuli of identical verbal content; decontextualization of stimuli; and arbitrary selection of rating scales with undetermined reliability. Giles and Bourhis (1973), replying, stressed (1) that matched guise results had been confirmed by various methods free of Lee's first two criticisms; (2) that rating scales had been selected through pilot studies, though these were often unreported; and (3) that the results of comparable British MGT studies involving different materials and subject samples had been consistent. It could also be argued that the most usual treatment of data in such research, analysis of variance, incorporates a reliability check in the error term, so that genuinely unreliable measurement would lead to statistically insignificant results. What has enabled MGT to withstand these criticisms, though, is probably less the persuasiveness of its advocates than its sheer productivity in accumulating information useful in building theories about social evaluation and speech.

Naturalistic adaptation of verbal guise techniques

Although verbal guise techniques have been used mainly in laboratory research, removed from real social situations, these techniques are increasingly being adapted for use in the decision-making situations of everyday life, so that subjects take the experimental tasks more seriously and find them more meaningful. Extrapolation from the laboratory to the outside world also has practical consequences. For example, Seligman, Tucker, and Lambert (1972), in their work with Canadian schoolchildren and their teachers, using unmatched verbal guises (since children are seldom able to record matched guises), showed that voice cues predominated over physical appearance and actual schoolwork in student-teachers' assessments of the children's abilities, a finding recently supported by the work of Eltis (1980) with Australian children. In a different social domain,

Fielding and Evered (1980) reported an MGT study with an independent-groups design that investigated the significance of the patient's accent in a simulated medical consultation. They found that the same symptoms were more likely to be attributed to psychosomatic than physical causes by medical-student listeners when presented in Received Pronunciation, as opposed to a British regional accent.

A number of investigators have used verbal guise techniques to study speech style in the employment interview. In the United States, Hopper and Williams (1973) presented a simulated job interview to personnel officers, reporting that semantic differential factor scores derived from ratings of the recorded speakers strongly predicted hiring decisions for high-status, but not low-status, jobs. However, in this aspect of their study, the contribution of speech itself to the predictor variables in the multiple regression analysis used is unclear: individual judges' hiring decisions were significantly related to their assessments of speakers on the semantic differential factors, but it is likely that this would be so whatever means of stimulus presentation were used. The same writers also reported another part of their study in which the effect of ethnic speech was assessed, concluding that whether speakers had black American or southern white accents did not affect hiring decisions. Nevertheless, Giles, Wilson, and Conway (1981) found in Great Britain that an ethnic, nonstandard accent (Welsh) received judgments of higher suitability for low-status jobs and of lower suitability for high-status jobs than Received Pronunciation. This was from a matched guise experiment with accent and vocabulary diversity manipulated in a factorial design, in which university students were asked to act as personnel officers after hearing recordings of supposed job interviews. High vocabulary diversity was judged to indicate unsuitability for low-status work. In Canada, Kalin and Rayko (1978) reported that foreign-accented speakers (Italian, Greek, Portuguese, West African, and Slovak) were rated more suitable for low-status jobs and less suitable for high-status jobs than English-Canadian speakers, using similar procedures with unmatched verbal guises. Kalin, Rayko, and Love (1980), extending this work, reported judgments of job suitability for four other foreign-accented types of speaker in Canada: for high-status employment, the (descending) order was English, German, South Asian, and West Indian, and this was reversed for low-status work. Moreover, De La Zerda and Hopper (1979) showed, using MGT, that hiring decisions in Texas were affected by *degree* of Mexican accentedness (though pronunciation may have been correlated here with speech rate, hesitancy, and other variables that genuinely predict job capacity).

In all these studies, except for Hopper and Williams (1973), nonstandard or non-native speech appeared to handicap speakers at the upper levels of employment. Another study of black and white American English by Hopper (1977), using MGT modified to exclude repetition of verbal content, produced an interaction between speaker ethnicity and speaker standardness: blacks who spoke standard American English were more likely than all others to be hired. These blacks were all at an *advantage* in applying for supervisory or sales jobs but not for technical positions. Hopper's results (Hopper & Williams, 1973; Hopper, 1977) differ some-what from the rest of the findings in this field and also from our intuitive expectations, since his studies suggest that black or white American ethnicity alone is not a major determinant of judged employability in Texas. It may influence perceived employability, however, in interaction with actual speech characteristics. Results obtained from such research in the future, combining speech and nonspeech characteristics in factorial designs, will probably reveal further inconsistencies according to local community relations and their ongoing changes. This will demand sophisticated theoretical treatment, drawing upon intergroup theory and applying it extensively to employer and applicant tactics in the job interview.

Distorted perception of speech style

Everything mentioned so far has concerned inferences about people's non-linguistic qualities based on how they speak, but another recent develop-ment in research examines how listeners perceive speakers' speech styles as a result of exposure to other information about them. One phenomenon repeatedly observed in psychological experiments on person perception has been the "halo" effect (Thorndike, 1920), that is, people's tendency to allow their general positive or negative impressions of others to influence their ratings of specific traits or attributes.

Three recent studies have demonstrated halo effects in impressions of speech style. Ryan and Sebastian (1980) found that standard-American English speakers described to subjects as being lower class were reported to be easier to understand and to make listeners feel more comfortable than when the same speakers were described as middle-class, whereas perception of Hispanic-accented speech was unaffected by this manipula-tion. The first result is almost the opposite of what would be expected and was even found for non–speech-related measures. The authors suggest that the reason for it was that standard speakers given high social status sounded affected to listeners, whereas the discrepancy between the actual speech and listeners' expectations of lower-class speakers made ratings more favorable.

Thakerar and Giles (1981) showed that a halo effect in speech perception can also operate retroactively, reporting an experiment in which listeners received information about a speaker's academic performance *after* hearing the speaker and just before making their ratings. When described as highly successful, the speaker was recalled as speaking faster and with more standard pronunciation than when described as unsuccessful. This has been replicated by Ball, Byrne, Giles, Berechree, Griffiths, McDonald, and McKendrick (1982), who presented a recording of a female speaker discussing a job interview and informed listeners that the speaker had, or had not, been offered the job. The same authors also found that a speaker with a "General Australian" speech style (Mitchell & Delbridge, 1965) was perceived as more "foreign-sounding" when described as belonging to a Greek immigrant family rather than an Anglo-Australian family. These studies illustrate the complex process by which new information is assimilated into old, with distortion of either or both, as the social perceiver constructs an understanding of events and people that is stable enough to be acted upon. This involves information flowing in all directions, with speech characteristics being both a primary source of information, conveying impressions of social attractiveness and competence (which, in turn, determine decisions to employ, convict, or diagnose) and themselves being perceptually affected by information about status, employability, or ethnicity.

A two-part laboratory demonstration

As mentioned in the introduction, this exercise demonstrates the use of MGT in research on the role of speech in the employment interview and combines it with illustrating a halo effect in the perception of speech style. Through this you will become familiar with (1) the matching of subject groups as a means of experimental control; (2) experimental manipulation of single social cues; (3) the use of two contrasting types of dependent variable; and (4) several different content areas in social psychology, including social markers in speech, impression formation, and stereotyping.

The exercise has two parts. In Experiment 1, on the retroactive halo effect in the perception of speech style, subjects hear someone talking about a job application and rate the candidate on four scales. Subjects next receive information about the candidate's success or failure in the job interview and then are asked to retrospectively estimate several features of the person's speech. This experiment serves as a warm-up for Experiment 2, which is about the effect of speech style itself on impression formation. Subjects are asked to play the role of employment agency personnel officers and listen to a job interview, with different subject groups hearing the same speaker as a candidate but in matched speech guises that differ in pronunciation and rate. Related written material is content-analyzed, and all of the resulting data is statistically analyzed. On the basis of previous evidence, we hypothesize for Experiment 1 that somebody who is decribed to subjects as a successful job applicant will be recalled as sounding more competent but not more socially attractive, and as having spoken faster, more grammatically, with more standard pronunciation and in a more easily understood way than somebody described as an unsuccessful applicant. In Experiment 2, we hypothesize that an applicant who speaks with a standard accent will be rated more favorably on competence than one who does not but will not be rated more favorably on integrity or social attractiveness. Such an applicant will be judged more suitable for high-status employment, but less suitable for low-status employment, and no more socially attractive or trustworthy than a slower-speaking applicant. The predictions regarding speech rate are the only ones that do not follow straightforwardly from findings already discussed. The basis for making them is a series of studies by Brown and his colleagues (Brown, Strong, & Rencher, 1973, 1974; Smith, Brown, Strong, & Rencher, 1975; Brown, 1980) that show competence judgments to be positively related to speech rate but indicate a more complex relation between speech rate and "bene-volence" (i.e., "goodness") ratings, with perceived "benevolence" peaking at intermediate speech rates.

Method

Sample materials and instructions for the experiments are in the appendixes to this chapter and will be referred to from time to time in this section.

Resources and materials

Space. Four rooms are desirable, each accommodating a group of subjects who can hear the stimulus recordings and make ratings without being disturbed. Otherwise, groups might be run successively in one room, or else simultaneously in either a language laboratory or a large room with group listening stations.

Instruction and response booklets. Separate booklets are needed for the two experiments, so that the first booklet can be used for group matching before Experiment 2 begins. Suggested scales for Experiments 1 and 2 are found in appendixes 4 and 5, respectively. It is essential to include the scales, in order to validate the experimental manipulations (*successful/ unsuccessful* for Experiment 1 and *fast/slow* for Experiment 2). Suitability for jobs with differing prestige should be included, but make sure that all the jobs are compatible with the interview content. Rating scales should be randomized for positional response set, and enough space should be provided for the open-ended responses.

Scripts and recordings. These should be adapted to local circumstances and available skills and should be prepared, of course, prior to the experiment. Assuming that the surrounding speech community has an accent-prestige continuum, two speakers at neither high nor low extreme are desirable, and a third who can shift realistically and noticeably across the range. This speaker plays the candidate role in the interview of Experiment 2. Recordings should ideally be made by people with acting experience and checked for authenticity by establishing that the recordings cannot be detected to differ from recordings of genuine spontaneous speech. The example scripts in appendixes 1 and 2 were prepared by editing transcripts of spontaneous speech obtained through role-play, a procedure recommended if scripts are written from scratch and transcripts of real interviews are unobtainable. Editing should not correct grammar, remove hesitation, and so forth, since this reduces authenticity. Recordings should be made under noise-free conditions, with high-quality tapes.

One speaker records the Experiment 1 script (see appendix 1), speaking normally, and the others record the Experiment 2 script (see appendix 2) four times, with the employer speaking normally and the candidate varying his or her style to produce all four combinations of high- or low-prestige accent and fast or slow speech. Special care is needed with the following: (1) keeping employer speech constant between recordings (particularly avoiding unintended convergence upon the candidate's speech); (2) controlling aspects of the candidate's speech that are not factors in the experimental design (especially avoiding projection of popular stereotypes); and (3) achieving orthogonal manipulations of the independent variables (i.e., both fast guises should be equally fast, both nonstandard guises equally nonstandard, etc.). Speech rate may be checked with a stopwatch, and versions of the Experiment 2 recordings, with each speaker erased in turn, can be pretested on a panel of raters for equivalence of accent and extraneous variables, since judgments of a candidate's speech can be influence by contrast with his or her interviewer (Ball, Giles, Byrne, & Berechree, 1984). It is, in fact, possible to hold the employer's speech completely constant by making a single master recording of it and then rerecording the employer's utterances from this, interleaving them with the candidate's remarks, to make up the dialogue for each of the candidate's guises.

Procedure

Although described here as two separate experiments, the exercise is meant to be presented to *subjects* as a single experiment with a warm-up period.

Experiment 1. Subjects should be assigned at random to two treatment groups, balanced for sex, at the start of the laboratory session. The experimenter then presents the verbal instructions in appendix 3, as the response sheets (appendix 4) are distributed, with the instructions face uppermost. These printed instructions are read aloud by the experimenter, and any questions are dealt with publicly, in front of the group, before the recording is played. Immediately after the recording, subjects complete Section A of the response sheet (which contains evaluative scales for later matching purposes), turn it over, read "Further Information" (which accomplishes the experimental manipulation), and complete Section B. They then hand in their sheets and take a short break, while assignment to groups for Experiment 2 is carried out.

Matching of groups for Experiment 2. Each subject's ratings on the scales in Section A of appendix 4 should be totaled, taking account of the direction of scoring for each scale, and subjects should be assigned to four groups of equal size, so that the group means are as similar as possible. One way is to arrange response sheets in rank order of evaluative totals and distribute them in rotation to four piles, beginning each rotation on the last pile of the preceding one, to prevent accumulation of differences between piles (i.e., if the piles are labeled *P*, *Q*, *R*, and *S*, the ranked sheets would be distributed thus: *P*, *Q*, *R*, *S*; *S*, *P*, *Q*, *R*; *R*, *S*, *P*, *Q*; *Q*, *R*, *S*, *P*; etc.). This scoring and matching procedure should take no longer than 15 minutes.

Experiment 2. Subjects are assembled as four experimental groups in their separate locations, ostensibly because they are to hear excerpts from different employment interviews, imagining themselves in the role of employment agency personnel officers. They are then handed the final set of response sheets (see appendix 5). The experimenters read aloud their printed instructions, ask for questions, and present one of the four stimulus recordings. Subjects then make their ratings of the candidate and provide open-ended reports before response sheets are collected.

Debriefing. The experimenters may begin by asking subjects what they imagine to be the aims and hypotheses of the exercise, adding, if necessary, the question "Was there perhaps more to it than there seemed to be on the surface?" This will help establish how transparent the experiments have been and how valid the data are, before subjects have the benefit of hindsight. The experimenter can then explain the aims and retrace the course of the experiments to show how the hypotheses were being tested.

Analysis and results

Using response sheets like the examples in appendixes 4 and 5 (for experiments 1 and 2, respectively), data are in numerical form and need no transcription before analysis. The data processing facilities available will determine the most appropriate analyses to choose from those suggested in the following sections.

Experiment 1. If analysis can proceed while Experiment 2 is in progress, some results should be available when it finishes.

Section A. Although the subject groups of Experiment 2 are matched for evaluation response set, those of Experiment 1 are not, so possible intergroup differences should be checked for with a *t*-test on Section A evaluation totals.

Section B. The main aim is to establish whether groups receiving interview-success and interview-failure information rated the speaker differently on these scales. *t*-tests for independent samples can be computed for individual scales. If analysis of the Section A data shows a group difference in evaluation set, analysis of covariance, with evaluation set as covariate, will control statistically for this. Another approach, if there is no difference in set, is to take all the Section B scales together in a multivariate analysis of variance, combined with discriminant function analysis, to establish how distinguishable by their ratings the treatment groups are and how the various scales contribute toward discriminability.

Since only two groups are compared in this analysis, results can be adequately presented in one table, with a row for every scale, and a column for each of the treatment means, for *t*, for the degrees of freedom (if they vary, owing to missed responses), and for the probabilities. The profile of each treatment group over all scales can be shown graphically, plotting the scale means vertically against the scale labels horizontally. With discriminant function analysis, scale poles could be marked as points along the function separating the two treatment groups.

Experiment 2. Analysis of these data concerns whether the standard and fast-speaking guises draw more favorable judgments than the nonstandard and slow guises on competence and suitability for high-status work, but not social attractiveness or integrity, as indicated by scale ratings and the content of free-response reports. The data comprise a 2×2 factorial design with independent groups. From the Section A data of Experiment 1, the mean evaluative response set can be computed for the four groups to demonstrate the success of matching, but nothing further is needed if groups have been matched. Otherwise, a one-way analysis of variance on the evaluative response set will establish whether it is contaminating treatments in Experiment 2 and, if so, its effect can be statistically nullified by making it a covariate in the subsequent analyses.

Conducting separate 2×2 analyses of variance for all scales is the easiest way of treating the rating data. The results can be displayed in one table, with columns for the four treatment means as well as for the F values for pronunciation, speech rate, and their interaction. Probabilities can be indicated with superscripts. Graphs can be drawn for the significant interactions. Multivariate analysis is again possible, with experimental conditions and scales plotted against two discriminant functions.

The student subjects should act as judges for content analyses and can proceed with this while the rating scales are being analyzed. Reports addressed to the candidate and another employment agency personnel officer must be scored according to predetermined content categories, and the scores can be subjected to the same type of analysis as the ratings or to appropriate distribution-free tests, if parametric statistical assumptions are violated.

Messages could be scored for a wide variety of content categories, but evaluative impact is the main concern. For whatever features messages are scored, account must be taken of message length, since the longer a message is, the greater the chance of it containing any particular feature. Message length itself should be analyzed as a dependent variable, since longer messages indicate favorability toward the recipient (Giles, Baker, & Fielding, 1975). Reports for the candidate and the other personnel officer can be combined or separated for analysis; separating them permits examination of potentially interesting differences in what the messages say.

An overall index of favorability can be obtained by applying to each report the formula

$$\text{favorability} = \frac{100 \times (\text{total } a - \text{total } b)}{\text{message length in words}}$$

(where a = number of positive terms and b = number of negative terms), weighted, if desired, to allow for intensifiers and deintensifiers ("very," "highly," "slightly," etc.). Scoring could be done separately for competence, social attractiveness, and so on. Since content scoring is a slow process, half the class could score reports to the candidate and the others score those to the personnel officer, possibly as a supplementary task to be done outside of class for later analysis. Statistical analysis is best based on composite scorings from all judges, but interjudge consistency should be estimated with a suitable reliability measure.

Discussion

To summarize the predictions: Experiment 1 is expected to show subjects forming a more favorable impression of the competence, but not the social attractiveness, of a speaker described as successful in a job interview than of the same speaker described as unsuccessful. The "successful" speaker will also be recalled as speaking faster and in a more socially approved manner. Experiment 2 is likely to show more favorable impressions for the standard- than for the nonstandard-accented candidate on competence-related scales, but not on integrity or social attractiveness. The standard-accented applicant will be judged more suitable for high-status work but less suitable for low-status work and will be more likely to be offered the job after the recorded interview. The same positive pattern of results was predicted for the fast as opposed to the slow speaker. These results should be corroborated by those from content analyses of free-response data.

For both experiments, the scales included to check the success of manipulations should show appropriate group differences (*successful/unsuccessful* in Experiment 1; *standard/nonstandard pronunciation* and *fast/slow speech* in Experiment 2). Without these differences, failure to obtain significant differences on other measures means nothing. Regarding Experiment 2, note here that a significant interaction would imply interdependence between perception of pronunciation and speech, provided that orthogonality of the two manipulations is confirmed when checked as suggested earlier.

Whether or not results uphold predictions, the four methodological aims listed at the beginning of the chapter will have been achieved, and the importance of speech characteristics in social encounters will inevitably be highlighted. That the connection between the speech cues and human qualities studied exists in the mind of the hearer, and not necessarily in the objective state of affairs, is demonstrated by the use of the same recording throughout Experiment 1 and the same speaker in Experiment 2. Nevertheless, it is also necessary to emphasize that interpersonal perception is more than simply bias and distortion, which are inevitable by-products of a finite cognitive system, integrating varied sources of information (including memory) into a basis for action in the social world. The human mind seems to be designed to respond not to unique stimuli directly but through systems of categories into which experiences are sorted by means of inferences that "go beyond the information given" (Bruner, 1957); that is, the mind responds to *interpretations* of stimuli. This gives social perception a heuristic character, highly efficient most of the time but subject to oversimplification (for example, halo effects) and distortions, so that mistaken inferences can be sustained through false validation (provided by other people, for example, in the form of stereotypes). Students can learn from this that bias and distortion in social perception reveal a great deal about how social perception normally functions and that research into these phenomena is the scientific way of exploiting this fact, not just the exposure of human naïveté and illogicality.

Experiments like these advance knowledge about reactions to speech and the kinds of behavior likely to result, contributing to an understanding of social interaction in general, but the results also suggest applications in business, education, and other spheres. Industrial personnel officers and employment agencies need a more informed analysis of their intuitive, everyday decision making to prevent bias in worker selection, besides improving their use of speech cues as legitimate sources of information. These experiments can help job seekers to learn about the realities of the working world and make them aware of self-presentation skills, both sociolinguistic and nonverbal, that they need to know if they are to receive full credit for whatever competence, reliability, and trustworthiness they actually possess. Research toward an applied science of how to win friends and influence people, in which students about to graduate and adults can be systematically trained, has already begun (Trower, Bryant, & Argyle, 1978) but has not yet taken advantage of theoretical developments arising from research on speech, even though it is sound theory, not isolated facts, that is needed to stimulate effective applications.

A good experiment is characterized not so much by the absence of limitations as by their being clearly defined. These two experiments deal with speech in a static fashion, whereas current research interest has shifted to speech dynamics and reactions to them. These techniques would be more complicated to demonstrate in the classroom, however, and the results would be less foreseeable. The sampling of subjects here is limited to students, and caution is needed in extrapolating findings to the rest of the community, though in the case of employment interviews less caution is required than one might expect (Bernstein, Hakel, & Harlan, 1975). Other independent variables could be added to extend the scope of these experiments, such as using, for Experiment 1, ethnic or religious information about the speaker or some kind of information about the situation (such as its formality) in which the recording was made. For Experiment 2, foreign accents or more varied native accents, besides other speech variables like vocabulary diversity, grammatical complexity, or idiomatic characteristics, could be added. Another possibility would be to vary the relative predominance of well-established masculine and feminine speech features between matched guises, using speakers of either or both sexes. Other dependent variables, in the form of different rating scales and sorts of free responses and various behavioral and physiological measures would also be possible in both experiments. Thus the sampling of manipulations and measures, although restricted in these experiments, is extendable if desired. Finally, as a laboratory exercise, this one is open to the commonly misapplied criticism of artificiality, which, if anything, is even less applicable here than usual, since the materials and procedures are designed to create in subjects a vividly realistic experience of involvement in employment selection practices.

The fact that subjects are likely to take the task seriously highlights the ethical issue of deceiving subjects by leading them to believe they are hearing genuine job interviews. This is, however, a very limited and nondistressing deception, and the explanation that the exercise is about impression formation in employment selection remains, of course, truthful. It may nevertheless be beneficial to discuss ethical aspects and compare this exercise with "third-degree" research like that of Bjerg (1968) or Milgram (1974).

Conclusion

From this laboratory exercise, it is possible to gain an acquaintance with the role of linguistic factors in social life, particularly in interpersonal perception, and an appreciation for several points of methodology in experimental social psychology, relating to control over stimuli, equation of samples on potentially contaminating factors, and confirming the success of manipulations, among others. Students will also become more aware of the types of information, other than verbal content, that flow to and fro during interpersonal encounters; the capacity such information has for creating socially stereotyped impressions; and the way in which even an interviewer's awareness of these cues can be colored by externally derived information. Students can thereby achieve a better understanding of the active integration of different sources and types of information in which social perceivers are occupied and of the types of error to which they are prone.

References

Agheyisi, R., and Fishman, J. A. (1970) Language attitude studies: a brief survey of methodological approaches. *Anthropological Linguistics*, 12, 137–57.

Ball, P. (1983) Stereotypes of Anglo-Saxon and non–Anglo-Saxon accents: some exploratory Australian studies with the matched guise technique. *Language Sciences*, 5, 163–83.

Ball, P., Byrne, J., Giles, H., Berechree, P., Griffiths, J., McDonald, H., and McKendrick, I. (1982) The retroactive speech halo effect: some Australian data. *Language & Communication*, 2, 277–84.

Ball, P., Giles, H., Byrne, J., and Berechree, P. (1984) Situational constraints on accommodation theory: some Australian data. *International Journal of the Sociology of Language*, 46, 115–29.

Bernstein, V., Hakel, M. D., and Harlan, A. (1975) The college student as interviewer: a threat to generalizability? *Journal of Applied Psychology*, 60, 266–68.

Bjerg, K. (1968) Interplay analysis: a preliminary report on an approach to the problems of interpersonal understanding. *Acta Psychologica*, 28, 201–45.

Bourhis, R. Y., and Giles, H. (1977) The language of intergroup distinctiveness. In H. Giles (ed.), *Language, Ethnicity and Intergroup Relations*. London: Academic Press.

Bourhis, R. Y., Giles, H., Leyens, J.-P., and Tajfel, H. (1979) Psycholinguistic distinctiveness: language divergence in Belgium. In H. Giles and R. St. Clair (eds.), *Language and Social Psychology*. Oxford: Blackwell Publisher.

Bourhis, R. Y., Giles, H., and Tajfel, H. (1973) Language as a determinant of Welsh identity. *European Journal of Social Psychology*, 3, 447–60.

Brown, B. L. (1980) Effects of speech rate in personality attributions and competency evaluations. In H. Giles, W. P. Robinson, and P. M. Smith (eds.), *Language: Social Psychological perspectives*. Oxford: Pergamon Press.

Brown, B. L., Strong, W. J., and Rencher, A. C. (1973) Perceptions of personality from speech: effects of manipulations of acoustical parameters. *Journal of the Acoustical Society of America*, 54, 29–35.

(1974) Fifty-four voices from two: the effects of simultaneous manipulations of rate, mean fundamental frequency and variance of fundamental frequency on ratings of personality from speech. *Journal of the Acoustical Society of America*, 55, 313–18.

Bruner, J. S. (1957) On going beyond the information given. In J. S. Bruner and E. Brunswik (eds.), *Cognitive Approaches to Psychology*. Cambridge, Mass.: Harvard University Press.

Byrne, D. (1971) *The Attraction Paradigm*. New York: Academic Press.

De la Zerda, N., and Hopper, R. (1979) Employment interviewers' reactions to Mexican American speech. *Communication Monographs*, 46, 126–34.

Eltis, K. J. (1980) Pupils' speech-style and teacher reaction: implications from some Australian data. *English in Australia*, 51, 27–35.

Fielding, G., and Evered, C. (1980) The influence of patients' speech upon doctors: the diagnostic interview. In R. St. Clair and H. Giles (eds.), *The Social and Psychological Contexts of Language*. Hillsdale, N. J.: Erlbaum.

Gardner, R. C. (1979) Social psychological aspects of second language acquisition. In H.

Giles and R. St. Clair (eds.), *Language and Social Psychology*. Oxford: Blackwell Publisher.

Gardner, R.C., and Lambert, W.E. (1972) *Attitudes and Motivation in Second Language Learning*. Rowley, Mass.: Newbury House.

Giles, H. (1970) Evaluative reactions to accents. *Educational Review*, 22, 211–27.

(1971) Patterns of evaluation in reactions to RP, South Welsh and Somerset accented speech. *British Journal of Social and Clinical Psychology*, 10, 280–81.

(1973) Accent mobility; a model and some data. *Anthropological Linguistics*, 15, 87–105.

Giles, H., Baker, S., and Fielding, G. (1975) Communication length as a behavioural index of accent prejudice. *International Journal of the Sociology of Language*, 6, 73–81.

Giles, H., and Bourhis, R.Y. (1973) Dialect perception revisited. *Quarterly Journal of Speech*, 59, 337–42.

Giles, H., Bourhis, R.Y., and Taylor, D.M. (1977) Towards a theory of language in ethnic group relations. In H. Giles (ed.), *Language, Ethnicity and Intergroup Relations*. London: Academic Press.

Giles, H. and Powesland, P.F. (1975) *Speech Style and Social Evaluation*. London: Academic Press.

Giles, H., and St. Clair, R. (eds.) (1979) *Language and Social Psychology*. Oxford: Blackwell Publisher.

Giles, H., and Smith, P.M. (1979) Accommodation theory: optimal levels of convergence. In H. Giles and R.St. Clair (eds.), *Language and Social Psychology*. Oxford: Blackwell Publisher.

Giles, H., Wilson, P., and Conway, T. (1981) Accent and lexical diversity as determinants of impression formation and employment election. *Language Sciences*, 3, 92–103.

Hogg, M.A. (1985). Masculine and feminine speech in dyads and groups: a study of speech style and gender salience. *Journal of Language and Social Psychology*, 4, 99–112.

Homans, G.C. (1961) *Social Behaviour: Its Elementary Forms*. New York: Harcourt, Brace & World.

Hopper, R. (1977) Language attitudes in the employment interview. *Communication Monographs*, 44, 346–51.

Hopper, R., and Williams, F. (1973) Speech characteristics and employability. *Speech Monographs*, 40, 296–302.

Kalin, R., and Rayko, D.S. (1978) Discrimination in evaluative judgments against foreign-accented job candidates. *Psychological Reports*, 43, 1203–9.

Kalin, R., Rayko, D.S., and Love, N. (1980) The perception and evaluation of job candidates with four different ethnic accents. In H. Giles, W.P. Robinson and P.M. Smith (eds.), *Language: Social Psychological perspectives*. Oxford: Pergamon Press.

Katz, D., and Braly, K.W. (1933) Racial prejudice and racial stereotypes. *Journal of Abnormal and Social Psychology*, 30, 175–93.

Lambert, W.E. (1967) The social psychology of bilingualism. *Journal of Social Issues*, 23, 91–109

Lambert, W.E., Hodgson, R.C., Gardner, R.C., and Fillenbaum, S. (1960) Evaluational reactions to spoken language. *Journal of Abnormal and Social Psychology*, 60, 44–51.

Lambert, W.E., and Tucker, G.R. (1972) *Bilingual Education of Children: The St. Lambert Experiment*. Rowley, Mass.: Newbury House.

Lee, R. (1971) Dialect perception: a critical review and re-evaluation. *Quarterly Journal of Speech*, 57, 410–17.

Milgram, S. (1974) *Obedience to Authority: An Experimental View*. New York: Harper & Row.

Mitchell, A.G., and Delbridge, A. (1965) *The Speech of Australian Adolescents*. Sydney: Angus & Robertson.

Robinson, W.P. (1972) *Language and Social Behaviour*. Harmondsworth: Penguin.

Ryan, E.B. (1979) Why do low-prestige language varieties persist? In H. Giles and R. St. Clair (eds.), *Language and Social Psychology*. Oxford: Blackwell Publisher.

Ryan, E.B., and Bulik, C.M., (1982). Evaluations of middle class speakers of Standard American and German-accented English. *Journal of Language and Social Psychology*, 1, 51–61.

Ryan, E.B., and Carranza, M.A. (1977) Ingroup and outgroup reactions to Mexican American language varieties. In H. Giles (ed.), *Language, Ethnicity and Intergroup Relations*. London: Academic Press.

Ryan, E.B., and Giles, H. (eds.) (1982) *Attitudes towards Language Variation: Social and Applied Contexts*, London: Edward Arnold.

Ryan, E.B., and Sebastian, R.J. (1980) The effects of speech style and social class background on social judgements of speakers. *British Journal of Social and Clinical Psychology*, 19, 229–33.

Scherer, K.R., and Giles, H. (eds.) (1979) *Social Markers in Speech*. Cambridge: Cambridge University Press.

Seligman, C.F., Tucker, G.R., and Lambert, W.E. (1972) The effects of speech style and other attributes on teachers attitudes towards pupils. *Language in Society*, 1, 131–42.

Shuy, R.W., and Fasold, R.W. (eds.) (1973) *Language Attitudes: Current Trends and Prospects*. Washington, D.C.: Georgetown University Press.

Simard, L., Taylor, D.M., and Giles, H. (1976) Attribution processes and inter-personal accommodation in a bilingual setting. *Language and Speech*, 19, 374–87.

Smith, B.L., Brown, B.L, Strong, W.J., and Rencher, A.C. (1975) Effects of speech rate on personality perception. *Language and Speech*, 18, 145–52.

Smith, P.M. (1985) *Language, the Sexes and Society*. Oxford: Blackwell Publisher.

Stewart, M.A., Ryan, E.B., and Giles, H. (1985) Accent and social class effects on status and solidarity evaluations. *Personality and Social Psychology Bulletin*, 11, 98–105.

Strongman, K.T., and Woosley, J. (1967) Stereotyped reactions to regional accents. *British Journal of Social and Clinical Psychology*, 6, 164–67.

Tajfel, H. (1962) Social perception. In M. Argyle and G. Humphreys (eds.), *Social Psychology through Experiment*. London: Methuen.

Tajfel, H. (ed.) (1978) *Differentiation between Social Groups: Studies in the Social Psychology of Intergroup Relations*. London: Academic Press.

Taylor, D.M., Bassili, J., and Aboud, F.E. (1973) Dimensions of ethnic identity: an example from Quebec. *Journal of Social Psychology*, 89, 185–92.

Thakerar, J.N., and Giles, H. (1981) They are – so they spoke: non-content speech stereotypes. *Language and Communication*, 1, 255–61.

Thakerar, J.N., Giles, H., and Cheshire, J. (1982) Psychological and linguistic parameters of speech accommodation. In C. Fraser and K.R. Scherer (eds.), *Advances in the Social Psychology of Language*. Cambridge: Cambridge University Press.

Thorndike, R.L. (1920) A constant error of psychological ratings. *Journal of Applied Psychology*, 4, 25–9.

Trower, P., Bryant, B., and Argyle, M. (1978) *Social Skills and Mental Health*. London: Methuen.

Useful introductory reading for students

Fishman, J.A., and Giles, H. (1978) Language in society. In H. Tajfel and C. Fraser (eds.), *Introducing Social Psychology*. Harmondsworth: Penguin.

Appendix 1. Script for Experiment 1

Uh ... well, I thought it'd be a good company to get into, because it's pretty big – it's got branches ... all over the country, and, uh, even some in England and Europe, and I wanna travel, 'n' I figured, like, they'd be ... that'd be a good opportunity ... and if I worked for them awhile maybe I'd get sent over there, so I'd get to travel a little. My girlfriend's worked for 'em a couple years now, and she says they're good people to work for, and ... they treat you ok ... 'n,' um, the job looks like it's just what I been lookin' for ...

Appendix 2. Script for Experiment 2

Employer: Now let's see ... Your high school counselor's report is good, and
your grades look pretty good too, I get the idea you must have liked
school, but I guess it wasn't just the studying ... What other activities did
you get into?

Candidate: Uh ... at lot of things, I guess. Like, my buddies and I used to play
basketball a lot, you know, like at lunch and after school. Uh, yeah, and
when I was a senior I was in *West Side Story!* You know, I didn't have to
sing by myself or anything, I just had to stand in a line with some other
guys, and we were supposed to look tough, and we sang some of the
chorus stuff, you know what I mean? ... and get in a fight sometimes ...
They just needed eight guys all the same height ... and uh, ... like, I just
was the right height! ... you know, me and seven other guys. I ... uh, it
was pretty good ... uh ... it was the first time I'd ever been in a show or
anything at school ... uh ...

Employer: Uh-huh ... anything else?

Candidate: Um ... I was on the planning committee for the dances. I got elected
... and I did it for two semesters, but ... my dad thought it was keeping
me from studying, so I gave it up, let somebody else do it ... um ... I
don't think I did much else at school ... except some studying ... like,
really the basketball used to take up most of my spare time ... I used to
play most Saturdays.

Employer: Is that so? ... Now you've quit school, do you still play?

Candidate: Well ... sometimes I play, but I don't play as much as I used to. I'm
into this nature thing, now – I go hiking, in the mountains.

Employer: Oh, really? ... So, do you belong to a club, ... or do you just go by
yourself?

Candidate: Oh no ... I mean, no, I didn't go by myself ... I joined the Sierra
Club, I go with some buddies.

Employer: Well, we better stop talking about your hobbies, because I like the
outdoors – if we get into that, we'll be here all night!

Candidate: Mmm.

Employer: Er ... um ... tell me, did you have any jobs while you were in high
school ... during vacations, maybe?

Candidate: Oh yeah ... um ... I used to work every summer. I got a part-time
job in a grocery store – you know, stocking shelves. I worked for a few
days before Christmas, too. I did that every year ... till I quit high school.

Appendix 3. Verbal instructions for Experiment 1

Interviews for jobs are important encounters, because of their effects on the subsequent courses of people's lives. This experiment is about the employment interview, and in a few minutes I'd like you to listen carefully to part of one, but before that we will have a practice session, to get you used to the kind of task you have to do.

It's important for all of us to go through every stage of the experiment in the right order, paying attention all the time – so please don't start to examine the material until I tell you, and listen carefully to what I say, so that you won't get confused.

Take the sheet of paper headed "Practice Trial," and, without turning it over, quietly read the printed instructions. If you do not understand anything, raise your hand, but don't discuss them. In fact, from now on, please don't talk at all, because it is important for everyone to do the task independently. I'll quickly run through the instructions with you now (i.e., instructions on appendix 4).

... Any questions? (Questions dealt with publicly)

Then let's begin the practice session now, but remember that even the practice must be taken seriously if it is to be useful.

Appendix 4. Instructions and scales for Experiment 1

Practice session

You are going to hear someone talking about a job opening. Listen carefully, and try to imagine what the speaker is like, just as you might if you were talking to a stranger on the telephone, overhearing a conversation behind you on a bus, or hearing somebody on the radio. Different people form different impressions, of course, and there are no "right" or "wrong" answers here.

On the next page is a set of rating scales, on which you will be asked to give your impression of the speaker. When you are told to do so, *but not before*, please turn over, go through the scales in their printed order, and circle the numbers that best represent your opinions: For example:

Unbalanced   1 ② 3 4 5 6 7   Balanced

The rating shown would indicate that the speaker was regarded as quite, but not extremely, unbalanced. If you think the speaker sounds completely neutral with respect to a scale, or you have no opinion at all, you may use a rating of 4 to indicate this.

Make your decisions carefully, but quickly. Taking a long time to think does not improve the quality of judgments in this experiment.

Do not omit any scales. If you have to make any alterations, make it clear which rating is being deleted and which is meant to remain.

If you do not understand anything, please ask now.

LISTEN TO THE RECORDING, THEN BEGIN

Section A

The speaker appeared to be:

Untrustworthy	1	2	3	4	5	6	7	Trustworthy
Incapable	1	2	3	4	5	6	7	Capable
Unkind	1	2	3	4	5	6	7	Kind
Dull	1	2	3	4	5	6	7	Lively

NOW TURN OVER AND CONTINUE

The speaker you have heard was one of three applicants interviewed for the job concerned. None of them was considered suitable, so the job has been readvertised.

OR

The speaker you have heard was one of 12 interviewed, out of a field of 60 applicants for the job concerned. He (she) was offered the post, but decided to go to college instead.

Section B

The person on the recording spoke with:
  Nonstandard pronunciation 1 2 3 4 5 6 7   Standard pronunciation
  A slow speech rate   1 2 3 4 5 6 7   A fast speech rate
  Monotonous intonation   1 2 3 4 5 6 7   Expressive intonation
  A narrow vocabulary range 1 2 3 4 5 6 7   A wide vocabulary range
  Bad grammar   1 2 3 4 5 6 7   Good grammar
  A hard style to understand 1 2 3 4 5 6 7   An easy style to understand
  An articulate manner   1 2 3 4 5 6 7   A hesitant manner
The speaker gave the impression of being:
  Unambitious   1 2 3 4 5 6 7   Ambitious
  Unsympathetic   1 2 3 4 5 6 7   Sympathetic
  Unintelligent   1 2 3 4 5 6 7   Intelligent
  Unkind   1 2 3 4 5 6 7   Kind
  Unsuccessful   1 2 3 4 5 6 7   Successful
  Not dependable   1 2 3 4 5 6 7   Dependable
  Unsure   1 2 3 4 5 6 7   Confident
  Insincere   1 2 3 4 5 6 7   Sincere

Now write here your AGE (   ), SEX (   ) and NAME _____
FINALLY, CHECK THAT YOU HAVE NOT MISSED ANYTHING.

Appendix 5. Instructions and scales for Experiment 2

Now that you are familiar with rating impressions of recorded speakers, you are going to hear part of an actual interview for a job as an executive assistant. It is one of four for which the employers and the candidates have given their consent for the recordings to be made for research and teaching purposes.

Imagine that you are an employment agency personnel officer who has to advise the candidate about his (her) prospects and self-presentation and to prepare a short report about him (her) for another officer. Normally, this would be done following an interview conducted by the employment officer him- or herself, quite similar to one conducted by an employer. Study the job applicant's behavior in the interview, and then carry out ratings as you did in the practice session, but this time think of them as ratings intended to form part of reports to be given to the candidate and your fellow personnel officer. After completing the ratings, elaborate your views on the two forms also provided – Form A for the candidate, and Form B for the employment officer – trying to indicate especially your opinions on aspects not covered by the rating scales. If you have any questions, ask them now.

LISTEN TO THE INTERVIEW, THEN TURN OVER AND BEGIN

Ratings

The candidate gave the
impression of being:

Poor at communication								Good at communica-
skills	1	2	3	4	5	6	7	tion skills
Insincere	1	2	3	4	5	6	7	Sincere
Unintelligent	1	2	3	4	5	6	7	Intelligent
Bad at working in a								Good at working in a
team	1	2	3	4	5	6	7	team
Irritable	1	2	3	4	5	6	7	Easygoing
Unambitious	1	2	3	4	5	6	7	Ambitious
Untrustworthy	1	2	3	4	5	6	7	Trustworthy
Impolite	1	2	3	4	5	6	7	Polite
Not dependable	1	2	3	4	5	6	7	Dependable
Unlikely to be offered								Likely to be offered the
the job	1	2	3	4	5	6	7	job

How suitable do you think the candidate was for the following jobs?
THIS JOB (EXECUTIVE ASSISTANT)

Very unsuitable	1	2	3	4	5	6	7	Very suitable

SALES CLERK

Very unsuitable	1	2	3	4	5	6	7	Very suitable

JANITOR

Very unsuitable	1	2	3	4	5	6	7	Very suitable

GRADE SCHOOL TEACHER

Very unsuitable	1	2	3	4	5	6	7	Very suitable

ACCOUNTANT IN A BUSINESS

Very unsuitable	1	2	3	4	5	6	7	Very suitable

How did you find the applicant's speech during the job interview?

Slow	1	2	3	4	5	6	7	Fast
Nonstandard	1	2	3	4	5	6	7	Standard
pronunciation								pronunciation

Form A: Advice to Be Given to Candidate

Indicate both strengths and weaknesses, make constructive suggestions about upgrading qualifications and self-presentation, and list the kind of openings the candidate should seek, as well as making any other comments you consider relevant.

_____

_____

_____

_____

_____

_____

Form B: Employment Agency's Internal Report (to be read by another personnel officer)

Indicate candidate's strengths and weaknesses, most suitable and most unsuitable types of work, any special considerations to be noted in future interviews with the client, and any precautions thought appropriate.

_____

_____

_____

_____

_____

_____

7   Recreational use of the street by boys and girls: an observational study

Antony J. Chapman and Frances M. Wade

Summary

This is an observational exercise within the field of applied social psychology in which a simple categorical system of recording behavior is used to collect information about how boys and girls use the streets for recreational purposes. The underlying problem concerns the sharp difference in pedestrian accident rates associated with the age and sex of children: it is the 5- to 9-year-olds, particularly boys, who are especially at risk. Specifically, the exercise investigates whether these children exhibit a greater degree of exposure to danger or a higher incidence of "careless" behavior relative to their less vulnerable peers, when engaged in everyday street activities. In the experiment student observers (Type A) patrol a predetermined suburban route and, on preprinted data sheets for each child encountered, they note the following information: estimated age; sex; whether the child is on the street or sidewalk; activity of the child, according to eight prescribed categories; and street name. Other student observers (Type B), independently of Type A observers, collect information relating to the traffic volume in the streets in the study area. Type A and Type B observers are paired with one another, and they switch roles halfway through the observation period. The data are collated by the students and pooled at a later class session. In each age and sex category the ratio of observed to resident children is calculated, in order to assess the extent to which the sex difference in the accident rate is reflected in the disproportionate use of the street by young boys. Percentage scores are used to examine age and sex differences in "heedless" behaviors. Data can be represented pictorially and/or subjected to chi-square analysis. Discussion of the exercise relates to the degree of support obtained for the hypotheses and is expanded to debate several issues, including the following: the validity of studying routine behavior in the context of accident analysis; the temptation to impute accident causality to exposure factors; and the ethics of observing subjects without their knowledge or informed consent.

150

Introduction

Child pedestrians tend to use the streets near their homes for three reasons: for trips to and from school, for running errands, and for general recreational activities. In recreational activities, streets serve as playgrounds and meeting places. For this exercise information is collected about recreational use as a function of age and sex. Children are observed in selected streets and their activities noted. The extent of street usage is assessed by relating the number of observed children to the number of resident children (the resident child population is obtained from school district or census records). Students are introduced to an observational technique and to a simple classification system for coding observed behavior. They become aware of problems such as possible observer influences on the observed children and the difficulties of categorization, as well as a variety of issues relating to reliability, validity, and the nature of data.

The exercise is an example of research within the field of applied social psychology. Applied research and theoretical research are often discussed as though they were at opposite ends of a continuum. Polarized in this way, theoretical research is said to emphasize the accumulation and synthesis of knowledge about principles of behavior, whereas applied research emphasizes the solving of problems. Applied social psychology is social psychology oriented toward problem solving. Ultimately social psychology seeks to provide a fuller understanding of social behavior and experience, and applied social psychology seeks to alleviate social problems. But inevitably, any such polarization is misleading: research is not either theoretical or applied; most contributes to both knowledge of principles and solutions to problems.

The social problem of interest to us is child pedestrian accidents, and the ultimate goal of research along the lines of this exercise is to reduce accidents through understanding how, when, and why children use streets. From description we move toward theoretical models and policy recommendations. For example, it is commonly held that children cause traffic accidents by dashing heedlessly into the street, giving drivers no chance to take effective evasive action (cf. Chapman, Wade, & Foot, 1982). We might expect, therefore, to find that children often run, in the course of their street activities. But if running were rarely observed, then our theories about accidents, and our opinions about how legally to apportion blame for accidents, would have to be substantially revised.

Like much applied social research, this exercise is conducted in an everyday setting: naturally occurring public events are observed systematically. Observational methods have been defined by Weick (1968) as the "selection, provocation, recording, and encoding of that set of behaviors and settings concerning organisms 'in situ' [in their own contexts] which is consistent with empirical aims." By design, his definition is all-embracing, and it blurs any distinction between observational and experimental methodology, on the grounds that observation and experimentation differ from one another on only a few dimensions. Crano and Brewer (1973), for example, identify three principal dimensions: participant–nonparticipant, structured–nonstructured, and response restriction dimensions. These are outlined later in the chapter.

In practice there is wide variation in observers' participation in the social situations within which the behaviors under study occur. Participation ranges from complete membership of a group to distancing in time and/or space from those being observed. Hence in "participant observation" the observer might be accepted as a member of the group: obtaining membership for research purposes may be achieved either openly, so that the observer's status as a researcher is common knowledge, or covertly, so that the observer's research function remains unknown to other group members. Of course an observer's presence may interfere with the natural course of events, but this interference can be minimized by various methods, the most extreme of which is concealment. Total concealment implies a form of nonparticipant observation but, short of that, the concealment can be partial, or subjects may falsely believe that others in the group, and not themselves, are the focus of the study (cf. Weick, 1968).

In a thorough review of the issues in observational research, McCall and Simmons (1969) noted that participant observation is a blend of methods and techniques characteristically employed for studying informal groups (for example, factory workers and deviant subcultures); complex organizations (for example, hospitals, unions, and industrial corporations); social movements; and communities. It can include both formal and informal interviewing and collecting documents. It always involves some direct recording (or tape-recording) of events, although there can be a time lapse between the occurrence of those events and the creation of a permanent record. With respect to the choice of measures, participant observation studies are often open-ended, with the range of measures perhaps narrowing as studies unfold over weeks or months. Hence participant observation is characterized by McCall and Simmons as a research enterprise in which several methods are combined in the pursuit of a broad objective – namely an "analytic description" – and that is a form of description that excludes, for example, journalistic reports.

Where this exercise lies on the participant–nonparticipant continuum is a moot point. (It is also an obscure point of no practical importance: any label – for example, "participant observation" – does not in itself offer any practical insights into an issue under investigation.) Observers, in independent pairs, patrol selected streets on foot, passing close to child pedestrians whose activities are surreptitiously recorded, using prescribed categories: one member of a pair records the children's activities as the other records traffic volume. The method thereby resembles a typical participant observation in several respects: first, it involves direct observation of events: second, some principal events are recorded (immediately) after, rather than during, their occurrence: third, the observers are visible to the observed, and there is interaction to the extent that pedestrians (observers and children) comply with rules to limit or avoid social and physical encounters with strangers. If observers did not resemble ordinary pedestrians, other kinds of interaction might be sought: For example, passers-by might ask what an observer was doing, or they might initiate what they considered to be appropriate conversation, having first assigned him or her to a particular role (such as market researcher). The project also involves consulting documents to establish the sex and age profiles of the population in the study area: The documents can be census data obtained from the local school district. As in nonparticipant observation, subjects are not interviewed, and there is no intention that the study should develop over days, weeks, or months: There are precisely formulated short-term procedures and a small set of possible outcomes.

Turning now to the "structured–nonstructured" dimension: On the structured end, data are tightly systematized, using coding schemes that focus on a limited number of precisely defined behaviors. The behaviors are determined primarily by the hypotheses under investigation. At the nonstructured end of the continuum, observers supposedly conduct their research with no theoretical preconceptions as to the patterns that their data will eventually take. Again, for convenience of discussion we are speaking of this polarization as though it were real, and therefore we want to repeat that the various techniques lie on a continuum of structuredness and that there is no such dichotomy. The more structured approaches allow for reliability checks and for data analysis involving inductive statistical procedures, whereas neither reliability checks nor inductive analysis is usually feasible when data are collected through unstructured observation. Inevitably the researcher is confronted with a trade-off or series of trade-offs: for instance, one may decide that statistical precision should be sacrificed in the interests of data richness, or vice versa. A decision to record the frequency of specific behaviors (within a set time period and for a particular target group), as in this exercise, implies that one has chosen to make an intensive inquiry into a particular set of behaviors, rather than an extensive inquiry attempting to detail all group events.

With many coding systems the decision to record a behavior is a two-part one: The behavior is judged to have occurred or not to have occurred. Some systems, however, also require the observer to judge the intensity of the behaviors: For example, a category such as "walk" might assume three values: slow, medium, and fast. Other systems include items that are measured with standard laboratory equipment such as stopwatches or sound-level meters, but problems about judging the onset of behaviors, for example, can remain in an essentially identical form, and their solutions can be just as arbitrary (for example, how loud does a noise have to be before it is recorded as present by the researcher?).

The data in this exercise are restricted to a small, predetermined set of activities, which include "walking," "running," "sitting," "standing," "playing," and "talking." As already noted, we will therefore be engaged in an intensive inquiry concerning the classification of behaviors into these few categories. Yet, because the categories of behaviors are broadly defined, the inquiry is extensive with regard to street usage: all aspects are coded. As outlined, the system requires a simple frequency count of behaviors observed within samples of subjects. No rating scales or duration measures are used.

The "response restriction" dimension identified by Crano and Brewer relates to the constraints placed upon subjects' behaviors by the environment within which the observations are made. Toward the more restricted end of this continuum are studies that make use of specifically designed settings and props to bring out or facilitate particular types of responses. In some of our research, for example, children have been brought to a mobile laboratory equipped as a playroom, where they watch cartoons (cf. Chapman, Smith, & Foot, 1980). Responses are videotaped with concealed cameras and microphones, and the tapes are then transcribed by small groups of independent judges, using a computerized event recorder. This experiment lies toward the opposite end of the continuum: The physical setting is neither designed nor manipulated for the research, and the observers try to exert no influence over subjects' behaviors.

Specific background to the exercise

We turn next to the specific background behind this research. In the United States and elsewhere the problem of child pedestrian accidents is plain. Invariably there are marked age and sex trends in the statistics: It is alarmingly clear that 5- to 9-year-olds are especially likely to be involved in traffic accidents (National Safety Council, 1983) and that the rates for boys are almost twice those for girls (Wolfe & O'Day, 1981). The trends may result from a combination of factors, but on the face of it the most plausible causes are age and sex differences in exposure to traffic hazard, and age and sex differences in behavior. Perhaps young schoolchildren, and boys particularly, are outdoors more, and perhaps some forms of behavior (such as playing ball) result in more serious conflict with vehicles than others (such as jumping rope).

There is surprisingly little research on children's road safety, and it is also rather fragmented and nontheoretical. What research there is has, at least, used the full range of techniques. A few of the more relevant studies are mentioned later in the chapter, and all are cited in the book by Chapman et al. (1982). From observing children on their trips to and from school, Howarth and colleagues (for example, Routledge, Repetto-Wright, & Howarth, 1974) have reported that exposure to traffic risk increases with age and that there are developmental changes in street-crossing strategies, but no corresponding sex differences have been noted. Playing outdoors has been investigated, using survey, interview, and observational methods. In a survey of accidents, Preston (1972) found that more boys than girls were injured at play, and from interviews with mothers Sadler (1972) and Newson and Newson (1976) have reported that boys play in the street more than girls. Sandels (1975) observed more 5- and 6-year-olds than younger children playing in places that she regarded as unsuitable, but there were no sex differences regarding either the suitability of play locations or their distances from home. In our own observational work (for example, Chapman, Foot, & Wade, 1980), we have seen many more boys than girls using streets for recreational purposes but few differences between boys and girls in choice of activity.

To reduce observer bias, we will not state the specific hypotheses to be tested in this experiment until the "Data Analysis" section.

Method

Roles and deployment of student observers

The project is conducted over two consecutive laboratory sessions. In the first session, half the students in the class begin by observing children (Type A observers) and half begin as observer-enumerators of traffic (Type B observers). The two types of observer are paired, and individuals switch roles halfway through their patrol. Each observer pair is assigned a small sector of streets, and members of a pair seldom find themselves together in the one street. There is no overlap of sectors, and, taken all together, they should include all streets in a geographical area whose resident population can be determined fairly easily.

The main resource is a set of sections of a large-scale map divided into sectors, the number of sectors equaling the number of observer pairs. The instructor annotates the sections with sector boundaries and route directions. In addition, for collecting data each observer pair needs five or six Pedestrian Data Sheets (appendix 1) and two Traffic Density Sheets (appendix 2): extra sheets will be necessary for the laboratory session. For processing their own data, students need a Pedestrian Collation Sheet (appendix 3) and a Traffic Density Collation Sheet (appendix 4). Clipboards are useful, but they make the observers more visible.

The second session involves pooling observers' collated data. Unless the first session is scheduled during the school vacation, it should include an afternoon. This is because for this experiment children are observed on the streets but specifically not on trips to school (when, for example, boys and girls would necessarily be present in approximately equal numbers). Observations are made in residential areas during the late afternoon of the first session, when children are on the streets after returning home from school. All observation routes should start within a short walk from the introductory session. It is best to run the project when the weather and light are likely to be good: This is not only for the observers' comfort and safety but because otherwise the streets may be just about deserted.

Prior to the first session the instructor has performed several tasks. First, using the map, the selected study area is divided into the sectors. Everything else being equal, a sector ought to comprise about 1 mile of streets, so that it requires approximately 30 minutes to patrol. When feasible, long shopping streets, having many pedestrians, are divided into two or more segments and then shared between adjacent sectors, and, in general, arrangement of sectors should be such that they all include both quiet and busy streets. Each observer pair should be given a map of the area (or a copy), with a single sector clearly marked. Once they have completed observations in the streets at the start of their patrol, it is possible that observers may need to walk along some of those same streets again in order to get to others. Therefore, the directions of patrols are marked on the students' maps. Crossroads and intersections serve as useful boundary markers for sectors.

Choice of study area and subjects

For ease of obtaining population information (i.e., the numbers of resident boys and girls in the three age groups), the geographical study area must coincide with the area of a local public school (or school district). School districts cooperate in such research and usually can supply details about district boundaries and about age and sex distributions of children in their records. Local governments may also be able to provide the information. The youngest age category (under 4) would clearly have to be omitted if school records were used, but, as we have said earlier, these children are seldom outdoors unless accompanied by adults. Naturally some children from neighboring districts will intrude into the study area, and resident children will also migrate into those neighboring regions. For this exercise it is reasonably assumed that there are no systematic imbalances in these movements with respect to either boys or girls or children in the three age groups.

The instructor also needs to prepare four sets of data sheets for distribution to all students at the start of the exercise. These are shown in the appendixes.

Schedule

During the opening part of the first session the instructor (1) gives the background context to the exercise; (2) issues the maps and data sheets; and (3) instructs students how to be observers/observer-enumerators. Members of the class then disperse in pairs to their assigned sectors. It is strongly recommended that they do a practice period of at least 15 minutes before they begin the observation. It is important, as we have said, that formal observations are not scheduled to begin until after children have come home from school. There is no need for students to return to the instructor when they have finished their observations. However, at the end of the session (or at least between sessions), individual observers should each enter their own data on the Pedestrian Data Sheet (appendix 1) and Traffic Density Sheet (appendix 2). During the second laboratory the data for all students are pooled (through the instructor), and analyses are carried out by individual students.

Instructions for observers

The preobservation instructions focus on observational techniques, the category scheme, and procedures to be adopted by the observers. Observers begin their observations at, say, half past four (but earlier in winter), starting their patrols at the points indicated on the maps. Each pair follows its prescribed route, with observers using three criteria for selecting subjects. First, they are children estimated to be 14 years old or younger; second, they are pedestrians; and, third, they are not accompanied by an adult. To be regarded as "pedestrians" they are required to be on the sidewalk or street, either on foot or sitting or lying down; they do not qualify as pedestrians if they are riding, or are mounted on, bicycles or other wheeled toys/vehicles (such as scooters, roller skates, and skateboards). This operational definition includes as pedestrians any children who are seen standing with bicycles or other wheeled vehicles or who are pushing rather than riding them.

Type A observers proceed at a casual walking pace, watching the activities of the nearest boy or girl who is under 14. They look away to record information as unobtrusively as possible on a Pedestrian Data Sheet, and then the next subject is sought as their patrol is continued. Information is classified following the row headings, left to right, in appendix 1. As an observer moves into the various streets, the street names are listed in turn. When the sex and age of an observed child has been noted, the row entries are continued by making a single entry in one of the four primary information categories: a check mark is placed under "run," "walk," "stand," or "sit." These mutually exclusive behaviors are defined as follows:

- *Run* (includes athletic behaviors such as those commonly called "jumping," "turning cartwheels" "somersaulting," and "skipping" without rope): forward, backward, or sideways motion of the legs, during the course of which both feet are sometimes off the ground simultaneously
- *Walk:* forward, backward, or sideways motion of the legs, in which at no time are both feet off the ground
- *Stand:* no regular motion of the legs, and the body weight is borne primarily or exclusively by the feet
- *Sit* (includes actions commonly termed "kneeling" and "lying"): body weight borne principally by parts of the anatomy other than the feet, and no change of body location

Data recording for the one child continues with secondary information being entered in the same row. In the "road/sidewalk" column, the letter *R* is entered if the subject is in the road (or in the center of the road on a raised, curbed area), whereas the letter *S* is entered if the subject is on the sidewalk (being defined as a raised and curbed strip at the side of the road).

Other secondary information relates to playing, eating/drinking, and talking. *Play* is defined as interaction with a person or object (except drinkable and edible items) and is subdivided into "active play" (which potentially involves the child's moving more than 2 meters) and "passive play" (which involves less movement, perhaps no noticeable movement). Examples of active play are fighting and playing ball games. Examples of passive play are handling snails and cradling dolls. Clearly, subjective judgments are demanded for this classification. Hence, observers may find it helpful, and it may be more reliable, to note play behaviors in "longhand" (as illustrated in appendix 1), and then introduce the active–passive subdivision at the end of the observation period. Eating/drinking are defined by the process of placing food or drink in the mouth and swallowing; and talking (which includes shouting or singing) is defined in terms of discernible vocal sounds or, for more distant subjects, displays of lip movements. Having completed this classification, the (Type A) observer moves to the next subject and the next row on the Pedestrian Data Sheet. This procedure continues to the halfway stage in the observation session when, at a prearranged point on the route, Type A observers meet their Type B partners and exchange roles. With just a little practice most observers, as they approach a small group or procession of subjects, are able to register the activities of those subjects with ease; they readily develop a knack of putting their observations on paper without calling attention to themselves. It is vital that observers try not to record any child twice; children are disregarded if they reappear on an observer's route. From traffic observations, the volume classifications (quiet or busy; see appendix 2) are later transferred to the Pedestrian Data Sheet in a segment of the first column for each street.

Although they start from the same points and walk the same routes, Type B observers, as traffic enumerators, proceed at an irregular pace, and they conduct their traffic counts independently of Type A observers' activities. As already indicated, individuals switch Type A and Type B duties halfway through the observation period, having met their prescribed routes. In their traffic-enumerating role, students record 3-minute traffic counts of vehicles (including bicycles) traveling on five or more roads in their sector. (By standing at intersections, marked on their maps by the instructor, they can usually do counts for two or more roads at one time). For each of these roads, information is entered under the first two headings of the Traffic Density Sheet illustrates in appendix 2; these headings are "street name" and "number of vehicles in 3 minutes." "Vehicles per hour" (the third column) is calculated by multiplying the observed 3-minute number (i.e., the figure in the second column) by a factor of 20. In the final column the observer puts a Q (for quiet street: 0–120 vehicles per hour) or B (for busy street: 121 or more vehicles per hour). Entries in columns 3 and 4 can usually be made in quiet moments during the observation, but they can also be done after the observation period is completed.

Data tabulation

Before the second laboratory session, each observer transfers his or her pedestrian data to the Pedestrian Collation Sheet illustrated in appendix

3. This groups data according to subjects' ages and sex. Taking each row in turn from the Pedestrian Data Sheet, the student places a check mark in each appropriate cell in the collation sheet. For example, from appendix 1, the first observation is of a 7-year-old boy running and talking while playing ball on the road; hence checkmarks are placed on the collation sheet in the row for "Boys 5–9" under the columns headed "run" (R), "active play," and "talk." The street, Richmond Street, has been classified as "quiet" (Q). Football is classified as "active play" because potentially it involves more than two meters of movement: If this child had been "standing," his activity would still be classed as "active play." The collation process is not complicated; the only possible uncertainty is in the active – passive play classification. In appendix 3, numbers have been entered (instead of check marks) to illustrate how the collation works. Thus, 1 refers to the first subject, 2 to the second subject, and so on to the final (twelfth) subject. Next the numbers of subjects, corresponding to the age and sex categories, are entered in the first column, headed "N." The grand total equals the number of all children observed (12, in this illustration). Finally, the check marks are added up in the other cells and entries made beside the check marks. In appendix 3 these totals are shown in dark print; in the student's sheet only one number would be entered in any one cell.

In their enumerator roles the student observers use the Pedestrian Data Sheet to record traffic density for each street. By this point the density data have been condensed to two categories, giving two classes of street: Q = "quiet"; B = "busy." On the Pedestrian Data Sheet, a Q or B is entered (shown in appendix 1) for each of the streets listed. Entries are also made in the Traffic Volume Collation Sheets (appendix 4), indicating the numbers of boys/girls in each age group who are observed in busy and quiet streets. In appendix 4 the traffic volume collation exercise has been completed from the data given in appendix 1; again numbers have been used to represent each subject, and the bold numbers are cell totals. We would recommend that where there is bold print in appendixes 3 and 4, students use a second ink color or circle the numbers. Some internal checks on collation accuracy are available: Each of the subsample sizes, and the grand totals, remain constant from the Pedestrian Collation Sheet (appendix 3) to the Traffic Volume Collation Sheet (appendix 4).

Data collection, analysis, and results

Analyses of data pooled from all students (i.e., for the entire study area) are recommended, rather than analyses for individual students (i.e., for sectors or half sectors). Hence data for the class are pooled in the opening part of the second session. Six student assistants are appointed, one for each of the age/sex categories, to pool data from Pedestrian Collation Sheets, and six more assistants are appointed to collect the traffic volume information. Each assistant has a master collation sheet (or transparency for an overhead projector, with rows and columns already labeled) and transfers onto it the various cell totals from each student. For example, one assistant collects scores for boys under 4, a second collects the data for 5- to 9-year-old boys, and so on. Students visit each assistant in turn until all the data have been pooled, including the assistants' own data. Each assistant then enlists other students to add up the scores within each age/sex category and for each activity. The accumulated information relates to child pedestrians in the whole observation area, with behavior frequencies given for the six age/sex categories. The next step is to transfer the clerks' summed scores to a large board (or to project them onto a screen), so that students can note down the class data.

Testing predictions

Prediction 1. The first prediction states that boys have higher exposure to traffic danger than girls do: Specifically, it is predicted that the ratio of observed to resident children (the observation ratio, *OR*) is higher for boys than girls. Ratios are derived by dividing the number of children observed by the number of children resident in the area, calculating each age group separately. Hence,

$$\frac{\text{5-to-9-year-old boys observed}}{\text{5-to-9-year-old resident boys}} = \frac{48}{144}$$

Therefore, OR = 1:3 (or 33.33%)

$$\frac{\text{5-to-9-year-old girls observed}}{\text{5-to-9-year-old resident girls}} = \frac{23}{118}$$

Therefore, OR = 1:5.13 (or 19.49%)

Hence OR is numerically higher for boys than for girls. In other words, proportionally more boys than girls were observed to use the streets.

Prediction 2. The second prediction states that, relative to girls, boys engage in more heedless behaviors; that is, boys run more, play more active games, and are found in the street more. For the pooled data in the

Pedestrian Collation Sheet (i.e., for the class as a whole), a percentage is calculated for each of the "run," "active play," and R cells by dividing the observed number in the cell by the number of subjects in the subsample and then multipling by 100. These percentages should be entered on a blank Pedestrian Collation Sheet (or written directly on a blackboard or overhead transparency). Taking each of the three activities separately, statistical associations and the statistical significance of sex differences can be established using chi-square tests.

Prediction 3.   The third prediction is that OR is higher for 5- to-9-year-olds than for older children: ratios are compared for 5- to-9-year-olds and 10- to-14-year-olds.

Prediction 4.   The fourth prediction is that 5- to-9-year-olds exhibit more heedless behaviors than older children. This prediction is examined in similar fashion to Prediction 2. Taking "run," "active play," and "R" separately, frequency scores are cast in three tables for chi-square statistical analyses.

Further prediction.   The traffic count data can be used to investigate sex differences in exposure to traffic. From pedestrian accident statistics, it might be expected that more boys than girls would be observed in "busy" streets (i.e., those with more than 120 vehicles per hour). This prediction is tested in much the same way as the others: Percentage scores for boys and girls in quiet and in busy streets are subjected to chi-square tests.

Presentation of data

The chief features of the data can be brought out in graphs, as in Figure 7.1, which depicts sex and age trends in running and active play. (Note that the data represented in Figure 7.1 are fictitious pooled data and are not derived from the fictitious data in appendixes 1–4.)

Discussion and evaluation

From our own research (for example, Chapman et al., 1980) we expect to find support for all four predictions. Almost certainly boys will be found to use streets for recreational purposes more than girls do. Sex differences in "heedless" behaviors are likely to be found for some of the age groups, showing more heedless activity for boys. However, it is unlikely that all these differences will be statistically significant, especially if subsamples

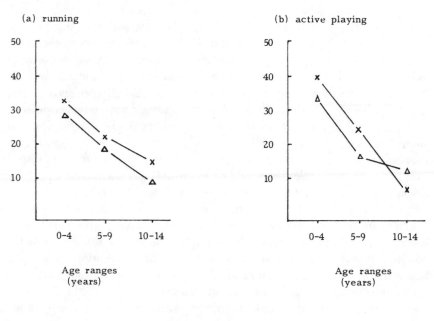

(a) running (b) active playing

Age ranges (years)

Age ranges (years)

Key: Boys ✗

Girls △

Figure 7.1 Age variations in boys' and girls' (a) running and (b) active playing. *Note*: the data depicted in these graphs are not based on the data given in the appendixes.

are small. Some trends may even run counter to prediction: That is, girls may be observed to engage in some heedless behaviors more than boys. Regarding age trends, running and active play will probably be found to decrease as subjects' ages increase, whereas walking and talking will probably be more prevalent in older children.

This project raises three conceptual questions. The first concerns how appropriate it is to study routine behavior in the context of accident analysis. In extrapolating from everyday behavior to accidents, there is an implicit assumption that we need to examine critically – namely, that accidents and routine behavior are located on one continuum (see Chapman et al., 1982). But it could be, for instance, that patterns of sex differences observed in routine situations reveal little or nothing of importance about abnormal, accident situations. Thus, having little or no external validity in relation to accidents, exercises such as this may be of very little practical significance.

Let us assume, though, that the exercise is indeed valid and move to the second question, which has to do with statistical significance. We have said that the aim of applied social research is to provide answers to social problems, and then to make recommendations to alleviate those problems. In any research that has practical implications, the question of statistical significance becomes very important. If large sex differences were observed in the so-called heedless behaviors – say, if boys engaged in much more running and active games – policymakers might decide that boys should take traffic-safety courses, perhaps through informal groups like Boy Scout troops and youth clubs. Under these circumstances the responsibility of the social scientist would be to ensure, as far as possible, through empirical means that there was a true sex difference: that is, to demonstrate beyond reasonable doubt that the findings were not due to empirical artifacts or to sampling error. To err on the conservative side, before committing themselves researchers might choose to set the statistical confidence level at a more demanding level than conventionally set (i.e., below 0.05). Then again, before making any recommendations having far-reaching consequences, the experiment described here might be considerably enlarged and conducted in various towns and cities, under various temporal and environmental conditions.

The third issue concerns the temptation to identify exposure factors as the cause of accidents (Sheehy & Chapman, 1985). Even if we find a sex difference in exposure to traffic hazards, it is not sound reasoning to assert that accidents are "caused" by exposure to traffic hazard per se: at most we can merely suggest that differences in exposure probably contribute to the sex difference in accident rates. It cannot be emphasized too much that the *reasons why accidents happen* have not been dealt with in the course of this procedure.

There are two major design limitations. One concerns the assumptions underlying the use of the chi-square test, and the other concerns the reliability of the method. Testing with chi-square requires that each subject has been observed only once, but sometimes this condition is not met in full. This is mostly because children may cross sectors and because, within each sector, students share the observation-of-children duties. The extent of the problem can be estimated by following subjects, in the style of Routledge et al. (1974). It would be interesting to know the time and route of trips, the number of sectors entered, and the number of observers encountered on the way.

The reliability of any coding system is primarily dependent upon making sure that the categories within the classification scheme are distinct from one another and upon adequately training the coders. In this project these aspects of reliability can be both assessed and optimized. Estimating age and sex can be difficult, especially when children are wearing unisex clothes, coats with hoods, and so on. For a major project, observers lacking experience with children should spend some time beforehand in nursery and elementary schools. Short of that, it helps inexperienced observers to see films and photographs portraying children in their various age groups. Some reliability estimates can be gained by having observers within pairs independently assess the ages (and/or sex) of particular children and then make comparisons of their assessments. The efficient use of the category system can easily be improved through prior training and practice. The reliability of its use can also be evaluated, again by comparing observers' categorizations for particular children.

Finally, it should be noted that subjects are observed without their (or their caretakers') knowledge or consent. This practice is contrary to the basic principle of informed consent, whereby subjects understand the nature and extent of their participation and freely consent to it. This principle may be considered particularly important when the subjects are members of the community who are especially vulnerable to exploitation by others: for example, children. Psychologists are divided in their opinions about the necessity for unobtrusive observation of naturally occurring behaviors. Most psychologists regard the practice of concealing observations as acceptable when behaviors are public and/or when the settings are open to public scrutiny. However, a minority regard any form of unaware participation in research as an intolerable invasion of the individual's right to privacy. Clearly the definition of "public behavior" is crucial to the debate. Even though some settings obviously permit public observation, the issue of privacy remains when individuals in those settings do not expect to be observed or perhaps expect not to be observed.

Conclusion

Through this exercise students become aware of several key factors relating generally to the choice and use of observational techniques. They are introduced to the participant–nonparticipant dimension; they contemplate the degree of structure in the classification scheme and the necessary compromise between an intensive and extensive scheme; they analyze the extent to which behaviors are restricted by the observer bias and observer interference; and they debate the ethics of unobtrusive observation. In addition they gain some insight into the extent to which validity and reliability can be established in relation to this particular applied social problem.

Report guidelines

The introduction in the students' reports should include three main features. First, it should include a description of the observational method, in terms of the participant–nonparticipant, structured–nonstructured, and response restriction dimensions. Second, the introduction should mention the research relating to recreational use of the street by boys and girls. Third, the specific predictions should be clearly and fully stated. The "Method" section should detail the following: choice of study area and subjects; procedures adopted by observers and traffic enumerators, including the detail of behavior-category definitions; and a description of the method of recording behavior (i.e., using the coding and collation sheets). In the "Results" section, each hypothesis is presented in turn, using the pooled class data giving details of the Observation Ratio (OR) and the results of chi-square analyses. Graphing of data is recommended. Discussion of the results is held until the final session, where the student should discuss fully the extent to which the predictions have been supported. Here, too, matters relating to the validity, reliability, and ethics of the exercise can be explored. Finally, students are encouraged to suggest ways in which the research might be improved or extended.

References

Chapman, A.J., Foot, H.C., & Wade, F.M. (1980). Children at play. In D.J. Oborne & J.A. Levis (eds.), *Human Factors in Transport Research*, vol. 2. New York: Academic Press.

Chapman, A.J., Smith, J.R., & Foot, H.C. (1980). Humour, laughter and social interaction. In P.E. McGhee, & A.J. Chapman (eds.). *Children's Humour*. New York: Wiley.

Chapman, A.J., Wade, F.M., & Foot, H.C. (eds.). (1982). *Pedestrian Accidents*. New York: Wiley.

Crano, W.D., & Brewer, M.B. (1973). *Principles of Research in Social Psychology*. New York: McGraw-Hill.

McCall, G.J., & Simmons, J.L. (eds.). (1969). *Issues in Participant Observation: Text and Reader*. Reading, Mass: Addison-Wesley.

National Safety Council (1983). *Accident Facts, 1983 Edition*. Chicago: National Safety Council.

Newson, J., & Newson, E. (1976). *The Seven Year Old in His Home Environment*. London: Allen & Unwin.

Preston, B. (1972). Statistical analyses of child pedestrian accidents in Manchester and Salford. *Accident Analysis and Prevention*, 4, 323–32.

Routledge, D.A., Repetto-Wright, R., & Howarth, C.I. (1974). A comparison of interviews and observation to obtain measures of children's exposure to risk as pedestrians. *Ergonomics*, 17, 623–38.

Sadler, J. (1972). *Children and Road Safety: A Survey amongst Mothers*. Report SS450. London: HMSO.

Sandels, S. (1975). *Children in Traffic*. London: Elek.

Sheehy, N. P., & Chapman, A. J. (1985). Adults' and children's concepts and perceptions of hazard in familiar environments. In T. Gärling and J. Valsiner (eds.), *Children within Environments: Towards a Psychology of Accident Prevention*. New York: Plenum Press.

Weick, K. E. (1968). Systematic observational methods. In G. Lindzey & E. Aronson (eds.), *The Handbook of Social Psychology* (2nd ed.), vol. 2. Reading, Mass.: Addison-Wesley.

Wolfe, A. C., & O'Day, J. (1981). Factbook on U.S. Pedestrian accidents. Ann Arbor: Highway Safety Research Institute, University of Michigan, Report no. UM-HSRI-81-05.

Appendix 1. Pedestrian data sheet

Street name and classification	Sex	Age	Primary information				Secondary information			
			Run	Walk	Stand	Sit	Road/ sidewalk	Active/ passive play	Eat/ drink	Talk
Q Richmond Street	M	7	√				R	Football		√
Q Richmond Street	M	7		√			S	Football		√
Q Richmond Street	F	14		√			S		√	
Q Norfolk Street	M	6		√			S			√
Q Norfolk Street	M	4			√		S			√
Q Newport Street	F	10		√			S			
Q Newport Street	F	10		√			R	Stilts		
B Suffolk Street	F	14		√			R			√
B Suffolk Street	M	14		√			R			√
B Suffolk Street	M	8				√	S	Photo-graphs		√
B Petersburg Street	F	8			√		S	Photo-graphs		√
B Portsmouth Street	M	9			√		R	Photo-graphs		√
Q Lynchburg Street										

Appendix 2. Traffic volume sheet

Street name	Number of vehicles in 3 minutes	Number of vehicles per hour	Street classification
Richmond Street	1	20	Q
Norfolk Street	3	60	Q
Newport Street	3	60	Q
Lynchburg Street	6	120	Q
Suffolk Street	80	1,600	B
Petersburg Street	8	160	B
Portsmouth Street			

Appendix 3. Pedestrian collation sheet

Subject group	N	Primary information					Secondary information				
		Run	Walk	Stand	Sit	R	S	Active play	Passive Play	Eat Drink	Talk
Boys, 0–4	**1**			5 **1**			5 **1**				5 **1**
Boys, 5–9	**5**	1 **1**	2, 4, **2**	12 **1**	10 **1**	1, 12 **2**	2, 4, 10 **3**	1, 2 **2**	10, 12 **2**		1, 2, 4, 10, 12 **5**
Boys, 10–14	**1**		9 **1**			9 **1**					9 **1**
Girls, 0–4											
Girls, 5–9	**1**		11 **1**				11 **1**		11 **1**		11 **1**
Girls, 10–14	**4**		3, 6, 7, 8 **4**			7, 8 **2**	3, 6 **2**	7 **1**		3 **1**	8 **1**
Grand Total (N)	**12**										

Note: Cell totals and sample sizes are in bold print.

Appendix 4. Traffic density collation sheet

Subject group	*n*	Quiet	Busy
Boys, 0–4	**1**	5 **1**	
Boys, 5–9	**5**	1, 2, 4 **3**	10, 12 **2**
Boys, 10–14	**1**		9 **1**
Girls, 0–4			
Girls, 5–9	**1**		11 **1**
Girls, 10–14	**4**	3, 6 **2**	7, 8 **2**
Grand Total (*N*)	**12**		

Note: Cell totals and sample sizes are in bold print.

8   Social skills training

Paul Robinson and Peter Trower

Summary

This exercise demonstrates how relatively small changes in individuals' social behavior can dramatically influence interactions they engage in. Two students, selected as "actors," enact a series of roughly scripted role-plays, while other students observe and record a number of objective and subjective measures of behavior. Later analysis of these measures should show how interaction has been affected by variation of behavior on the part of each participant. This can be related to the analysis of social behavior in terms of skills, with its implication that social problems may arise when individuals lack such skills and that specific skill training may help deal with the problems.

Preliminary Note

This exercise requires students to work in groups of at least four, and preferably six or seven. Right at the start, two students from each group should be selected by the group or the instructor to act a number of role-plays. They will be given brief scripts by the instructor, which they should familiarize themselves with before the exercise starts, but for the time being it is best if they *avoid reading through the rest of the chapter until the exercise has been completed.*

Aim

In this chapter we present an exercise designed to show participating students something of the psychological power and complexity of elements of social behavior, and to demonstrate just how handicapping a deficit in one or more aspects of social skills might be for an individual. More specifically, the aim is to show how altering one or two basic behavioral elements can have major effects on social interaction.

172

Introduction

Social behavior is arguably the most central and important characteristic of human beings, and yet social behavior as such has remained a relatively neglected subject in psychology and related disciplines until recent years. In the last two decades or so, however, researchers have focused increasingly on the topic, and today there is a substantial body of scientific information. Research has unraveled the components and processes of interpersonal relationships to the point where we can now identify some of the complex behavior patterns involved in friendship, love, domination, and other psychological qualities in social interaction (Argyle & Trower, 1979). From this information a striking picture emerges, showing that people possess social skills that are very complex and sophisticated.

The model behind the approach to social behavior presented in this exercise is that of skills learning, centered on the idea that human behaviors are mostly learned and can be developed by means of structured learning opportunities. A natural and valuable extension of this work is to analyze the behavior of people with problems (including psychiatric patients) in terms of skill deficits and to devise ways of overcoming these by training (Bellack & Hersen, 1979).

What then, are the important aspects of social behavior? The first and most obvious answer is that social behavior does not occur in a vacuum, but rather as part of an interaction and a context. First, an interaction has a *purpose* or goal, whether it is loosely stated, as in two old friends reminiscing over the past, or more clearly stated as in, say, a marriage ceremony. If this purpose is to be achieved, then the individuals involved in the interaction must *perceive the cues* given by the others involved with regard to which behavior it is appropriate for them to show. These cues may indicate other people's expectations, attitudes, or feelings or refer to unwritten rules of conduct generated by the social community.

Second, the individual must show *appropriate behaviors* for the situation. These must be such that they not only allow the person to achieve his or her particular aim in the interaction but also conform to the rules of the situation and the needs of others involved. For example, in a conversation between friends, one purpose of which is to maintain and perhaps extend the friendship, it is unlikely that if one person does all the talking, this will be seen as acceptable behavior by the other person.

Finally, if individuals are going to act as self-correcting systems, they must be aware of the *feedback* that they receive from others in the social setting. Equally important, they must also provide feedback for the others in the interaction. For example, if an individual is enjoying a conversation with a friend, then adequate cues of this fact should be provided.

The exact summary of these stages depends on the model one is using. Thus the Argyle and Kendon (1967) model labels these stages *perception, translation, performance*, and *feedback*. A behavioral model labels them antecedents (or setting conditions), *behavior*, and *consequences* (or social reinforcement/punishment). Which model is chosen is not crucial. The important point is to realize that an interaction can break down due to problems encountered at a variety of different stages: For example, people may behave inappropriately due to lack of skills in their repertoires or because they have misperceived the cues in the situation.

It can be seen that although we normally take the execution of social behavior for granted, it consists of a large number of complex skills. The task of research is partly to examine social behavior closely and discover what elements it consists of and what constitutes "normal" behavior under a variety of conditions (see Siegman & Feldstein, 1978).

For example, the amount and patterning of eye gaze have been shown to play a variety of important roles (Argyle & Cook, 1976). In normal two-person interactions between peers it has been shown, for example, that the person speaking looks at the listener less than the listener looks at the speaker, so that as the individuals change roles they change their gaze time. Roughly, the speaker looks at the listener for about 30% of the time spent talking, and the listener looks at the speaker for about 50 to 80% of that time. Furthermore, the speaker tends to look at the listener at the end of his or her turn (i.e., as he or she finishes speaking and changes to become the listener), and so this look often functions as a "hand-over" cue.

By deviating markedly from the normal pattern for one's cultural group, an individual affects the interaction in striking ways. Let us take an imaginary pair of people, John and Rachel. They meet for the first time at a party, and Rachel starts talking to John. All the time they are talking, John never once looks at Rachel. This makes Rachel feel very uncomfortable, since she feels either that John is not interested in her or what she has to say, or that John is very shy. Whatever explanation she uses, she does not find the interaction rewarding and is likely to keep it quite short and to move on to someone else.

What would Rachel's reaction have been if John had behaved at the opposite extreme, namely with 100% eye contact? She starts a conversation and finds that John, who is a stranger to her, never takes his eyes off her. She is likely to consider him rude and offensive, and possibly even sexually offensive, because she compares his behavior with normal male behavior in these circumstances. She might also wonder whether something dreadful had happened to her makeup or her hair ("What on earth is he staring at me like that for?"). The interpretation she makes will affect her emotional reaction. In the first place she is likely to get annoyed, and in the second place embarrassed. Either way she is likely to end the interaction quickly and move on.

These examples demonstrate how a change in a single element of behavior can radically affect social interactions, and how the other person's interpretation of the behavior will also have a major effect. Furthermore, it illustrates the importance of the context of the behavior. If Rachel and John were lovers, it would be perfectly acceptable to Rachel for John to stare into her eyes for 5 minutes continuously, while softly saying "sweet nothings." Similarly, a long pause in the conversation is likely to be felt as very awkward on a first meeting but quite normal between two lovers.

Another example of a behavioral component bound by normative rules is the question. Too many precise questions ("Who are you? Where do you live? What do you do? What do your parents do?", etc.) which allow only short answers fired off in rapid succession will make the person feel interrogated rather than conversed with; this approach is appropriate, perhaps, in an interview but hardly between potential friends. A normal interaction uses a few introductory questions to establish identity and a common area of interest from which a general conversation is developed. Contributing unequally to the interaction will create difficulties: Either individuals are seen to be monopolizing the conversation and only wanting to talk about themselves or, at the other extreme, they appear shy and withdrawn, with nothing to say for themselves.

The number of behavioral elements is considerable and, in the nonverbal domain alone, includes gaze, facial expression, gesture, posture, proximity, touching, vocalization, and physical appearance (Knapp, 1978). Such elements do not occur in isolation but are organized in many complex ways; for example, we can look at the frequency of questions, the timing of disclosures, the pattern of pauses, interruptions, and the turn-taking "system" (Duncan & Fiske, 1977).

In the following exercise we shall focus mainly on a few of these specifiable and quantifiable behaviors. Participants may also like to look at the more interpretive aspects, however, in ways to be suggested later. The exercise will attempt to show how altering one or two of the basic behaviors can have major effects on interaction, as discussed in our imaginary examples involving John and Rachel. It is to be hoped that this will bring students' attention to a variety of points. It should sensitize them to the complexity of social behavior and the possibilities of fine-grained analysis. It should also illustrate how handicapping it might be for an individual to exhibit social behavior that deviates too far from the normal. This type of approach helps clinical psychologists and others to identify those aspects of an individual's behavior that might be contributing to a problem and may enable them to train that person in a more socially acceptable manner.

Method

Subjects

The main activity is a series of role-plays by two students, which is observed by other students. This allows a lot of flexibility; the minimum number needed is a working group of four – two actors and two observers, but it is best to have at least four observers and two actors. With larger numbers, more observers can be added to record a wider range of behaviors, or the class can be split up into a number of independent groups so that data can be pooled later for analysis.

Resources

Basic resources can be minimal: two chairs facing each other, for the actors: paper and pencil, for recording by the observers; and a minimum of two stopwatches (or at least a clock with a sweep second hand). However, the availability of other equipment, in particular more stopwatches or event recorders, allows a greater degree of refinement in data collection. Ideally then, a video or audio system is set up to record the interaction, and these provide a record with which observations can be compared or new observations made afterward.

If there are a number of groups, each will need a separate space or room to work in. If video equipment is used, then groups may need to arrange some sort of schedule to share it.

Procedure

The exercise essentially involves having two actors enact a series of four role-plays of about 5 minutes each, while the rest of the group observes and records aspects of their behavior, so the first thing here is to consider and decide on the behavioral measures to be used. The main emphasis is on objective measures of behavior, as will be seen later in this chapter, but a subjective measure is also included to reflect more impressionistic responses to interactions.

Objective measures.   The measures suggested here have been chosen on the basis of ease of measurement and analysis. The amount and type

Table 8.1. *A selection of measures and the equipment they require*

Type of measure	Behavior to be measured	Clock with sweep second hand	Stop-watch	Event counter	Audio tape recorder	Video tape recorder	Minimum number of observers
		Equipment					
F	Questions	X	√	√	√		1
F	Turn changes	X	√	√	√		1
F	Smiling	X	√	√		√	2
F	Posture shift	X	√	√		√	2
F	Eye gaze	X	√	√		√	2
D	Speech		X		√		1
D	Smiling		X			√	2
D	Eye gaze		X			√	2
D	Gesturing		X			√	2

Note: For full definitions of behavior and explanations of the table, see text.
Key: F = frequency count
D = duration
X = essential
√ = extra equipment that would be useful

of equipment available is also a factor in choosing the measures, and we have therefore put this information, together with the list of measures, in Table 8.1.

Two of the basic types of objective measures are frequency counts and measures of duration. For frequency counts you add up the number of occurrences of each behavior of each interactant over a specified period of time. We suggest a period of 5 minutes, starting from the beginning of each interaction. The period chosen is arbitrary, the main essentials being a defined starting point, a period long enough to give a reasonable sample of behavior, and that the period is kept constant for each interaction, both in the student group and between groups (for ease of analysis, see the discussion of data analysis in the section of this chapter entitled "Results").

There is also the problem of what constitutes one occurrence of the behavior chosen. Although we could provide definitions, we feel that this would sacrifice an important part of the learning involved in having to decide on definitions prior to making observations. No one definition is necessarily a correct one: Different researchers can, and do, use different definitions, although they may try to use the same ones for consistency and to make it easier to compare the results of different studies. The question

178 TECHNIQUE APPLICATIONS

of definitions, then, is left open for discussion in the class, but we give some guidelines later.

"Asking a question" is a fairly easily defined behavior, but how will two different pieces of information requested in one sentence be counted: as one question or two? Turn changes are also often clearly distinguishable, but what if the speaker stops, and there is a pause during which the other person makes a noise (such as "er" or "um") but does not say any words, and the original speaker starts again? A clear definition can help avoid these problems, although it may not cover every circumstance. A tape recording can be particularly useful here to allow for analysis afterward. The recording can be stopped and replayed in order to check how a particular instance fits with the definition decided upon. Similarly, with smiling, posture shifts, and eye gaze, it can be difficult to decide whether or not there has been a short break, making one long occurrence of a particular behavior into two or three shorter ones. Again, a recording for later playback can help overcome these difficulties.

The number of occurrences can be noted either by using a prepared record sheet on which a tally count is kept or by using an event recorder. The second method is preferable, especially with potentially high-frequency behavior such as eye gaze, since it can be done more quickly and without the observers having to take their eyes off the subjects.

Another problem in measuring frequencies is that some behaviors may be exhibited by both subjects simultaneously (for example smiling). This is reflected in the column for "minimum number of observers" in Table 8.1. Clearly, to get an overall total for, say smiling, it is necessary to have two observers, each watching separate actors. Interesting information can be found by analyzing the behavior of each of the actors separately, but since this can lead to a massive amount of analysis, we suggest combining both subjects' totals into a single score.

The duration measures require similar considerations. These are records of the total duration of the behavior within a given period (for example, with the same 5 minutes of interaction). Definitions of when the behavior is or is not occurring will have to be decided upon (do within-speaker pauses count as speech or not?). The recording procedure will involve using a cumulative stopwatch that is started and stopped at the same time as the behavior, with totals for each actor being combined to provide a single figure.

One final point on recording is that the number of observers suggested is the bare minimum needed to obtain a result. Due to the difficulty in recording these types of behavior it is desirable at least to double the number of observers for each behavior. In this way it is possible to check the accuracy of the observation. It is also possible to calculate such things as inter-rater reliability coefficients, although we do not consider this essential here, since there is likely to be plenty of information for analysis. It is suggested, though, that if two or more observers differ markedly they reobserve the behavior on the video or audio tape recording. If this is not possible or if the discrepancy is small, the mean figure can be taken. This requirement highlights one value of a tape recording (either audio or visual): It allows analysis of any number of other behaviors at leisure, after the interaction has occurred, and permits any one observer to check his or her own (intra-rater) reliability.

Subjective measures. For a subjective measure we suggest the use of a semantic differential such as that used by Trower, Bryant, and Argyle (1978), which is shown in appendix 1. This is used in the normal way, with raters scoring each interaction on a 7-point scale for each adjective pair. Each actor, at least, should fill in the semantic differentials for him- or herself and separately for the other actor. This allows you to compare judgments of self with those of the participant observer. Discrepancies between the two will help highlight the fact that subjective judgments about self often differ in significant ways from the judgments of others. In addition, observers can rate each actor, thus permitting further comparisons to be made.

We therefore suggest the following procedure. After each interaction has been role-played, the actors are each given two copies of the semantic differential to complete before they start the next role-play.

Exercise organization. Since there are a large number of tasks to be carried out when the role-plays take place, groups of students will need to be well organized before they start. If video or audio tape recording equipment is available, it will have to be set up and checked for quality (particularly of the sound and lighting). A standard shot of two people in the same frame, orientated at about 45 degrees to each other, is quite sufficient, without panning and zooming: It should not be necessary to have all the students acting as film crew!

One person can be in charge of timing the 5 minutes from the start of interaction and signaling it to the observers. (A simple call of "time" would also mark it on the tape.) The remaining four students (using a standard group of seven, for example) can then record the various measures decided upon. Since we suggest doubling the minimum numbers of observers, this means that two behaviors having a minimum requirement of one observer can be observed and checked, or only one behavior having a minimum requirement of two observers. Clearly, this emphasizes the advantage of making a tape recording. For example, if only an audio tape recorder is available, it will be possible to have the four students observing and recording eye gaze during the "live" interaction and then measuring three behaviors from the audiotape (i.e., frequency of questions, turn changes, and duration of speech). Indeed, with a little ingenuity they might manage to measure both frequency and duration of eye gaze by holding a stop-watch in one hand and an event recorder in the other. They will then have to press both when eye gaze starts, and only the stopwatch when it finishes (or it might be easier always to press both and divide the resulting fre-quency by two). In this way the four observers could measure five elements of behavior, and the actors would also produce a semantic differential for each role-play.

Observational measures to be used should be discussed and agreed on. If a number of different groups are involved, it is best if all agree on the measures being employed so that data can be pooled for analysis.

Finally, when the group is ready, the "actors" can be brought in and asked to enact each script, stop when signaled, fill out a semantic differen-tial form, and get ready for the next role-play.

Results

Each group of students should have collected a set of measures on each of four role-plays (under varying constraints), which lasted 5 minutes each. For each measure they should preferably have two results, which can be averaged, provided they are reasonably close. If not close they should be remeasured or, if this is impossible, an average will have to be accepted, but recognized as being of doubtful validity. The method of analysis will be the same for each measure, so we will refer only to one set of data from now on.

Once the group members have finished collecting their results, they can be allowed to see the actors' scripts for a debriefing. Then they should graph their results for each measure. The graphs will have four points, with the differing role-plays (A, B, C, D) along the x-axis and the amount of the behavior (in terms of either frequency or duration) along the y-axis. Similar sketch graphs can be drawn for each of the adjective pairs in the semantic differential, with one for each of the actors.

For a more quantitative analysis, all groups should pool their results. This then gives a number of values for each measure under each condition, and an analysis of variance can be carried out (see Keppel & Saufley, 1980). (This is the reason for requiring consistent definitions and timings across groups.) A similar approach can be used with each adjective pair of the semantic differential, although here the pair of values obtained from each actor pair should be kept separate rather than averaged. (For this analysis an extra factor could be used of self-ratings versus participant observer ratings.)

In this manner an analysis of variance can be carried out for each measure taken, and the results of these analyses will show whether or not variations in observable behavior have occurred under the differing situational constraints. The analysis of results from the semantic differential will show a similar effect for subject impressions.

Discussion

This exercise is designed to demonstrate that a relatively small change in behavior from that which is socially "normal" can have a striking effect and indeed even seriously impair social interaction. We would expect a considerable change on subjective impressions between the role-play where normal behavior was specified for the actors and the other three where alterations were required (see now the actors' scripts). We would also expect variations in observable behavior, although, depending on the behavior change specified and the measures used, this may not show up so clearly. One of the important points that we hope will emerge is the difficulty of pinning down subjective impressions of impaired social behavior in terms of changes in observable, quantified behaviors.

Since variations in behavior can lead to impaired interactions, it is important that we have an understanding of what constitutes "normal" behavior if we are to help those with difficulties in social interactions. This type of difficulty (i.e., impaired social skills) has been implicated in a wide variety of social problems, and there has been a considerable upsurge of interest and literature in using social skills training to help overcome such problems.

The behavioral changes and suggested measures were chosen with this body of knowledge in mind to demonstrate some of the important variables in social behavior. They were also chosen as being some of the simpler behaviors with which to work. However, we think that students may find difficulties in working with these behaviors, and this will demonstrate the complexity of the problem. This is likely to be particularly true where video equipment is unavailable; students will realize just how many different types of behavior are occurring, but they can only focus on one or two at a time.

When a video tape recording has been made, students might like to replay it and notice how various other behaviors are used in a social inter-action and how they fit together to form a system. Using the turn-taking system as one example, the observer may find some or all of the behaviors listed in appendix 2.

The complexity of a social interaction has meant that, for this exercise, we have had to limit ourselves to easily specified and easily observed behaviors. More complex analysis requires a greater familiarity with ob-serving social behavior, plus sophisticated methodology and equipment. Nevertheless, we hope that this limited analysis will demonstrate our basic point clearly, namely that it requires only small variations in social be-havior from the norm to affect an individual's interaction significantly, and the result can be serious social problems.

References

Argyle, M., & Cook, M. (1976). *Gaze and Mutual Gaze.* Cambridge: Cambridge University Press.

Argyle, M., & Kendon, A. (1967). The experimental analysis of social performance. In L. Berkowitz (ed.), *Advances in Experimental Social Psychology*, vol. 3, pp. 55–98. New York: Academic Press.

Argyle, M., & Trower, P. (1979). *Person to Person: A Guide to Social Skills.* New York: Harper & Row.

Bellack, A.S., & Hersen, M. (eds.) (1979). *Research and Practice in Social Skills Training.* New York: Plenum Press.

Duncan, S., & Fiske, D.W. (1977). *Face to Face Interaction.* New Jersey: Erlbaum.

Keppel, G., & Saufley, W., Jr. 1980. *Introduction to Design and Analysis: A Student Handbook.* San Francisco: Freeman.

Knapp, M.L. (1978). *Nonverbal Communication in Human Interaction*, 2nd ed. New York: Holt, Rinehart & Winston.

Siegman, A.W., & Feldstein, S. (1978). *Nonverbal Behavior and Communication.* New Jersey: Erlbaum.

Trower, P., Bryant, B., & Argyle, M. (1978). *Social Skills and Mental Health.* Pittsburgh: University of Pittsburgh Press.

Appendix 1. General ratings

Cold	—	—	—	—	—	—	—	Warm
Assertive	—	—	—	—	—	—	—	Submissive
Socially anxious	—	—	—	—	—	—	—	Calm
Happy	—	—	—	—	—	—	—	Sad
Rewarding	—	—	—	—	—	—	—	Unrewarding
Poised	—	—	—	—	—	—	—	Awkward
Socially skillful	—	—	—	—	—	—	—	Socially unskillful

Source: P. Trower, B. Bryant, & M. Argyle, *Social Skills and Mental Health* (Pittsburgh: University of Pittsburgh Press, 1978).

Appendix 2. Turn-taking signals

Handing over.

Meaning: "I've finished; your turn now."
Asks question and continues looking. Leans forward.
As A finishes talking, looks at B and then looks down or away.
Stops gesturing.
Changes voice pitch on last word or two.
Uses concluding phrase.
Doesn't start new phrase.

Taking up.

Meaning: "Please finish; I want to speak."
Prepares other that he or she is going to speak.
Withholds any response until other stops speaking, and then takes up conversation.
Uses simple reflection, picking up a word or phrase, but then keeps the floor.
Interrupts and speaks strongly, avoids speech errors and keeps talking.
In group, gets speaker's attention by body shifts and orientation.
Interrupts B during pause for thought.

Suppressing a turn claim.

Meaning: "I'm not stopping."
As A reaches a point, doesn't pause, doesn't look back at other, continues gesturing, talks louder.

Resisting a handover.

Meaning: "You keep talking."
Uses a listener response, and keeps looking at other.
Asks question to turn other's question around, then continues looking at other.

Source: Adapted from P. Trower, B. Bryant, & M. Argyle, *Social Skills and Mental Health* (Pittsburgh: University of Pittsburgh Press, 1978).

9 Person perception

Mark Cook

Summary

The accuracy with which we make judgments about other people is a topic
of considerable practical importance, but research in this area has been
hampered by methodological difficulties. In the present exercise some of
the methodological problems encountered in measuring accuracy of person
perception are discussed and a means of overcoming them is suggested,
using a rank order method.

A personality inventory is used to provide an external criterion against
which subjects' perceptions about others' personality, gained from interaction in a group discussion, are compared. This provides a measure of
accuracy and allows the testing of a number of hypotheses about factors
affecting the accuracy of person perception.

Aim

The aim of this exercise is to introduce some of the problems involved in
measuring how accurately people perceive each others' personalities and to
examine a number of hypotheses about factors affecting accuracy of person
perception.

The specific hypotheses are (1) that judges' accuracy differs with
different personality traits being judged (for example, that extroversion
will be perceived more accurately than neuroticism); (2) that accuracy of
perception is related to personality (for example, that extroverted judges
will be more accurate and neurotic judges less accurate); (3) that there
is no sex difference in accuracy of person perception. Possible additional
hypotheses concern the effect of length and topic of group discussion on
accuracy of members' judgments.

Introduction

Many people pride themselves on being very good judges of others; many
social psychologists thought the study of such judgments was an easy area
to research. Both have been proved wrong. Research on the accuracy of
person perception has been hampered by methodological problems, so
much so that the impression was created, in the years following publication of Cronbach's (1955) critique, that research was virtually impossible.
Indeed, the apparent difficulties led many workers in the field to argue, by
a familiar process of rationalization, that the issue was not important, or
even that it did not exist. This conclusion was obviously false: People do
make decisions about each other; these decisions are often wrong; and the
consequences of such wrong decisions are often serious. Hence, ways of
finding out if someone's opinions about others are accurate are vitally
needed, and refinements in experimental method since Cronbach's critique
have provided them.

The accuracy of people's judgments of each other is a significant topic
at a number of levels. It has obvious practical value, in that people are
constantly forming opinions of each other and acting on those opinions. A
person who habitually forms wrong impressions of others will find life
difficult. Consider, for example, the decision about whether to accept the
offer of a ride late at night; ask someone to marry you or accept such an
offer made to you; ask someone to help you get a job by writing you a good
reference; intervene in a quarrel between two friends. A similar range of
decisions occurs in professional contexts where an individual may have to
decide whether to employ this person or that person; release this person
from prison or not; accept this person's plea for special treatment or reject
it.

At a more general level, person perception is one of the starting points
of social psychology. Talking to someone, joining the person's group, staying in the group, leaving the group, and conforming, bargaining, persuad-
ing, all presuppose you have perceived the individual, summed the person
up, judged the person, and formed an impression of him or her. It is a
truism that people react to the world as they see it, not to the world as it
really is, yet it is a very important truism, for the discrepancy between the
seen social world and the real social world is often very great.

Finally, accuracy of person perception is relevant to a broad class of
theories of social psychology. Phenomenological theories emphasize
heavily the point that people react to what they see; therefore, the way
people see the world is the most important issue, if not indeed the only
issue, in psychology. Since the most important things people perceive are

generally other people and their moods, intentions, and thoughts, accuracy of person perception is a key issue.

Trait-rating studies and their problems

The history of the study of the accuracy of person perception falls into three phases; the period of "naive empiricism," the period of neglect, and the period of revival. The date of the ending of naive empiricism can be given precisely: 1955; the date of the revival of interest might be set more vaguely in the early 1970s. Before 1955, numerous studies of accuracy of person perception appeared, the majority using one of two favorite paradigms: "trait rating" and "empathy." In a trait-rating study, the judge expresses an opinion of the subject, using a multipoint scale; thus, Taft (1955) required his judges to rate each other, on 5-point scales, for persuasiveness, social assertiveness, sociability, carefulness, drive, and conformity. The judges' ratings were then compared with a set of criterion ratings, and difference scores were calculated. The smaller the summed difference between a particular judge's ratings and the criterion ratings, the more accurate a judge of others that person was taken to be. There are two main snags with this paradigm – one obvious, one more subtle. The obvious snag is the criterion: What is the "correct" value of the subject's social assertiveness, drive, and other qualities? Taft used "expert opinion"; other researchers used self-ratings by the subject or some form of group consensus. All, however, are obviously themselves judgments of the subject, and there is no reason to think that they are any better than the judge's opinion.

The less obvious snag arises from the use of difference scores, which prove to be statistically complex and potentially very misleading. These statistical complexities have come to be known as *Cronbach's components*. Cronbach's (1955) paper analyzed difference scores based on ratings of a number of traits, across a number of subjects; this yields seven "components," but the simpler case of ratings of one trait yields three components. These are "mean," "spread," and "correlation."

Mean, or "levels." If the mean of a judge's ratings is higher or lower than the mean of the criterion scores, the difference score will be higher, and the apparent accuracy consequently lower; if a constant error were subtracted from, or added to, all the ratings, the judge's apparent accuracy would be improved. The constant error is an artifact of the use of numerical scales and may not reflect the judge's accuracy of perception. The judge may match the mean of the criterion ratings by chance or may match them through a more or less conscious decision to use the middle of the scale, as opposed to actually thinking about the target person's personality, as the experimenter intends him or her to.

Spread.   The spread of a judge's ratings may correspond to the spread of the criterion scores, or it may be greater or smaller. If the judge's spread is greater than the criterion spread, the judge's difference score will be greater, and his or her accuracy score correspondingly lower. Again the judge may match the spread of the criterion ratings by chance or by semiconscious strategy, rather than by a conscious decision about the subjects' personalities.

Correlation.   The judge's ratings may correlate with the criterion scores. That is, the judge may have correctly perceived which subjects score higher than the mean and which subjects score lower than the mean. In other words, the judge may have placed the subjects in an approximately correct order of possession of the trait being judged.

Cronbach's analysis was very valuable and penetrating, but its scope has tended to be overestimated. His observations apply only to trait-rating studies and not to other ways of studying accuracy of person perception. The problem arises in trait-rating studies because the judge is required to express an opinion in terms of an arbitrary numerical scale; different judges may represent the same estimated level of a given trait – for example, extroversion – by different numbers. This is a fault of numerical rating scales that has been noted in the study of personality and attitudes for years. In fact, the same problem exists in most school and college grading systems, and some teachers deal with it by carefully comparing samples of papers marked by different examiners.

Empathy studies and their problems

In the empathy paradigm, the judges predict how the subjects will complete a personality questionnaire; the criterion – how the subject actually completed the questionnaire – looks sound but is not. The difficulties arise from two types of assumptions: "stereotype accuracy" and "assumed similarity." When asked to say whether the subject agrees that "his/her mother is (or was) a good person," the judge may not consider that subject as an individual, seeking evidence that he or she seemed to think well of his or her mother; the judge may attempt instead the easier tasks of deciding either how most people would answer such a question (stereotype accuracy) or how the judge would answer such a question (assumed similarity). In the former case the judge is in effect giving an opinion about the questionnaire item – that most people would say their mother is (or was) a good person – and in the latter case the judge is giving his or her own opinion: Yes, my mother was a good person. But in neither case is the judge doing what the experimenter actually wanted: thinking about the subject. These problems are termed collectively *response set artifacts*.

Such artifacts arise in any study of the accuracy of person perception that uses a multiple choice format, not just ones that use personality questionnaires. Whenever the judge has to choose between two or more outcomes, he or she can "cheat" by considering which of them is more likely, not which of them the particular subject chose. Thus, recently devised tests of the accuracy of person perception include Schroeder's filmed binary choice procedure, in which the judge has to decide which of two responses the subject will make (for example, break a light bulb or water a potted plant), and Fancher's "programmed case" method, in which judges decide, retrospectively, what choice the subject made at a crucial moment in his life – for instance, at the outbreak of World War II, did he join the army, go to college as planned, or become a journalist? In both of these tests, as in any multiple choice test, the possibility exists that one response will be more likely than the others and that some judges will be able to use this information to get higher scores, without considering the subjects as individuals.

Similarly the judge can assume similarity and choose, as the subject's choice or outcome, the judge's own choice or outcome; there is evidence from a wide variety of experiments that judges commonly do precisely that. Byrne and Blaylock's (1963) study of married couples found that they assumed considerably more similarity of opinion – to the extent of husband –wife correlations of .69 and .89 – than was justified by the actual similarity of their opinions, represented by correlations of .30 and .44.

The ranking method as a solution to artifacts

Cronbach's (1955) discovery of complicated and seemingly insoluble problems in apparently straightforward experiments discouraged researchers so much that they largely abandoned the topic and came perhaps by rationalizing, to consider it unimportant or even nonexistent. The issue is, however, a real and important one, and there are ways of studying it that are not methodologically suspect.

Various attempts have been made to avoid the problems created by Cronbach's components. Data can be analyzed more carefully, separately identifying Cronbach's components; several complex methods of analyzing trait ratings have been devised. Another solution is to calculate correlations between the judge's ratings and the criterion ratings; a correlation necessarily eliminates the level and spread components of the accuracy score.

However, these methods do not solve the problem of response set artifacts, and, in any case, they apply only to rating studies. The response set problem can be solved only by altering the judge's task so that the judge cannot use response sets. The experimenter can do this by altering the questions asked, or, more drastically, by altering the structure of the task itself and using matching or sorting methods. Another way of restructuring the task is to require the judge to give his or her opinion in rank order form. This eliminates Cronbach's level and spread effects and gives a single score representing the judge's ability to distinguish among the subjects. Requiring judges to give their judgments in rank order form also eliminates response set artifacts. The essential point of such artifacts is that the judge makes an informed guess (or an uninformed but lucky guess) about what most subjects will say or do or think. If the judges are required to rank order the subjects they are forced to differentiate among the subjects and cannot assume that all or most subjects are like the judges themselves or that all or most will make the usual, or socially desirable, response.

The present exercise, then, uses the rank order method to overcome the methological difficulties and to allow a meaningful investigation of some of the factors affecting accuracy in judging others' personality. The specific hypotheses have already been given in the "Aim" section.

Method

Subjects

This exercise requires for each experimenter or group of experimenters a group of between 7 and 14 subjects. Subject groups should, where possible, be balanced for sex, and members should not know one another too well.

Materials

Materials needed are copies for each subject of a suitable personality questionnaire, which should be provided by the instructor, together with a scoring key and information about population norms. For present purposes it is assumed that the questionnaire being used is the Eysenck Personality Inventory (EPI), which measures extroversion and neuroticism, but the instructor may decide to use a different scale. A supply of Perceived Rank Order forms and Criterion Rank Order forms (one of each, per subject, for each trait being studied) will also be required (see appendixes 1 and 2 for examples of these forms).

During the exercise, subjects need to be identified by letters, *A* through *N*, avoiding numbers, since they might create confusion during judgment and scoring. This requires a supply of name tags to be worn by subjects, or cards to be placed on a table in front of them, so that they can identify and refer to each other when asked to make judgments about others.

Finally, each group will need a comfortable place in which to hold a brief discussion.

Procedure

It is best, if possible, first to administer the personality questionnaire, score it to provide the criterion data, and then set up groups that include the largest possible spread of criterion scores for the dimensions under consideration. If this is not possible, all the testing can be done at the same time with a preselected group of subjects, but it may then turn out that there is little actual spread of criterion scores in the group, and so the experimental task becomes more difficult.

Either way, the personality inventory is distributed to subjects and completed by them first, according to the printed instructions on it. This should pose no problems unless some subjects have difficulty understanding some of the items, in which case they should be given assistance.

When the criterion data has been collected, subjects are then assigned to groups and asked to discuss a topic such as "student social life" for say, 15 minutes. Each group should have an experimenter or assistant present at the start of the discussion. To help get the discussion started and ensure that every group member speaks at least once, the experimenter should ask each person in the group to say in turn what he or she thinks about the topic. Once the discussion is under way, the experimenter should withdraw. When the 15 minutes have passed, discussions should be stopped and subjects given the Perceived Rank Order forms (appendix 1), and the instructions printed at the top of the form should be read out to them. Subjects are then asked to complete the form, and experimenters should circulate to ensure that the instructions have been understood. When subjects have completed their forms, they should note their identifying letter and sex on the forms, and then these can be collected.

Analysis and results

For each subject there will be an inventory form and a Perceived Rank Order form. The first thing to do, if it has not already been done, is to score the inventories and rank order the results to construct the criterion rank order for each dimension under consideration.

Using the Criterion Rank Order form in appendix 2, students can calculate, for each subject, rank order correlations for each pair of perceived and criterion rank orders. From each subject, therefore, students should have available (1) identifying letter, sex, and a rank order correlation value for each trait studied, and (2) the sets of perceived ranks.

The correlation values are, in effect, accuracy scores indicating how successful subjects were in ranking group members according to their personality scores. Data should be collated for each group, and, if desired, results can be pooled from a number of groups.

To aid subsequent analysis, it is useful to draw up a matrix such as the one presented in Table 9.1, listing an arbitrary number for each subject: sex, extroversion, and neuroticism scores; and correlation coefficients for predicting extroversion and neuroticism.

The experimental hypotheses set out at the beginning of the exercise can be tested, using the tabulated data for each group or for a number of groups, as follows:

Comparing accuracy of judgment of different traits. The accuracy of ranking extroversion is compared with the accuracy of ranking neuroticism, across whole groups or a number of groups, using the t-test for related groups.

The generality of ability to perceive personality accurately is determined by correlating accuracy scores for extroversion with accuracy scores for neuroticism, across the whole group. (But first look at the mean and standard deviation of accuracy scores for each trait: if subjects' accuracy scores for neuroticism are consistently near zero, no correlation with accuracy scores for extroversion can be obtained).

Sex differences in accuracy. Accuracy scores of males and females for each trait are compared, using t-tests for unrelated groups, or two-way analysis of variance, with sex of subject as one factor and trait ranked as the second (repeated) factor (see Kirk, 1968).

Personality correlates of accuracy. This analysis employs the criterion data as a measure of the subjects' personality. This analysis may be performed in one of two ways. Subjects can be divided into two groups according to their extroversion or neuroticism scores, and t-tests for unrelated groups, or two-way analysis of variance, can be calculated, as was done in comparing accuracy of judgment of different traits. Alternatively, the criterion data may be correlated with the accuracy scores.

Topic of group discussion, length of group discussion. These factors, if included in the design, are compared across groups, again using t-test for

Table 9.1. *Layout for tabulating main personality and accuracy data*

Subject number	Sex	EPI		Accuracy	
		E	N	rE	rN
1					
2					
3					
4					
5					
6					
7					
8					
9					
10					
11					
12					
13					
14					

Key:
E = Extroversion score
N = Neuroticism score
rE = Correlation coefficient for extroversion
rN = Correlation coefficient for neuroticism

unrelated groups, or two-way analysis of variance, in which trait is the second (repeated) factor.

Some other analyses are also possible. For these a second matrix should be shown up, listing the subject's arbitrary number and the subject's perceived rank order of the whole group for each trait studied (see Table 9.2).

Implicit personality theory. For each subject, calculate a rank order correlation (see Siegel, 1956) between the perceived rank order for extro-

Table 9.2. *Layout for analysis of consensus on perceived rank order*

	Rank for subject													
	A	B	C	D	E	F	G	H	I	J	K	L	M	N
1														
2														
3														
4														
5														
6														
7														
8														
9														
10														
11														
12														
13														
14														

version and the perceived rank order for neuroticism. A positive correlation indicates that the subject expects extroverted persons to be neurotic, whereas a negative correlation indicates that the subject expects extroverted persons to have stable personalities. A zero correlation indicates the subject sees no link between extroversion and neuroticism; extroversion and neuroticism as personality traits are in fact uncorrelated.

Consensus judgment. Use the data of a whole group, for each trait separately, to determine whether a group consensus exists; even if subjects are unable to rank each other according to the criterion personality scores, they may agree among themselves about who is most extroverted, least extroverted, and so forth. Kendall's Coefficient of Concordance (see Siegel, 1956) gives an index of overall consensus among members of the group. If a significant consensus is obtained (see Siegel), calculate the mean rank attributed to each subject by the group, and examine these means in the light of the criterion data.

Discussion

The results of the exercise should show that people can judge at least some aspects of personality, while at the same time finding that they cannot judge others. My own observations suggest that it is likely that subjects will be found to judge extroversion somewhat better than neuroticism. If this is so, it might be argued that sufficient relevant information can be communicated in the course of a fairly short discussion for subjects to make an informed estimate of a person's sociability and impulsiveness but not of their neuroticism.

Trope and Bassok (1983) show that subjects who have been told to test a hypothesis about another person ask more penetrating, diagnostic questions. In the present exercise, subjects do not know until the end of the group discussion that they will have to judge the others' personality; Trope and Bassok's results suggest that telling people *before* the group discussion would both alter the nature of the discussion, and perhaps improve accuracy.

If subjects do achieve some accuracy in ranking more than one trait, it is possible to determine whether any transfer from one task to the other occurs; that is, whether the accurate judge of extroversion is also an accurate judge of neuroticism. Previous research found no evidence of generality of accuracy, although Cline (1964) did find some limited transfer when judgment tasks were all based on the same set of filmed interviews.

The exercise bears some resemblance to the sort of decisions often made during the course of job interviewing, in which candidates are ranked in order of perceived suitability, before the lucky one or more at the head of the rank order are offered the position being competed for. It is reassuring to know that such decisions have some demonstrable validity, but they also have considerable limitations. As the exercise is likely to demonstrate, some traits cannot be judged with above-chance accuracy, and even the traits more accurately judged should show only a limited accuracy.

Positive results from the exercise can be taken to show that the ranking method is free of the artifacts found in other types of research on accuracy of person perception, which allow the subjects to get above-chance accuracy scores without really thinking about the target people. The results also, incidentally, provide some evidence of the validity of the personality measures. If the personality measures were unreliable or lacked validity, judges' rankings would presumably bear no resemblance to criterion rankings derived from the measures.

Limitations of the study

There are two main limitations to this study: inadequate control of the sample of behavior used for the judgment of personality, and the low reliability and subjectivity of the criterion.

The group discussion leaves the sample of behavior poorly controlled in two ways. It is impossible to ensure that every person in the group makes an equal contribution to the discussion, and some may contribute so little that their silence is the only information that the rest have to judge them by. It is difficult to ensure that the subjects have no other information about each other besides that made available in the discussion. (Also since each group of subjects had a different discussion, it is difficult to generalize across groups or to pool data from different groups). These difficulties are common to all research using small groups, whose essential spontaneity makes rigorous experimental control difficult. One possible compromise between control, and richness and diversity of information, is the use of video recordings. It would be possible, for example, to video-record a group discussion and play the recordings to as many experimental subjects as required.

The criterion of extroversion and neuroticism in this study was the Eysenck Personality Inventory, which imposes two sorts of limitations on the results. The first is simply that judges' perceived rank order correlations cannot, in theory, exceed the retest reliability of the extroversion and neuroticism scales (.82 and .84, respectively), though higher correlations than these figures might occur by chance.

The second limitation is that the inventory, like other criteria in research on accuracy of person perception, turns out, in the last analysis, to be just another opinion about other people. The extroversion and neuroticism scores derive from the answers that the target people gave to sets of 24 questions about themselves; they are, in a sense, self-judgments or self-perceptions made by the target people, which the experiment compares with judgments of perceptions made by the subjects. Depending on one's view of personality, one might see this as an inevitable limitation, or just a reflection of the current limitations, of personality measurement. Obviously many traits are socially defined and exist only in the eye of the beholder; it would be absurd to suppose there could ever be a way of measuring "politeness," for example, that did not depend somehow on other people's opinions. But if everyone thought a particular person was unintelligent, it would be possible to prove them wrong by showing that person had a high IQ. According to Eysenck's theories of the biological basis of personality, it might be possible eventually to measure extroversion or neuroticism by behavioral or psychophysiological methods, without relying on people's opinions at any stage. Recently McArthur and Baron (1983) and Swann (1984) have suggested that accuracy of person perception in real life is generally higher than in laboratory studies, because social norms and expectations, the social context, and the "negotiation of social identities" all make people's behavior more predictable.

Conclusions

Assuming, for the sake of argument, that the method used here is a satisfactory test of individual skill in forming judgments of others, it will be apparent that most people are much poorer at this task than they like to think. Judgments of extroversion – a highly visible characteristic, after all – are likely to have some accuracy, although not a great deal. Attempts to judge people in terms of neurotic tendency generally prove to have little if any validity. Yet people often make judgments about traits like these, with significant practical implications, for example, in the context of job interviews, case conferences, reports on school behavior, or job performance assessments. All these types of judgments, often made with great faith in their accuracy, are likely to be imperfect reflections of what the person being judged is really like. In addition to learning to deal with methodological problems of research in this area, you may also learn from this exercise to be somewhat more cautious, less sweeping, and less confident in your assessments of others.

References

Byrne, D., & Blaylock, B. (1963). Similarity and assumed similarity of attitudes between husbands and wives. *Journal of Abnormal and Social Psychology, 67,* 636–40.
Cline, V. (1964). Interpersonal perception. In B.A. Maher (ed.), *Progress in Experimental Personality Research*, vol. 1. New York: Academic Press.
Cronbach, L.J. (1955). Processes affecting scores on "understanding of others" and assumed similarity. *Psychological Bulletin, 52,* 177–93.
Kirk, R.E. (1968). *Experimental Design: Procedures for the Behavioural Sciences.* Belmont, Calif.: Brooks Cole.
McArthur, L. Z., & Baron, R.M. (1983). Towards an ecological theory of social perception. *Psychological Review, 90,* 215–38.
Siegel, S. (1956). *Non-parametric Statistics for the Behavioural Sciences.* New York: McGraw-Hill.

Swann, W.B. (1984). Quest for accuracy in person perception: A matter of pragmatics. *Psychological Review, 91*, 457–477.

Taft, R. (1955). The ability to judge people. *Psychological Bulletin 52*, 1–23.

Trope, Y., & Bassok, M. (1983). Information gathering strategies in intuitive interviewing. *Journal of Experimental Social Psychology, 9*, 560–76.

Further reading

Cook, M. (1982). Perceiving others. In M. St. Davids & M. Davey (eds.), *Judging People*. New York: McGraw-Hill.

Appendix 1. Perceived rank order form

Instructions:

Decide who is the most extroverted person in your group; then enter the number *1* next to his or her letter on the form. Decide who is the second most extroverted, and enter the number *2* next to his or her letter at rank position 2. *Extroversion can be defined as a combination of sociability and impulsiveness.* Continue this process until every person in the group has been given a rank. Include every member of the group in the rank order, and remember to include yourself in the rank order. Ties are not permitted; for example, you cannot put two or more persons down as third. You can start at the other end of the rank order if you prefer, deciding who is the least extroverted, second least extroverted, and so on, or you can use any other strategy you prefer. Repeat the procedure for *neuroticism*, which *can be defined as a general tendency to become anxious or upset about things.*

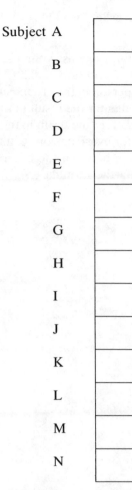

Subject A
B
C
D
E
F
G
H
I
J
K
L
M
N

Note: 1. For neuroticism, use a similar list but on a separate sheet, or the back of this sheet, to prevent subjects comparing rank orders.

2. Where the group size is less than 14 and the experimenter does not have time to prepare sheets with the correct number of rank positions, surplus subjects' ranks should be crossed out at the bottom of the list.

Appendix 2. Criterion rank order form

Instructions:
Line up the edge of the form against your list of perceived rank order positions, so that the set of criterion ranks (N) is alongside the set of perceived ranks. For each person in the group, subtract the perceived rank from the criterion rank, and enter the result in the second column, headed d. Square each d score, and enter the result in the third column, headed d^2. When you have done this for every person, you are in a position to calculate a rank order correlation between the criterion rank order, and your perceived rank order, using the formula

$$1 - \sqrt{\frac{6 \Sigma d^2}{N^3 - N}}.$$

Criterion Rank	Subject	d	d^2
2	A		
5	B		
1	C		
9	D		
11	E		
10	F		
4	G		
8	H		
3	I		
6	J		
12	K		
14	L		
7	M		
13	N		

(Extroversion)

Note: The neuroticism rank uses the same layout.

10   Social dimensions of industrial bargaining

Geoffrey M. Stephenson and Maryon Tysoe

Summary

The exercise is designed to examine the outcomes of negotiation as a function of the role and stance that the negotiators take in two union–management disputes concerning hourly wages and paid vacation time. The class is divided up into pairs of negotiators, and each negotiator is given information relevant to the position that he or she has to adopt. Outcomes are measured in terms of the frequency and nature of settlements, the level of satisfaction with the settlement achieved by the negotiators, and other indexes devised from Conference Process Analysis (CPA).

Introduction

Objective

This exercise shows that group decisions and the processes that lead up to them are influenced by both intergroup and interpersonal orientations. In addition, it (1) introduces students to the experimental technique of the role-playing debate and (2) illustrates the application of method and theory to problems of industrial relations.

General theoretical and methodological background

Stephenson (1981) suggests that social behavior can usefully be characterized in terms of both its intergroup and interpersonal significance. From the individual's point of view, an *intergroup orientation* involves acting and speaking as a representative of your own group and viewing the other person in the interaction as also representing a (different) group. An

The authors would like to thank Dominic Abrams and Russell Newcombe for their help with the experimental sessions required for the preparation of this chapter.

interpersonal orientation involves acting and speaking for yourself and viewing the other interactant as behaving in the same way. For instance, although our interactions with friends may have largely interpersonal significance most of the time, they can also have a strong intergroup dimension when our membership of different social groups – families, genders, generations, for example – becomes of significance. Then we may find ourselves having to cope with the fact that our roles as representatives of those groups will impinge on or interact in some way with our interpersonal interests, perhaps contradicting them.

Consider some of the problems that may arise from the differing intergroup loyalties of a couple who live together. Which of them does most of the housework may reflect intergroup assumptions about what is appropriate behavior for men and women, rather than interpersonal understanding about what is appropriate for them in particular, and this intrusion of the intergroup perspective may be very disruptive. Or, to move closer to the theme of this exercise, take the case of two fellow workers who are friends. If one of them is promoted to a managerial position, their friendship is put under a strain, because they are no longer just friends but members of groups whose goals are seen to be in conflict. The intergroup perspective affects their interpersonal relationship, probably doing some damage to it.

Although social behavior generally may usefully be viewed in this way, certain occupations and tasks pose particular problems for the effective reconciliation of interpersonal and intergroup interests. Let us consider the role of a union representative. Whereas in the previous example intergroup loyalties threatened interpersonal relations between friends, the union representative may develop friendships with managers that create problems when they bargain as representatives of their respective groups. Nevertheless, Batstone, Boraston, and Frenkel (1977) see close relations as a necessary requirement if effective bargaining is to take place:

A balance of power by itself is insufficient. There has also to be a relationship of trust. If the persons concerned are powerful, then they will be more likely to be able to resist pressures to break confidences. But beyond that there has to be a readiness to enter into trust relations. For the "informal chat," which is central to a strong bargaining relationship, involves a partial dropping of caution, since information private to one's own side is imparted. Both [union] leaders . . . and management are very aware of this trust relationship and the fact that it rests upon an acceptance of "the facts of life," that is, the basic conflict which exists between them. (p. 172)

Of course, union representatives who fail to make a convincing show of the "basic conflict" with management may find their interpersonal relations with management the source of distrust and accusations of betrayal from their fellow workers.

Specific research background

The work of Batstone and his colleagues indicates how the development of a "strong bargaining relationship" may enable union representatives and managers to deal with one another in a spontaneous way but without necessarily betraying the trust placed in them by their respective groups. This combination of strong interpersonal and intergroup orientations has been shown to be the best one for negotiation (Ben Yoar & Pruitt, 1985). However, such productive relationships, in which intergroup and interpersonal interests are in effect reconciled, may be comparatively rare, though it is interesting that they have emerged where the potential for intergroup conflict was greatest. More typical, in our experience, is an uneasy alternation or compromise between the competing intergroup and interpersonal interests.

Morley and Stephenson (1977) report a series of experiments in which the relative importance of interpersonal considerations was varied by manipulating the medium of communication in which (role-playing) negotiations were conducted. In those experiments, one side (management or union) or the other was given a stronger case (as judged by independent assessors of the background literature used by the role-players), so that, other things being equal, the outcome should have favored the side that had been given the stronger case. When subjects, in pairs, negotiated an agreement, it was found that the agreement was more likely to reflect the relative strength of case when subjects negotiated by "telephone" (audio communication only) than face-to-face, regardless of whether the management or the union had been given the stronger case. Face-to-face, the bargainers usually compromised meeting each other halfway. This finding was attributed to the fact that when negotiating face-to-face, the interpersonal orientation of the bargainers was stronger than when they were communicating by telephone. In the relatively impersonal situation of the phone call, the emphasis was more upon negotiators' roles as party representatives, and the outcome presumably favored the side with the stronger case. Two reasons were given for this: First, greater concentration on the negotiation issues and relevant arguments should lead to a more objective assessment of the issues; and second, the interpersonal considerations that might otherwise keep a negotiator from exploiting his or her advantage are not felt so much in a phone conversation.

In those experiments, and in subsequent replications (for example,

Short, 1974), the interpersonal orientiation was varied indirectly by changing the mode of communication, using mostly audio rather than face-to-face. Other investigators – for example, Milgram (1974) in his studies of obedience – have also used the medium of communication to "deindividuate" or "depersonalize" social relationships. In effect, the telephone makes people more anonymous than does face-to-face interaction or, indeed, any other medium (such as a video link) that combines both vision and hearing. Advantage can be pursued more thoroughly without too much interpersonal distraction.

Aim

All members of the class will be role-playing participants in this exercise on negotiations. The exercise takes the form of an experiment on negotiation processes. Expectations concerning negotiation processes and negotiators' perceptions will also be examined. Where possible, a comparison of male and female negotiators may be incorporated into the design.

Method

The experimental model to be used in this exercise is called the "role-playing debate" paradigm (Morley & Stephenson, 1977). Participants play the roles of representatives of opposing groups. They have to negotiate an agreement concerning disputed issues by unrestricted verbal communication and are provided with relevant background information. Morley and Stephenson have argued that this is a more appropriate way of studying negotiations than by using one of the more popular but simplistic techniques such as matrix games and the Bilateral Monopoly game (Siegel & Fouraker, 1960).

Students are divided into pairs according to directions given by the instructor. The pairs are then distributed among four groups.

At the start of the exercise the four groups should meet separately to study their appropriate background material (see Bass, 1966), a copy of which is given to each person. This contains

- Townsford Textile Company: background information (appendix 2)
- Negotiating assignment (management or union) (appendix 3)
- Issue 1 for bargaining: pay increase (appendix 4)
- Issue 2 for bargaining: paid vacation time (appendix 4)
- Negotiating instructions (given by the instructor)

After an introduction by the instructor, the pairs proceed with their negotiations. Thirty minutes is adequate time for pairs to achieve agreement, although deadlocks may occur.

When a pair has completed its negotiation, one member will notify the instructor, who will then ask each member of the pair to complete the postnegotiation questionnaire (appendix 7). There should be no discussion or collaboration between the two members of a pair at this point. The instructor will collect questionnaires and final contracts, clearly record names and experimental conditions, and ensure that all questions have been answered.

Results

Analysis of outcomes

The instructor will inform you how to calculate the cost of your settlement. Any deadlocks that occur present a problem. How should the outcome be described in such cases? Following Morley and Stephenson (1977), the most effective strategy is to take the midpoint between the last offers made by each side to represent the final contract. However, it is rare that both issues are not settled, so this strategy should not normally be needed.

It is appropriate to perform a statistical analysis of the *time taken to reach agreement*. If all the negotiation groups have come to agreement within the allotted time, parametric statistics should be employed to test the significance of the differences between the conditions as specified by the instructor; the *t*-test can be used for this purpose. However, when dead-locks occur, negotiations are artificially shortened. To compensate for this, either some arbitrary time should be assigned (such as the maximum permitted negotiating time), or, preferably, nonparametric statistics should be employed. For example, using Mann-Whitney U, deadlocks can be assigned the highest rank, and the times of the other settlements can be used to rank order the rest.

Analysis of postexperimental questionnaires (appendix 7)

As a quick check on perceptions of the strength of case of the two sides, the responses to question 7 can be examined. If only 1 week is available for the exercise, there will be little time in class for further analysis of the questionnaire results, but at this point the data from all the groups should be collated and made available to all participants for analysis (as indicated later in this chapter) during the week. However, the instructor will at least discuss in class how those in the different conditions should have responded to the other questionnaire items and how differences could be examined statistically. (If 2 weeks are available, the analyses can be conducted the following week.)

Analysis of the effects of other manipulations and factors will depend upon the teacher's instructions after the postnegotiation questionnaire has been completed. The teacher will inform students in detail concerning other comparisons that can be made and the tests that should be used.

Further design considerations: bargaining teams

Formal wage bargaining normally takes place between teams of representatives, although meetings between individual representatives may take place privately and secretly. If there is a shortage of students or of classrooms to use, then bargaining teams of two or three persons each can be formed and used in place of individual representatives.

Use of teams will have other consequences. Almost certainly the variability of the settlement points will be reduced, because the impact of personality differences between the sides, which might otherwise affect the process, will be limited. Teams are also more likely to deadlock owing to the difficulty each will have with what Walton and McKersie (1965) term *intraorganizational bargaining* – that is, the process of creating and maintaining in-group cohesiveness. Use of teams will also raise the question of the appointment of a principal spokesperson for each side. If this is done, it would be likely to decrease the risks of deadlock but also would probably leave other members of the teams dissatisfied. Although it may not be possible to examine systematically the effect of negotiation between teams, nevertheless the use of one or two teams for demonstration purposes is worth considering. One such negotiation could be videotaped and used to illustrate issues concerning the interplay of intergroup and interpersonal forces in negotiation.

References

Bass, B. M. (1966). Effects on the subsequent performance of negotiators of studying issues or planning strategies alone or in groups. *Psychological Monographs: General and Applied*, 80, whole no. 614, 1–31.

Batstone, E., Boraston, I., & Frenkel, S. (1977). *Shop Stewards in Action*. Oxford: Blackwell Publisher.

Ben Yoar, O., & Pruitt, D. G. (1985). Accountability to constituents: a two-edged sword. *Organizational Behavior and Human Decision Processes*, 34, 282–95.

Milgram, S. (1974). *Obedience to Authority*. London: Tavistock.

Morley, I. E., & Stephenson, G. M. (1977). *The Social Psychology of Bargaining*. London: Allen & Unwin.

Short, J. A. (1974). Effects of medium of communication on experimental negotiation. *Human Relations*, 27, 225–34.

Siegel, S., & Fouraker, L. E. (1960). *Bargaining and Group Decision Making*. New York: McGraw-Hill.

Stephenson, G. M. (1981). Intergroup bargaining and negotiation. In J. C. Turner & H. Giles (eds.), *Intergroup Behaviour*. Oxford: Blackwell.

Walton, R. E., & McKersie, R. B. (1965). *A Behavioral Theory of Labor Negotiations: An Analysis of a Social Interaction System*. New York: McGraw-Hill.

Appendix 1. Management–union questionnaire

The questionnaire yields two subscales: *Attitudes toward management* and *Attitudes toward unions*. The 16 items should be made up in conventional form in random order, and subjects should be required to respond to each item on a 9-point scale, as follows:

Attitudes toward industrial relations

Please indicate with an X, on each scale, the extent to which you agree or disagree with each of the following statements:
1. The company should have the absolute right to discharge a worker it thinks is unsatisfactory.
     Agree ___:___:___:___: ___:___:___:___:___ Disagree
2. In negotiations, the management side is often rigid and inflexible.
     Agree ___:___:___:___: ___:___:___:___:___ Disagree
and so on. The full list of 16 items is as follows. Items are grouped according to their pro- or antimanagement position, or as prounion or antiunion.

Items in management–union questionnaires

Management (anti-)

   1. In negotiations, the management side is often rigid and inflexible.
   2. Management is too aloof and remote from day-to-day activity on the factory floor.
   3. Management often resists legitimate claims from representatives of workers.
   4. It is frequently managerial policy that provokes industrial unrest.

Management (pro-)

   5. We need new industrial relations laws to give management the weapon it needs to take the initiative away from unions.
   6. Most managers are sufficiently concerned about the health and safety of the work force.
   7. It is a manager's absolute right to manage his or her company's affairs without interference from unions.
   8. The company should have the absolute right to discharge a worker it thinks is unsatisfactory.

Union (anti-)

9. Unions represent the interests of top union executives rather than the interests of working people.
10. Unions have too great a say in the running of the country.
11. Unions rarely adopt a positive attitude but merely obstruct the intentions of management.
12. Unions are more to blame for inflation that management.

Union (pro-)

13. Unions should be given equal representation with management on the board of directors that governs the company.
14. Workers have an absolute right to withdraw their labor in times of dispute.
15. It is only through union activity that higher standards of living are achieved.
16. Industrial democracy can only be achieved by the active pursuit of union principles.

From responses to the above items, two scores should be derived: (1) for attitudes toward management, and (2) for attitudes toward unions. In deriving these scores, from items scored on a 1 (disagree) to 9 (agree) scale, remember that negative items are scaled in reverse.

The median should be used to divide the group into those who should definitely be management representatives (i.e., those who are promanagement and antiunion) and those who are definitely union representatives (being antimanagement and prounion). (If the negotiations of men and women are to be compared, this procedure should be followed separately for both sexes, given that the attitudes of men and women toward industrial relations are likely to differ somewhat.) The remaining subjects can be allocated to roles using combined (total) scores on the two subscales (for example, attitudes toward unions *minus* attitudes toward management). Allocation would have to be random in the case of ties.

Appendix 2. Townsford Textile Company: background information

The Townsford Company is a small textile company located in a large town in the Northeast. Townsford is respected for the consistent quality of its work in the dyeing and finishing of raw woven fabrics. It employs approximately 100 people, at the middle range of skill for the area.

General business conditions in the town are good, but the financial condition of Townsford is becoming more and more precarious. The number of back orders has fallen, and profits have decreased because of the rising costs of raw materials and shipping.

The company has raised its prices to cover a recent wage increase, but it is unable to pass full costs on to customers if it is to maintain a competitive position with other sections of the industry. The company's financial position would improve in the long run if the union were willing to encourage the workers to accept the installation and manning of more modern equipment. The union has, however, refused any discussion of work reorganization or restricting output.

The personnel policies at Townsford are better than those of most plants the same size. The past president of the company, who retired 3 months ago, valued the reputation of Townsford as a "good place to work." His successor intends to continue with the same objectives.

For the last 25 years, a majority of employees have been members of the union. Relations of the union with the company have been quite good, with grievances promptly discussed and settled. The first strike occurred, however, 3 years ago and lasted 15 days. The workers obtained a sizable wage increase.

Townsford's wage scale compares very favorably with most other textile companies'. It is about 5% below textile firms that employ workers of a higher level of skill, producing a higher-quality product, but ranks higher than firms employing workers of a similar level of skill. Wages in the industry have increased in proportion to increases in other industries and, to a large extent, with increases in the cost of living. With regular wage increases over a period of years, Townsford's workers have remained on a high pay scale relative to that of equivalent workers in other industries.

Unemployment is at an average level in the area: It should not be very difficult to obtain replacements of similar skill. Management is, however, reluctant to dismiss employees who have worked for the company for some years. *Any* wage increase at the present time would, in management's view, necessitate cuts in the size of the labor force, in addition to price increases, and increases in the number of vacation weeks allowed would merely increase the present financial difficulties. Townsford gives 7 paid holidays and 3 weeks of paid vacation to all workers with at least 1 year of service.

The previous contract has now run out. Negotiations for a further 1-year contract broke down in the final week, with both sides stubbornly holding to their positions. The only agreement reached was that each side would select a new chief negotiator to represent it, scheduled to meet today in an attempt to avoid the strike that is due to begin tomorrow.

Appendix 3. Assignments for negotiators

Assignment as company negotiator

You have been selected by the Townsford Company to represent it in its negotiations with the union. Negotiations for a new 1-year contract broke down last week. The union demands for general wage and benefit increases are completely unreasonable.

Employees' hourly rates compare very well with others in the area. If labor costs are increased, it would necessitate further price increases, which could seriously damage the company's competitive standing. The union has refused to discuss the introduction of more modern machinery, which would improve efficiency, reduce present practices of restricting output, and therefore, lower costs to some degree.

Although no compromises were reached in either side's position, it was decided that each side should appoint new negotiators in an effort to settle the contract and halt the strike, which begins tomorrow.

Each week on strike would cost the company heavily in lost profits.

You are to do the best possible job you can to get a good settlement on the contract on each of the two issues for the company. The number of back orders has fallen, and the company will probably lose its major customers if increased labor costs necessitate further significant price increases. The finances of the company are rapidly becoming a serious source of concern.

It is important to the company that the issues be settled in the given bargaining period. We realize that this involves compromises on both sides, and you are appointed to carry out binding negotiations for us. Remember, your job is to reach a settlement on the issues that is good for the company.

Assignment as union negotiator

You have been selected by the union to represent it in its negotiations with the Townsford Company. Negotiations for a new 1-year contract broke down last week. You feel this refusal on the part of the company to grant your demands is another illustration of their failure to understand the difficult problems you face in a time of rapidly rising prices. Management has been very uncooperative recently, trying to introduce more modern machinery that might lead to fewer jobs, when unemployment in the area is already at a high level.

The union is aware of the financial difficulties of the company, with rising costs of raw materials and a decreased level of orders. It is, however, irritated by the company's refusal to grant the workers wage and benefit increases. Although no compromises were reached in either side's position, it was decided that each side should appoint new negotiating agents in an effort to settle the contract and halt the strike, which begins tomorrow.

Each day on strike would cost the workers heavily in lost wages and overtime pay.

You are to do the best possible job you can to get a good settlement of the contract on each of the two issues for labor. It is important to the workers, however, that the issues be settled in the given bargaining period. We realize that this involves compromise on both sides, and you are appointed to carry out binding negotiations for us. Remember, your job is to reach a settlement on the issues that is good for the workers.

Appendix 4. Bargaining issues

Issue 1. Pay increase

PAST CONTRACT: $4.75 per hour
CURRENT POSITION: Union demands an increase of 40 cents per hour; management refuses outright.

	Increase per Hour (Cents)	Total Value over 1 year ($)
Management aim	.00	0
	.02	5,000
	.04	10,000
	.06	15,000
	.08	20,000
	.10	25,000
	.12	30,000
	.14	35,000
	.16	40,000
	.18	45,000
	.20	50,000
	.22	55,000
	.24	60,000
	.26	65,000
	.28	70,000
	.30	75,000
	.32	80,000
	.34	85,000
	.36	90,000
	.38	95,000
Union aim	.40	100,000

DATA FROM AN INDEPENDENT COMMUNITY SURVEY (last year): Information is given below comparing wages at Townsford, with wages at other textile plants and average wages for nontextile industries in the country. The Moss Company and the Rose Company are the only ones employing highly skilled workers.

	Townsford	Moss	Rose	Baxter	Kraft	Average for other industries in the country
Number of workers	100	300	90	150	300	60
Hourly pay	$4.75	$4.95	$4.95	$4.35	$4.45	$5.20

Issue 2. Paid vacation time

PAST CONTRACT: 3 weeks' paid vacation for all workers with 1 year's service.

CURRENT POSITIONS: Union wants 4 weeks' paid vacation for workers with 2 years' service; management rejects.

	Management Aim					Union Aim
	3 weeks for 1 year's service	3 weeks for 1 year's service; 4 weeks for 18 years' service	3 weeks for 1 year's service; 4 weeks for 14 years' service	3 weeks for 1 year's service; 4 weeks for 10 years' service	3 weeks for 1 year's service; 4 weeks for 6 years' service	3 weeks for 1 year's service; 4 weeks for 2 years' service
Total value over 1 year ($)	0	$2,400	$6,000	$9,600	$24,000	$40,000

DATA FROM AN INDEPENDENT COMMUNITY SURVEY (last year): Information is given below comparing paid vacation time at Townsford, with vacation time at four other textile plants and averages for nontextile industries in the country. The Moss Company and the Rose Company are the only ones employing highly skilled workers.

	Townsford	Moss	Rose	Baxter	Kraft	Average for other industries in the country
Number of workers	100	300	90	150	300	60
Paid vacation time	3 weeks for 1 year	3 weeks for 1 year	3 weeks for 1 year	3 weeks for 1 year	3 weeks for 1 year; 4 weeks for 14 years	3 weeks for 1 year; 4 weeks for 10 years

Appendix 5. Negotiating rules

There are two issues to be negotiated. You can discuss them in any order or at any time. You can agree on both issues at the same time. Thirty minutes is the maximum time allowed for the negotiation. If agreement has not been reached on both issues at the end of that time, a deadlock must be declared.

When you and the other negotiator are ready to negotiate, you can begin. Start the stopwatch when you begin, so you can time your negotiation.

You will see that you have a tape recorder. Please use it to record your negotiation, beginning your recording as you start the stopwatch and begin the negotiation.

When you reach agreement on an issue, circle the appropriate settlement on the "Final Contract" sheet, and you must both initial the agreement in the spaces provided. Once an agreement has been initialed, you cannot reopen negotiations about it.

When you have initialed your agreement on the second issue, stop the stopwatch immediately, and write down the time taken to reach agreement in minutes and seconds in the space provided on the "Final Contract" sheet for issue 2. If you have not finished by the time 30 minutes are up, you must stop immediately and write *D*, for deadlock, in the space provided for time taken to reach agreement.

After you have reached agreement on both issues, or 30 minutes is up, please stop the tape recorder and call the instructor.

IF YOU DO NOT UNDERSTAND ANY PART OF THE INSTRUCTIONS AND MATERIAL YOU HAVE BEEN GIVEN, CALL THE INSTRUCTOR.

Appendix 6. Final contract agreement

Final contract: Issue 1, pay increase

CENTS INCREASE PER HOUR (circle agreed amount):
.00   .02   .04   .06   .08   .10   .12   .14   .16   .18
.20   .22   .24   .26   .28   .30   .32   .34   .36   .38   .40
   INITIALS OF NEGOTIATORS
Management _____
Union _____

Final contract: Issue 2, paid vacation time

Put a check mark in the appropriate box:

3 weeks for 1 year's service	3 weeks for 1 year's service; 4 weeks for 18 years' service	3 weeks for 1 year's service; 4 weeks for 14 years' service	3 weeks for 1 year's service; 4 weeks for 10 years' service	3 weeks for 1 year's service; 4 weeks for 6 years' service	3 weeks for 1 year's service; 4 weeks for 2 years' service

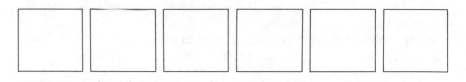

INITIALS OF NEGOTIATORS
Management _____
Union _____
   State time taken to reach agreement on the two issues:

Appendix 7. Postnegotiation questionnaire

State party represented (management or union):

Questionnaire

Please put a cross in the appropriate space on each scale to indicate how strongly you feel one way or the other about each question.
  Do not spend too long over each item.

1. How satisfied are you overall with the agreements reached?
   Dissatisfied __:__:__:__:__:__:__:__ Satisfied

2. How satisfied are you with your own performance in the negotiations?
   Dissatisfied __:__:__:__:__:__:__:__ Satisfied

3. How accountable did you feel to the party you were representing?
   Unaccountable __:__:__:__:__:__:__:__ Accountable

4. How important to you was it to look strong to the other negotiator in the negotiations?
   Unimportant __:__:__:__:__:__:__:__ Important

5. How committed did you feel to your party's position during the negotiations?
   Uncommitted __:__:__:__:__:__:__:__ Committed

6. Please describe both yourself and the other negotiator during the negotiations on the following scales. Mark an *X* in the space best describing yourself on *each* dimension and an *O* in the space describing the other negotiator. You have to judge whether the person you are rating lies at one extreme of a scale, or in the middle, or somewhere in between.

Rigid	—:—:—:—:—:—:—:—	Flexible
Constrained	—:—:—:—:—:—:—:—	Free
Influential	—:—:—:—:—:—:—:—	Uninfluential
Competitive	—:—:—:—:—:—:—:—	Cooperative
Successful	—:—:—:—:—:—:—:—	Unsuccessful
Helpful	—:—:—:—:—:—:—:—	Unhelpful
Hostile	—:—:—:—:—:—:—:—	Friendly
Hard	—:—:—:—:—:—:—:—	Soft
Yielding	—:—:—:—:—:—:—:—	Stubborn
Productive	—:—:—:—:—:—:—:—	Destructive
Unemotional	—:—:—:—:—:—:—:—	Emotional
Strong	—:—:—:—:—:—:—:—	Weak
Cautious	—:—:—:—:—:—:—:—	Impulsive
Formal	—:—:—:—:—:—:—:—	Informal
Aggressive	—:—:—:—:—:—:—:—	Defensive
Rejecting	—:—:—:—:—:—:—:—	Accepting

7. Who did you think had the stronger case? Please put a cross in the appropriate box.

Management ☐   Union ☐   Cases approximately ☐
                            equally strong

Appendix 8. Sample coding of "accept" category

The following excerpt is taken from Chapter 10 of I. E. Morley and G. M. Stephenson's *Social Psychology of Bargaining* (London: Allen & Unwin, 1977). That chapter, entitled "Conference Process Analysis," describes in detail how to divide a transcript into "acts" and to describe each act in terms of its "mode," "resource," and "referent." The category *accept* is one of four modes (offer, accept, reject, and seek), and is defined as follows:

CATEGORY 2: ACCEPT (POSITIVE REACTIONS)[1]

Each of the units underlined below is coded as "accepts": for example,
U: So I think we are justified in claiming the 100 per cent/.[2]
M: I would agree that in time if things go as they should do, then this would be a

good thing for both company – and the workers/.

U: That requires a direct yes or no/.
M: That's true/.

M: How would you suggest then that we deal with this now/ as a company/? I mean, you're part of the community in this respect/.
U: Yeah/. Yeah/.

U: I would say now that we've got to reach agreement on the exact percentage/.
M: Yes/.

M: We have to think of this before lashing out on 85 per cent/.
U: Well, yes/. I entirely agree with you/.

[1] Statements indicating agreement with what the other has stated.
[2] A slash (/) denotes the end of each separate codable speech act.

Part III

Problem investigations

11   Eyewitness accuracy

Ray Bull

Summary

This exercise is concerned with accuracy of eyewitness reports. Both male and female members of the public are approached by a confederate in a public place and asked a question. Shortly afterward they are approached by an experimenter and asked to recall a number of details of the confederate's appearance. Results are scored for accuracy, and comparisons are made between male and female withnesses to determine whether females are more accurate eyewitnesses than are males. Optional additional variables for examination are the sex of the confederate and the duration of the interaction. As well as providing evidence about factors affecting eyewitness testimony, the exercise introduces a number of methodological problems, particularly those concerned with conducting experiments not in the laboratory but in public.

Aim

This exercise is designed to examine some of the factors that influence the accuracy of eyewitnesses' recollections and to highlight the problems encountered when attempting to collect and quantify such recall. Since we typically can recognize our friends and acquaintances easily, most people seem to think that witness memory should also be good. On the other hand, psychologists' field studies have shown that eyewitness recognition can, in many circumstances, be poor. This may be because witnesses often see, only briefly, a stranger, and therefore somewhat different processes may be involved in these two types of recognition task. Although laboratory-based studies of facial recall have often found the subjects' recollections to be highly accurate, field studies made in public places have frequently found much poorer levels of performance. Since the present exercise is to be conducted not in the laboratory but in a public place, it can

225

be considered both as a worthwhile piece of research itself and also as a useful training exercise in how to conduct field studies and to approach members of the public in order to gather meaningful information from them.

The specific hypothesis to be investigated is that female witnesses are more accurate than male witnesses. Possible additional hypotheses are that the sex of the person the witnesses try to recall will affect their response and that the length of time for which the witness sees the person to be recalled may influence how much he or she remembers.

Introduction

Even though a few early psychologists (for example, Munsterberg, 1908) argued that the senses cannot always be trusted, recall depends on the individual, and eyewitness testimony is basically unreliable, their views were almost entirely ignored by the legal world. Until very recently, jurors, judges, and lawyers placed a great deal of faith in eyewitness testimony, and it has been regarded as the most influential evidence that can be presented in court. However, recent psychological research (for example, Clifford & Bull, 1978; Loftus, 1979; Wells & Loftus, 1984) has suggested that a more critical look needs to be taken at eyewitness testimony and its use in the legal system. For example, Wells and Murray (1983) noted that in an influential case the U.S. Supreme Court identified five criteria to be considered in judging eyewitness evidence. In their review of psychologists' work concerning these criteria, Wells and Murray concluded that "the Court's intuitions may need reassessment in the light of recent psychological research evidence." In addition, a number of cases have come to light where people have been wrongly convicted on the basis of eyewitness testimony: For example, a man called William Jackson spent five years in prison for rape after being identified by victims as their assailant – wrongly, as it was later proved (Loftus, 1984). Clearly what is needed in this critical area are rigorous and ecologically valid investigations to evaluate eyewitness evidence.

Laboratory versus field studies

One issue that arises here is that of the use of laboratory and field studies in psychological research in this area. Ecologically valid studies are ones that investigate behavior in its true context, as opposed to an artificial situation (such as a laboratory can sometimes be). In laboratory research in psychology, controlling of variables may be overdone, resulting in findings that have no application to real life. Sometimes the dependent variable is chosen for its convenience, rather than its importance. Finally, stimuli are sometimes artificial and presented in an unrealistic way. Socially relevant research on real-life problems, on the other hand, has tended to be avoided, perhaps because such research is difficult to design, conduct, analyze, and discuss. Much laboratory-based research on people's powers of visual recognition suffers from these limitations. Though the results of laboratory-based studies seem to support the view that most people have excellent powers of recognition, this conclusion is not necessarily warranted.

In the laboratory, Shepard (1967) asked people to look at 600 pictures of various objects, landscapes, and scenes. They were then shown 60 pairs of pictures. Only 1 of the pictures in each pair had been seen in the original 600. The participants were simply asked, for each pair, to pick out the previously seen picture. This situation is quite similar to going through a series of mug shots. Correct identification was made in 97% of the cases. In a similar experiment, Nickerson (1965) showed 800 photographs of objects to a group of people and then showed them another set of 400 pictures, and they had to say which of these 400 pictures had appeared in the first batch of photographs they had seen. Nickerson found 92% correct recognition. Standing, Conezio, and Haber (1970) showed to a group of students the amazing total of 2,500 photographs of unfamiliar paintings, scenes, and magazine photographs for 5 to 10 seconds. At the end of about 7 hours' viewing, the observers still achieved 90% correct identification of photographs they had seen, even with an interval of a day and a half between first seeing and later identifying.

Although the power of visual memory seems amazing, it could be objected that it is quite easy to distinguish between different *objects*: A cat is very different from an airplane. Recognition of faces may be quite a different story, because the pattern of features are very similar across all faces. What are the facts? Hochberg and Galper (1967) asked people to look first at a series of 35 and then at a series of 60 pictures of faces. They then presented 15 pairs of photographs – one of each pair had been seen previously; the other had not – and asked for identification of the previously seen face. The subjects' recognition performance was better with 35 faces than with 60 faces, but even with 60 faces to store, they still recognized them 90% of the time. In this study the faces were of women. Yin (1969) observed 96% correct identification of male faces presented as photographs.

The results of these laboratory-based studies could be taken to suggest that eyewitnesses will usually produce high levels of recognition performance. However, one should remember that in such studies (1) the subjects are aware that their ability to recognize the pictures will be tested later; (2) their attention is focused on the stimuli to be recognized later; (3) each stimulus is static or stationary and is viewed for at least several seconds; and (4) the same pictures of target faces as presented at first are used again for the recognition test. (For further discussion of these points, see Goldstein, 1977; Wells & Loftus, 1984.) In contrast to this, in field studies that attempt to simulate criminal episodes, the usual procedure is to stage an incident in front of unsuspecting witnesses. This experimental approach is a big advance over static inspection and recognition of photographs, in the sense that the action is dynamic, it reproduces real life in content, and the subjects are unprepared for becoming witnesses. However, field studies of witness memory owe much to research conducted in the laboratory in terms of the theories and notions used to explain their outcomes. (Students interested in contrasting the value of field and laboratory studies can consult Bruce, 1985; Mook, 1983).

In order to study eyewitness accuracy in a realistic setting, Brigham, Maas, Snyder, and Spaulding (1982) asked cashiers working alone in convenience stores in Tallahassee to identify from photograph "lineups" prepared by the local police department two male customers who had been in their store 2 hours earlier. The 73 cashiers made correct identifications only one-third of the time, though this level of accuracy was significantly above that expected by chance.

For the purposes of the exercise, a procedure somewhat similar to that of Brigham et al. will be employed. In a local public place with a high volume of pedestrian traffic, a colleague (or "confederate") of the experimenter will stop a passerby and ask one or more questions. When the confederate has moved on, the experimenter will approach the passerby and will gather from him or her some details of recall of physical aspects of the confederate. Both male and female passersby will be used, the experimental hypothesis being that there will be a significant difference in the recall of female and male passersby.

Male versus female witnesses

Most of the research concerning sex differences in eyewitness accuracy suggests that the accounts of female witnesses may often prove to be more accurate than those of men. Cross, Cross, and Daly (1971) found female observers to perform significantly better than male observers on female faces, with the male observers being equally good on the male and female faces. In a similar way Ellis, Shepherd, and Bruce (1973) found that although there was no significant difference between male and female observers for male faces, there was a significant difference for female faces, with women performing better. How can the weight of evidence in favor of women be explained? Cross et al. and Ellis et al. explained their findings of female superiority by the greater exposure of females to female faces in magazines and cosmetic literature, giving them more opportunity to learn to encode features of faces. This, though, is just a guess. However, other explanations (Clifford & Bull, 1978) seem equally unsupported by the evidence.

These sex-difference findings have been drawn from studies on schematic and photographic faces. Does female superiority also hold in real-life or simulated crime studies? Apparently it does not. Kuehn (1974) showed that female victims are poorer at giving complete descriptions of assailants, whereas Bahrick, Bahrick, and Wittlinger (1985) indicated that in nonemotionally charged atmospheres female superiority does reassert itself in recognition and recall of people who have been interacted with. Clifford and Scott (1978) showed that when a nonviolent episode is viewed for later recollection, female witnesses do better than males, but when a violent episode is viewed, later recall by males is superior to that of females. Thus females were found to perform poorly under stressful conditions, a finding that supports Kuehn's tabulation of real-life identifications made by male and female victims during police interviews. Generally speaking, females are better at recognizing previously seen faces in non-stressful situations. Under stressful viewing conditions, males may make better witnesses.

Method

Resources

No special equipment or materials are necessary for this study. Students will work in pairs. In a local public place, one of them (referred to here as the "confederate") will approach and ask a question(s) of a member(s) of the public who is walking along. Shortly after this interaction has ceased, the other student in the pair (referred to here as the "experimenter") will ask the member of the public some prepared questions concerning the physical appearance of the confederate. If only a little time (for example, less than 1 hour) is available for the data gathering, then the data from several pairs of students (working in slightly different localities) can be combined for the subsequent analysis. In total, data from a minimum of at least 6 witnesses from each sex must be available. If more than $1\frac{1}{2}$ hours is available to each pair of students, then each pair should be able to gather enough data (i.e., at least 6 for each sex of witness) for statistical analysis to be performed on their own data.

If you want to expand this exercise by including further independent variables, such as sex of stimulus person (i.e., confederate), duration of the interaction, or both, more time (up to 2 or 4 hours) will be required for the data gathering.

Procedure

Since whether the accounts of female eyewitnesses are more accurate than those of male eyewitnesses seems to depend upon the level of stress or emotional arousal created during the witness's viewing of the information to be recalled, you need to make a conscious decision about the way in which the experimental interaction will take place. It is advisable to make the interaction between witness and confederate nonstressful for the witness. Have the member of the experimental team (the confederate) who interacts with each witness ask them a simple, ordinary question, such as "Can you tell me the time, please?" The main independent variable in the experiment is the sex of the witness, and the dependent variable is how well the witness remembers the appearance of the confederate. The confederate should try to make the way he (or she) interacts with each witness as similar as possible from witness to witness (so that the confederdate's behavior becomes a controlled variable).

It is important to note that only those passersby who respond to the confederate's questions can act as subjects (i.e., are witnesses). Any passerby who does not stop when approached and questioned by the confederate will not later be asked to recall details about the confederate.

Instructions to subjects

Once the interaction between the confederate and a subject has ended and the confederate is out of sight, the experimenter should approach the subject and say something like, "Excuse me, we are making a study of how well people can remember a stranger that they have just spoken to. A few seconds ago a friend of mine came up to you and asked you for the time. May I ask you a few questions about his (her) appearance?" If the person agrees to this request, he or she now becomes a subject, and his or her recall accuracy is assessed.

When the experimenter has finished questioning the subject, a short explanation should be given. The experimenter should briefly describe the aims of the study (i.e., to investigate eyewitness accuracy and to see if females are more accurate eyewitnesses than males) and should thank the person for participating in the study.

Assessing recall accuracy

You will need to decide how to assess the accuracy of the witnesses' recall of details of the confederate's physical appearance. Would it be better to ask each witness to describe the confederate in his or her own words, or would it be better to have each witness answer a structured questionnaire? If the former method is used you will run into scoring problems: for example, one witness may correctly recall four different and important aspects of the confederate, whereas another, say a hairdresser, may correctly recall four details about the confederate's hair but nothing else. Should these two witnesses receive the same accuracy score? It is therefore advisable to make up a questionnaire before the experiment takes place. This questionnaire can take a variety of forms. A number of questions (say 12) can be asked, each either providing the witness with a restricted choice of response (for example, "Did he have light or dark hair?"), or each permitting the witness to use his or her own words (for example, "What was the color of his hair?"). This latter, alternative form of question will make the scoring of the recall problematical, since, for example, if the confederate had black hair and a witness said it was brown, how would such recall be quantified – as totally wrong, nearly right, or half right? To overcome such problems, it is, suggested that a "forced-choice" questionnaire be used. Table 11.1 provides an example of this.

If a questionnaire somewhat similar to this one is used, each witness's recall can be scored using a scale of 12. Note that the final question (no. 12) in the suggested questionnaire should ask about the presence of something that, in fact, the confederate was *not* carrying. This question is designed to examine whether witnesses will assume from the question that something was present when in fact it was absent.

For question 8, witnesses may say yes more often for male than female confederates. Such response biases make the gathering of eyewitness recall a complex affair. Furthermore, for question 10 there is the problem of what fat and thin mean to each witness. Would the witnesses' answers to these questions depend on how fat or thin they are themselves? (A similar point may apply to nose size, in question 11).

Summary of method

To summarize the methodology: In a local public place, a confederate (one of a pair of experimenters) will approach and ask a question(s) of someone

Table 11.1. *Forced-choice questionnaire*

---

1. Was the person who asked you the question(s) taller or shorter than 5'8" [5'3, for female confederates]?
2. Did he (she) have brown or blue eyes?
3. Was he (she) wearing dark or light pants?
4. Was he (she) wearing glasses?
5. Was he (she) wearing a jacket or a long coat?
6. Did he (she) have a moustache/beard? ["lipstick," for female confederates]?
7. Was his (her) shirt blue or green?
8. Was he (she) wearing a belt?
9. Was his (her) hair light or dark?
10. Was he (she) fat or thin?
11. Did he (she) have a large or a small nose?
12. Was he (she) carrying a note pad?

Note: For questions 2, 3, 5, and 7, one of the two alternatives should, of course, actually have been part of the confederate's true appearance: Otherwise the questions should be modified appropriately.

who is walking along. A few moments after this interaction has ceased (and the confederate is out of sight), the experimenter will approach the person and inform him or her that an experiment on the accuracy of memory is being carried out. The person will be asked if he or she is willing to answer a small number of brief questions. (The mention of brevity is likely to increase the rate of cooperation.) If the subject agrees, the subject then becomes an experimental witness, and his or her recall is gathered and scored for accuracy. If, in response to a recall question, a witness replies "Don't know," is this as clear a sign of inefficient recall as a witness who produces an incorrect response (for example, says eyes were blue when they were brown)? For the purposes of the experiment, either of these two forms of error will score zero, and each correct response will score 1. You may want to discuss in your report the extent to which giving each of the two types of error just described a score of zero is a satisfactory method of quantifying the witnesses' recall.

Data analysis and experiment design

Experiment with one independent variable

Data from several experimenter/confederate pairs can be pooled for the purposes of statistical analysis. Since the independent variable of sex of witness leads to an experimental design involving "independent measures,"

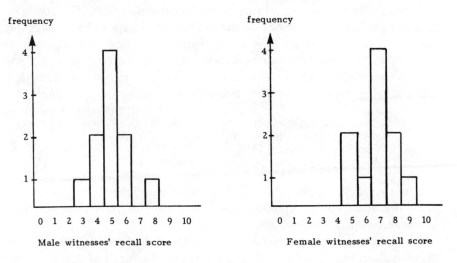

Figure 11.1 Histograms of raw data.

a statistical test of difference for independent measures should be used (either the independent *t*-test, if the data approximate a normal distribution, or the Mann-Whitney U test). (For details of these tests, see a book on simple statistics, such as Robson, 1973).

Graphs of the raw data can be drawn, as shown in Figure 11.1, one for the male witnesses' recall and one for the female witnesses' recall. These two histograms can be compared by eye to see whether or not they suggest a difference between the recall of male and female witnesses. The histograms can also be used as a guide to whether or not the raw data approximates a normal distribution.

Expanding the experiment: adding a second and third independent variable

For more advanced students, the basic single-variable exercise can be expanded into a more complex study.

A second independent variable that can be introduced easily into the design of the experiment is that of *sex of confederate*. This variable is worth investigating, since the literature reviewed in the introduction suggests that female witnesses may be most accurate when attempting to recall details of female, as opposed to male, stimuli.

If it is not possible or desirable to vary the sex of the confederate, then another very meaningful second independent variable can be that of the *duration of the interaction* between confederate and witness. The confederate can ask half the witnesses for the time (short duration) but engage the others in a longer interaction by asking them, for example, some questions about television. (In both duration conditions, the confederate would not be carrying a note pad.) In this latter (i.e., long-duration) condition, not one but several questions can be asked of each witness. For example:

1. "Excuse me, I'm conducting a survey. Do you think there are too many sports programs on television?"
2. "What is your favorite TV program?"
3. "Why do you like that particular program?"

The last of these three questions, because it is open-ended, will usually cause the witness to be exposed to the confederate for a longer period than in the short-duration condition.

The experimental hypothesis for the effect of the independent variable "short versus long duration" is that the witnesses' recall of details of the confederate will be more accurate in the long-duration condition. (Is this a two- or one-tailed hypothesis?) You may think that this hypothesis is simple common sense. Psychology is frequently accused of doing this, but psychology has an important role to play for society by scientifically confirming what common sense suggests. For instance, some previous research (Laughery, Alexander, & Lane, 1971) found that the longer the time for which a facial photograph had been viewed, the more accurate subsequent recognition was. Clifford and Richards (1977) found that policemen's recall of a person who asked them questions was more accurate for long- than for short-exposure durations. This latter study, however, found that members of the public on the other hand showed recall that was somewhat poorer under long- than under short-exposure duration conditions.

If a second independent variable (or factor) is introduced into the experiment (for example, sex of confederate or duration of exposure), then there should be an equal number of male and female witnesses in each of the two extra conditions (i.e., an equal number of witnesses in the four experimental conditions, as shown in Table 11.2).

The ideal statistical test for the experimental design illustrated in Table 11.2 is a two-way analysis of variance. If your instructor prefers, a number of independent t-tests can be used instead [for example, (1) one t-test comparing recall of male versus female witnesses, with the data from male and female confederates combined together; (2) one t-test comparing recall of male versus female confederates, with the data from male and female witnesses combined together; (3) a series of t-tests comparing each of the four cells of the experimental design with each of the other cells]. In

Table 11.2. *Allocation of subjects to conditions (two independent variables)*

Variable 2: Sex of confederate	Variable 1: Sex of witness			
	Male		Female	
	S1[a]	S4	S13	S16
Male	S2	S5	S14	S17
	S3	S6	S15	S18
	S7	S10	S19	S22
Female	S8	S11	S20	S23
	S9	S12	S21	S24

S = subject.

the two-way design, sex of confederate can be replaced by duration of exposure (short versus long). It is better to use a two-way analysis of variance, since this is less time-consuming and more statistically appropriate than a series of *t*-tests. Furthermore, the analysis of variance permits examination of the "interaction" between the two independent variables, as shown in Figure 11.2.

An "interaction" means that under different conditions of one independent variable, a second independent variable has different effects; For example, sex of witness may have a significant effect on results with female confederates but no effect with male confederates. Whether or not an analysis of variance is performed on the data, if the experiment contains two independent variables, then a diagram such as that in Figure 11.2 should always be drawn.

The experiment can also be expanded into a three-way design [i.e., three independent variables: (1) *sex of witness*, (2) *sex of confederate, (3) duration of exposure*]. A three-way analysis of variance should be performed on the data, there being an equal number of observations (say 3) in each cell (or experimental condition) of the design, as illustrated in Table 11.3.

Discussion

This exercise highlights some of the problems to be considered and overcome when gathering data not in the laboratory but in the field. It also explores various ways of assessing the accuracy of witnesses' memory, an issue that applies to all types of experimental study of memory performance. Students are able to see how the experiment can be expanded from the single independent variable design to a design employing two or even

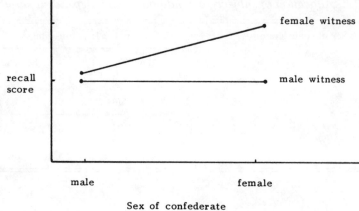

Figure 11.2 Diagram of interaction between two independent variables.

three independent variables, while keeping other factors constant as "control variables" (for example, the confederate's behavior).

The data gathered in this study will show whether there is a significant difference in the accuracy of recall of female versus male eyewitnesses. [This effects of the variables of (1) sex of witnessed person and (2) duration of exposure of the stimulus person to the witness may also have been examined.] The overall level of eyewitness accuracy found in the fairly naturalistic setting used in this study can be compared with the levels of accuracy found in the laboratory-based studies of facial-photograph recognition mentioned in the introduction.

The findings of the exercise have implications for the debate on whether eyewitness testimony is usually accurate or inaccurate. Legal and police practices and procedures can benefit from the results of research on this topic.

The exercise is not a perfect simulation of real-life criminal episodes, and in the introduction it was noted that the amount of emotional arousal created in a witness can influence whether females or males are better eyewitnesses. This factor needs to be taken into account when you are commenting on the data. Further, many aspects of the witnesses may not have been controlled for (for example, their age, or whether the male witnesses were in more of a hurry than the female). Other factors for consideration are (1) the extent to which the confederate behaved in exactly the same way with each of the eyewitnesses, and (2) the limitations of the questionnaire used to score accuracy of recall.

Table 11.3. *Allocation of subjects to conditions (three independent variables)*

Variable 2: sex of confederate	Variable 3: exposure duration	Variable 1: Sex of witness	
		Male	Female
Male	Short	S1[a]	S13
		S2	S14
		S3	S15
	Long	S4	S16
		S5	S17
		S6	S18
Female	Short	S7	S19
		S8	S20
		S9	S21
	Long	S10	S22
		S11	S23
		S12	S24

S = subject.

If the recall of female witnesses is found to be more accurate than that of males, is this due to their more efficient sensory input of physical details of the confederate, or to their better memory storage of such information, or to their more efficient retrieval of it from memory (or to a combination of these three factors)? When asked to recall, do some witnesses try harder than others to be good witnesses? Such questions reflect an important aspect of the method of social psychology: Gathering and statistically analyzing the data take us only halfway toward our goal; then we have to explain the data.

References

Bahrick, H., Bahrick, R., & Wittlinger, R. (1975). Fifty years of memory for names and faces: a cross-cultural approach. *Journal of Experimental Psychology: General, 104,* 54–75.

Brigham, J., Maas, A., Snyder, L., & Spaulding, K. (1982). Accuracy of eyewitness identifications in a field setting. *Journal of Personality and Social Psychology, 42,* 673–81.

Bruce, D. (1985). The how and why of ecological memory. *Journal of Experimental Psychology: General*, 114, 78–90.

Clifford, B., & Bull, R. (1978). *The Psychology of Person Identification*. London: Routledge & Kegan Paul.

Clifford, B., & Richards, G. (1977). Comparisons of recall by police and civilians under conditions of long and short durations of exposure. *Perceptual and Motor Skills*, 45, 503–12.

Clifford, B., & Scott, J. (1978). Individual and situational factors in eyewitness testimony. *Journal of Applied Psychology*, 63, 352–9.

Cole, P., & Pringle, P. (1974). *Can You Positively Identify This Man? George Ince and the Barn Murder*. London: Deutsch.

Cross, J., Cross, J., & Daly, J. (1971). Sex, race, age and beauty as factors in recognition of faces. *Perception and Psychophysics*, 10, 393–96.

Ellis, H. D., Shepherd, J., & Bruce, A. (1973). The effect of age and sex upon adolescents' recognition of faces. *Journal of Genetic Psychology*, 123, 173–4.

Goldstein, A. G. (1977). The fallibility of the eyewitness: psychological evidence. In B. Sales (ed.), *Psychology in Legal Process*. New York: Spectrum.

Hochberg, J., & Galper, R. (1967). Recognition of faces (I). An exploratory study. *Psychonomic Science*, 12, 619–20.

Kuehn, L. (1974). Looking down a gun barrel: person perception and violent crime. *Perceptual and Motor Skills*, 39, 1159–64.

Laughery, K., Alexander, J., & Lane, A. (1971). Recognition of human faces: effects of target exposure, target position, pose position and type of photograph. *Journal of Applied Psychology*, 55, 477–83.

Loftus, E. F. (1979). *Eyewitness Testimony*. Cambridge, Mass: Harvard University Press.

Loftus, E. F. (1984). Essential but unreliable. *Psychology Today*, February, pp. 22–6.

Mook, D. (1983). In defense of external invalidity. *American Psychologist*, April, 379–83.

Munsterberg, H. (1908). *On the Witness Stand: Essays on Psychology and Crime*. New York: Clark, Boardman.

Nickerson, R. (1965). Short term memory for complex, meaningful visual configurations: a demonstration of capacity. *Canadian Journal of Psychology*, 19, 155–60.

Robson, C. (1973). *Experiment, Design and Statistics in Psychology*. Baltimore: Penguin.

Shepard, R. (1967). Recognition memory for words, sentences and pictures. *Journal of Verbal Learning and Verbal Behaviour*, 6, 156–63.

Standing, L., Conezio, J., & Haber, R. (1970). Perception and memory for pictures: single trial learning of 2560 visual stimuli. *Psychonomic Science*, 19, 73–4.

Wells, G., & Loftus, E. (1984). *Eyewitness Testimony: Psychological Perspectives*. Cambridge: Cambridge University Press.

Wells, G., & Murray, D. (1983). What can psychology say about the *Neil v. Biggers* criteria for judging eyewitness accuracy? *Journal of Applied Psychology*, 68, 347–62.

Yin, R. (1969). Looking at upside-down faces. *Journal of Experimental Psychology*, 81, 141–45.

12 Attribution processes

Mansur Lalljee

Summary

The exercise described in this chapter is designed to test Kelley's hypotheses concerning the influence of consensus, consistency, and distinctiveness information in making causal attributions within the context of attributions for success and failure. In keeping with much of the research on attribution processes, a questionnaire consisting of brief descriptions of hypothetical events is used as a way of pursuing the problem. Two different dependent variables are suggested: rating scales of attribution to personal and situation causes, and the respondents' open-ended explanations about why the event occurred. The exercise introduces students to the methodological problems involved in drawing up a questionnaire and provides some experience in content analysis and in conducting a factorial, repeated measures analysis of variance.

Introduction

The kinds of explanations that people offer for events have received little attention from psychologists until recently. However, explanations have not been neglected by other disciplines, especially philosophy, anthropology, and sociology. The philosopher's interest has focused primarily on the nature of scientific explanation, and anthropologists and sociologists have stressed that different frameworks of explanation are prevalent in different societies, and in the same society in different historical periods. The proper study of explanations by the psychologist must be the examination of explanations that are actually provided by people. The tendency to seek explanations for physical events, social processes, and human behavior seems as pervasive a human tendency as any other. An explanation serves to demystify an event, to impose a particular sort of stability and predictability upon the world, and to enable the individual to act toward it in a systematic manner. To the child a wide variety of events are considered worthy of explanation, and the child is apparently easily satisfied with any explanation. A vital part of the process of socialization includes learning what events the adults in the culture consider worthy of explanation and the kinds of explanations they consider acceptable. A child must learn not only the generally acceptable forms of explanation but also how to invoke the appropriate sort of explanation on a particular occasion. The child must also learn that different explanations have different intra- and interpersonal effects.

Of course, the area has not been entirely neglected. Piaget's work is an important example of the way in which different forms of explanation vary as a function of cognitive development. In some of his earlier work on the child's conception of the world and on the development of moral judgment, Piaget attempts to relate the type of explanation the child provides to more general characteristics of cognitive functioning (see Piaget, 1929, 1932). More recently the explanations that children provide have received some attention from Robinson and Rackstraw (1972), who have attempted to examine differences between middle- and working-class children within the context of Bernstein's (1973) notion that middle-class children have more ways of linguistically organizing and expressing their thoughts. There also is current interest in developmental changes, from young childhood through adulthood, in the rules that people follow in attributing causality (Schultz, 1982).

In current social psychology, interest in how people explain events can be traced to the work of Fritz Heider (1958). Drawing on Heider's writings, a number of researchers have put forward hypotheses about how the layman arrives at attributions of causality and what the consequences of such explanations are. This area, now called *attribution theory*, has been dominated by two general assumptions: first, it is concerned with *causal* explanations rather than, for instance, explanations in terms of regularity or categorization and, second, it draws a central distinction between explanations in terms of *personal* causes and explanations in terms of *environmental* causes.

The general issue that is explored by researchers concerned with attribution theory can be clarified through an example. Take, for instance, the case of a student doing poorly at school work. There may be agreement that he or she is doing poorly, but there may be considerable disagreement as to why. The unsatisfactory performance could be explained in terms of lack of ability, in terms of not trying hard enough, in terms of emotional stress, a crisis in personal relationships, uncertainty about future employment, the difficulty of the course, bad teaching, or in a variety of other ways. Given the wide range of possible causes, the next question concerns the systematization or organization of explanations. Attribution theory sees as central the distinction between explanations in terms of personal and environmental causes. Thus explanations in terms of cleverness or hard work are based upon aspects of the person, whereas explanations in terms of the nature of the task or the quality of the teaching are based upon causes external to the person.

The distinction between attributions in terms of internal and external causes is central to the theory put forward by Harold Kelley (Kelly, 1967, 1973) as to how we arrive at attributions. This distinction also will be central to the study suggested in this chapter, which explores some of Kelley's ideas. However, it is important to note that the internal–external distinction by itself is unlikely to be adequate. Presumably, one of the functions of attribution is to enable the perceiver to make predictions about the behavior of other people and to assist in detecting the underlying invariances. Indeed some investigators, such as Weiner (1980), have distinguished between explanations in terms of three dimensions: locus (i.e., internal versus external causes); stability; and control. An explanation in terms of a person's intelligence implies a stability that is not implied by an explanation in terms of effort, though they both are internal explanations. An explanation in terms of a person's mood or emotional state implies causes that are less under the individual's control than his or her intentions. In a sense the goal of the individual's attribution may be to seek out the more permanent dispositions of the other. It should be pointed out that attribution theory has less to say about whether these attributions are correct. It is a theory dealing with how the layman arrives at attributions and what the consequences of these attributions are, rather than a theory about whether or not these inferences are accurate. Mischel (1968), among others, has argued that the notion of personality traits is frequently misleading, since it implies a consistency of behavior across different social situations that is not supported by the available evidence. The central questions for our purposes here concern how people arrive at attributions, rather than whether these attributions are correct or not.

Since the work of Freud, the idea that our opinions of ourselves and others are highly biased by our motivations has formed a general part of psychological thinking. The work on interpersonal perception in the 1950s and in the early 1960s, too, stressed notions such as stereotypes and halo effects, which emphasized the irrationality and distortions of our thinking about other people. Attribution theory has attempted to correct this imbalance. Rather than emphasizing the distortion of incoming information in order to satisfy the wishes and needs of the organism, the general model underlying attribution theory is of a scientist, or perhaps an applied scientist, shifting and analyzing information in order to arrive at conclusions. The paradigm case of scientific explanation, as far as attribution theory is concerned, is that of causal explanation, and the way in which causal explanations are arrived at is by observing covariation between events. Quite simply, if two events are observed to covary, then one is seen as the cause of the other. More specifically, Kelley suggests that in order to make causal attributions, people use covariation information with reference to three dimensions: persons, entities, and time.

Covariation information with regard to persons is called *consensus* information. It is concerned with whether or not other people behave in similar ways toward the stimulus object. Thus, in the example of passing an examination, consensus information refers to the behavior of other people with reference to that examination. If most people pass, we have an instance of high consensus; if few people pass, we have an instance of low consensus. The second sort of information that is considered relevant is *distinctiveness* information. Distinctiveness refers to the behavior of the person with reference to other relevant entities. Thus if the examination that John passed was a history test, we might want to know whether his passing this history test was for him distinctive (i.e., whether he passed other tests). If he *did not* pass other tests, then his response to the history test is distinctive; if he did, then his response to the history examination is not distinctive. The third sort of information that Kelley claims is important is *consistency* information: that is, information about the particular actor's response to this particular entity on previous occasions. Does John always pass his history tests? If he does, then we have an instance of high consistency; if he does not, then we have an instance of low consistency. On the principle of covariation, Kelley suggests that in the case where there is high consensus, high distinctiveness, and high consistency (i.e., where most people pass the examination, where John fails other tests, and usually passes history tests), the outcome is attributed to the entity (to the history test) rather than to characteristics of John. We will return to this issue in the experiment described later in the chapter. Before we proceed to the details of the study and its particular background, two other issues should briefly be mentioned.

Attribution theory stresses the rational information-processing aspects of forming attributions about the causes of behavior. Where the attributor has information from multiple observations, information along the three dimensions of persons, entities, and time is used. But what of cases where the person does not have such information, where information about only single observations is available and a judgment is required on that basis?

This is particularly relevant to first encounters in professional contexts such as interviews. Here Kelley suggests that the person draws on a variety of "causal schemata," one of the most important of which has been called the "discounting principle." Where there are a variety of plausible causes for an effect, the role of any particular cause in producing that effect is discounted. This can be illustrated with reference to a range of well-known experiments. Kelley himself draws heavily on the ideas of Jones and Davis (1965), and a brief description of an experiment by Jones, Davis, and Gergen (1961) will illustrate the idea.

Each subject heard one tape recording, supposedly of a job interview. Some subjects listened to a recording of someone being interviewed for the job of a submariner, others to an interview for the job of astronaut. Those in the former condition were told that a good submariner is obedient, cooperative, and friendly, in short "other-directed." Some subjects heard a recording where the candidate did behave in an other-directed way, but other subjects heard a recording where the interviewee seemed "inner-directed" – independent, and with little need for social contact. Those who listened to interviews for the job of astronaut were told that a good astronaut was inner-directed. Again some of these subjects heard recordings where the candidate behaved in an inner-directed way and others where the candidate behaved in an other-directed way. The subjects were far more confident that the behavior in the interview reflected the personality characteristics of the interviewee if he or she behaved in a different way from the "ideal candidate" for the job.

Conceptually, the experiment is simple. For instance, if, in the case of the astronaut, the interviewee behaves in an inner-directed way, there are two highly plausible explanations for the behavior: (1) the person really is inner-directed; (2) the person is behaving in an inner-directed way to get the job.

When the interviewee behaves in an other-directed way, the latter explanation can be ruled out. Hence the perceiver will have more confidence that the behavior is due to the person's character, since in this case there are fewer plausible causes and therefore more certainty.

The same principle has been used, with interesting results, in the area of self-perception. In a study by Lepper, Greene, and Nisbett (1973), children who enjoyed drawing with felt-tipped pens were subsequently rewarded for drawing with them. These children showed a decrease in subsequent play with the pens, compared with a control group who went through similar experimental manipulations without expectations of reward. Here again the discounting principle may be at work. If a person performs some intrinscially interesting act for a reward, that person may become uncertain as to whether it was done primarily for the reward or because it was intrinsically interesting. If, however, it was done in the absence of any external reward, the intrinsic motivation is clear. In the former case there are two plausible causes, in the latter case only one. The notion of discounting applies to interpretation of our own behavior as well as to our interpretation of the behavior of others.

This discussion has centered on the processes involved in forming attributions. It should be stressed that attributions do have important consequences. Indeed the Lepper et al. study on self-attribution demonstrates a behavioral consequence. The children who were rewarded for performing an initially valued activity performed that activity less on a subsequent occasion.

Attributions have also been related to helping. In a field study by Barnes, Ickes, and Kidd (1979), student subjects were telephoned a few days before an examination by someone supposedly in the same class who asked to borrow their lecture notes. The caller explained the inadequacy of his or her own notes in different ways to different subjects. Explanations in terms of lack of ability to take good notes resulted in greater helping than explanations in terms of lack of motivation. Patterns of attribution have also been related to depression (Abramson, Seligman, & Teasdale, 1978). Abramson et al. suggest that, compared with others, depressed people tend to explain their own successful outcomes more in terms of external causes and their failures more in terms of internal ones.

Let us return to the set of ideas from which we will derive the experiment to be suggested in this chapter. Kelley maintains that when making an attribution of causality to personal or environmental forces, a person draws on information concerning consensus, consistency, and distinctiveness. If there is high consensus, high consistency, and high distinctiveness, a stimulus attribution will be made; when there is low consensus, high consistency, and low distinctiveness, a person attribution will be made. Both these predictions are based on the principle of covariation. In the first case, the effect always occurs when the stimulus is present (high consistency and high consensus) and not when the stimulus is absent (high distinctiveness). In the latter case, the effect occurs when the person is present (high consistency and low distinctiveness) and not when the person is absent (low consensus). Kelley's initial ideas were formulated with reference to covariation along all three dimensions. This is relevant in a number of instances. Take, for instance, the event of "Dr. Smith praised Jane's philosophy paper." Here we can ask whether other professors praised Jane's paper, whether Dr. Smith praises other work by Jane, and whether Dr. Smith usually praises Jane's philosophy papers. Kelley's ideas concerning the pervasiveness of these three types of information and their influence on the attribution of causality to forces internal or external to the person have attracted a great deal of attention.

A large number of studies have been conducted exploring these ideas. Two main categories of study can be distinguished. The first category includes studies where the information concerning consensus, consistency, and distinctiveness are presented and manipulated within a questionnaire. Typically, subjects are presented with a brief description of an event, as well as consensus, consistency, and distinctiveness information, and asked to rate the cause of the event along selected rating scales. For instance, McArthur (1972) presented subjects with items concerning the occurrence of an event (e.g., "John laughs at the comedian") and manipulated the other information presented to the subject through statements such as "Almost everyone who hears the comedian laughs at him" (high consensus) or "Hardly anyone who hears the comedian laughs at him" (low consensus). Similar manipulations were made for consistency and distinctiveness information.

The second category of study includes experiments where subjects have typically been asked to make attributions of a target person's behavior on the basis of information about his or her behavior as well as information concerning the behavior of others in the same situation. For instance, Wells and Harvey (1977) asked their subjects to read the report of the procedure of a psychological experiment, such as Nisbett and Schachter's (1966) study on receiving electric shocks, and presented them with information (not always authentic) about how other people had behaved during the experiment. Subjects are then told about how a particular person behaved and asked to make attributions concerning the causes of that behavior. The results of both sorts of experiments are broadly supportive of Kelley's hypotheses.

However, in many cases people may not have all this information, and in many other instances it may not even make sense to require it. For instance, if Jane was popular at the Christmas party, it may make sense to ask whether she is always popular at the Christmas party and whether she is popular at other parties, but does it make sense to ask if everyone was popular at the Christmas party? Again, if Jane got into college, what would count as consistency information? Or if Jane divorced John, we may want to know about how often she divorces her husbands or whether other people have divorced John, but would we want to know whether Jane had divorced him frequently in the past?

It seems that for some events only certain kinds of information seem relevant. Even where consensus, consistency, and distinctiveness are all relevant, a person may not have access to all three types of information. What if we take each of these dimensions separately? A later paper by Kelley and his colleagues (Orvis, Kelley, & Cunningham, 1975) claims that high consensus should lead to more stimulus attributions than low consensus, since the information suggests that the effect always occurs when the stimulus is present and does occur even in the absence of the particular person. Low distinctiveness should lead to more person attributions than high distinctiveness, since the effect is present when the person is present and does occur in the absence of the particular stimulus. Where there is low consistency, the effect cannot be explained in terms of the stable characteristics of either the person or the stimulus, since the effect is not regularly observed even when both are present and should lead to an attribution in terms of the particular circumstances of the event. The study by Orvis et al. provides support for these hypotheses. In the study to be conducted in this exercise, the influence of consensus, consistency, and distinctiveness information will be investigated. In order to simplify the analysis, the notions of attributions to stimulus and to the circumstances will be combined into a more general concept of situational attributions.

The most rudimentary way to investigate these hypotheses would be to specify one event (for example, "John got a high mark on his history paper") and then to present the relevant information (for example, "Most people got high marks on their history papers" as compared with "Few people got high marks on their history papers"). Attributions of causality could be obtained on a 7-point rating scale, ranging from "Entirely caused by the person" to "Entirely caused by the situation." One limitation of such a decision would be the uncertainty as to whether the results obtained are relevant to other events. This particular event has several distinctive characteristics: The agent is a male; the event has a positive outcome; the event is concerned with academic achievement – perhaps even more specifically with academic achievement of a particular sort (*history paper*). In order to have greater confidence in the generality of our results, it is important to use more events. There is no general system of classification of events from which they can be systematically chosen, but the events can be selected with reference to past literature, with reference to the theories of the investigator (which may be based on past literature), or with reference to a specific practical issue.

In order to introduce variety in the type of event, two subsidiary variables will be introduced. Several studies have shown that success is explained more in terms of internal than external causes, and failure more in terms of external than internal causes. It has been argued that this is because we assume that people embark on ventures in which they expect to succeed (Kelley & Michela, 1980). This finding has been substantiated with reference to the tasks involving intellectual abilities. Relatively little attention has been paid to interpersonal tasks. Orvis et al. (1975) and McArthur (1972) suggest that interpersonal tasks are seen as dependng more on both the agent and the stimulus person than other tasks. Extrapolating from this, we can conclude that the difference in the explanations for successful and unsuccessful outcomes will apply more to intellectual tasks than to interpersonal ones.

On the basis of the preceding discussion, several hypotheses can be tested:

1. High-consensus information will lead to more situation attributions than low-consensus information.
2. Low-distinctiveness information will lead to more person attributions than high-distinctiveness information.
3. Low-consistency information will lead to more situation attributions than high-consistency information.

A subsidiary hypothesis is that there will be an interaction between outcome (success versus failure) and type of task (intellectual versus interpersonal) such that success will lead to more person attributions than failure for intellectual tasks, but the same effect will not be obtained for interpersonal tasks.

The predominant research procedures in the attribution literature are as follows. Subjects are presented with questionnaires containing hypothetical events for which the subjects are asked to give the causes. The simplest questionnaire could use one intellectual event and one interpersonal event and manipulate all the information and all the outcomes with reference to these events. For instance, the intellectual event could concern John and his history paper. The successful outcome would be "John did very well on his history paper," and the unsuccessful outcome "John did very badly on his history paper." These two items could be presented with each of the two levels of the three types of information. Thus the basic theme (i.e., John and his history paper) would occur 12 times in the questionnaire. Similarly, an interpersonal event (for instance, Jim impressing or failing to impress Peter) could also be presented with each of the two levels of the three types of information and occur 12 times. These 24 items would have to be presented in at least two different random orders to ensure that the results obtained were not due to different responses on earlier items as compared with later items or to the succession of particular items.

Such a design would be theoretically complete, in the sense that the relevant experimental manipulations have been carried out in a controlled way. But problems would remain. Since only one item of each sort is included, the problem of generality raised earlier would reappear. Boredom and inattention may affect the subject, because of the sheer repetitiveness of the items. Further, since everything else is kept constant, the independent variable may be highlighted, so that the subjects easily guess the hypotheses. An alternative design would involve preparing multiple versions of the questionnaire. Several instances of intellectual and interpersonal events could be included, with one group of subjects receiving a "success" version of the event and another group receiving a "failure" version. Similarly, one group would receive the item with one sort of information, others with different sorts of information.

For instance, group A would receive a questionnaire with "John did very well on his history paper," and group B would receive a questionnaire with "John did very badly on the history paper." Group A1 would get the item with high-consensus information, group A2 the one with low-consensus information. Similarly, group B could also be subdivided into two groups with different versions of the questionnaire, and so in all four versions would be needed. The questionnaire suggested in appendix 1 attempts to strike a balance, for the purposes of the exercise, between the simplest design and more complex ones.

The questionnaire consists of six intellectual and six interpersonal events. The intellectual items are instances of a history examination, a geography paper, a biology lab, a crossword puzzle, an anagram test, and a radio quiz. The interpersonal items are instances of attempts to impress, encourage, gain respect, reassure, interest, and dominate.

Within each type of item, half were randomly assigned to positive outcomes and half to negative outcomes. All 12 items appear twice, once with high-consensus, high-distinctiveness, or high-consistency information, and once with low-consensus, low-distinctiveness, or low-consistency information. The final order of the items in the questionnaire was randomly determined, with the constraint that the two instances of the same event do not occur in succession.

One of the strengths of the design includes the variety of items. Since the type of information appears as high or low for the same item, the comparison of the effects of different levels of information can be made with confidence. Similarly, using several instances of intellectual and interpersonal tasks strengthens our confidence in any differences found with reference to this comparison. There are, however, difficulties and limitations. For instance, within each type of event the success–failure comparison refers to different items. Therefore, differences between the ratings of success items and failure items might be due to the particular items being used, rather than to their "success" or "failure" phrasing. This could, of course, be taken into account by developing an equivalent questionnaire interchanging the success and failure outcomes. Another difficulty is the lack of control for order effects. That is, the way subjects respond to later items may be due to the particular items they had encountered earlier. The suitability of different types of items should also be questioned. For example, only males have been mentioned in the items. Clearly the entire design could be replicated with female agents, and sex included as a between-groups factor in the analysis. But care must be taken in constructing alternative items. An item such as "John gave offense to Jack" may be unclear, since it may have been a successful or an unsuccessful outcome, and "David did not persuade Peter to buy the car" includes an additional element (the car). Think of other items that might have been used, and evaluate their suitability.

Analysis of rating scales

The main hypothesis to be investigated is that when high-consensus information is provided, people attribute causality more to situational factors than when low-consensus information is provided. Outcome (success and failure) and type of event (intellectual and interpersonal) were also included, and an interaction was expected among these variables. Thus we have three independent variables, each of which has two levels: consensus information level (high versus low); outcome (success versus failure); and event type (intellectual versus interpersonal), so that the design is a 2 × 2 × 2 factorial with repeated measures across all levels of all the factors. A data sheet is presented in Table 12.1.

The class may divide into groups of four for the coding of their responses. You should first familiarize yourself with the coding scheme in appendix 2 and then proceed to code your own responses. Do *not* code your responses on the questionnaire but on a separate sheet, since each questionnaire will be coded by several students. When you have completed the analysis of your own data, *exchange* the questionnaire with one of the other members of your group, and independently code the responses of that student. Next, you and the other student should discuss the coding of the two questionnaires, check your level of agreement, and resolve disagreements. This will enable you to have some preliminary practice before coding data that will be statistically analyzed. When you and your partner have completed discussion of your own two questionnaires, exchange questionnaires with the other two members of your group. Independently code the responses of the two questionnaires, and when this is completed, work out the per-

Table 12.1. *Raw data entries: effects of consensus*

	High consensus				Low consensus			
	Success		Failure		Success		Failure	
	Intel-lectual (I)	Inter-personal (H)	Intel-lectual (E)	Inter-personal (T)	Intel-lectual (R)	Inter-personal (C)	Intel-lectual (L)	Inter-personal (G)
Student								
1								
2								
3, etc.								

Note: Each student, numbered 1 through n, should call out his or her rating for each of the eight items listed in the table (cols. I, H, E, T, R, C, L, G: Each letter corresponds to an item on the questionnaire).

centage of items on which you and the original coder agreed. Then resolve your disagreements over the remaining items. The causes of difficulties in obtaining agreement and the limitations of the coding scheme can be discovered by asking what responses were particularly difficult to code, and why. A tabulation should be kept of the number of disagreements per item; items that accumulate large numbers of disagreements require modification in wording or clarification of their code.

The data should be examined for the effects of distinctiveness. If the behavior of the target person is not distinctive to the particular occasion described in the item, then a person attribution is expected. There are various ways of analyzing the data, but the simplest involves dichotomizing the dependent variables and performing an analysis of variance. The general format for the analysis is the same as that for the previous analysis. For each relevant item, each student can read aloud whether the explanation was coded as a person explanation. If it was, a score of zero is entered by a scorekeeper; if not, a score of 1 is entered. A $2 \times 2 \times 2$ analysis of variance is then calculated on the scores (see Table 12.2). For a complete description of this ANOVA, see Kirk (1968).

If the main hypothesis concerning the effects of distinctiveness information is confirmed, the average of the scores for high distinctiveness will be higher than the average of the scores for low distinctiveness. The interaction expected between outcome and type of event is identical to that expected in the case of consensus information (intellectual/failure items should yield the highest average score, intellectual/success items the lowest).

Table 12.2. *Raw data entries: effects of distinctiveness*

	High distinctiveness				Low distinctiveness			
	Success		Failure		Success		Failure	
	Intel-lectual (B)	Inter-personal (U)	Intel-lectual (D)	Inter-personal (A)	Intel-lectual (J)	Inter-personal (Q)	Intel-lectual (P)	Inter-personal (W)
Student								
1								
2								
3, etc.								

Note: Each student, numbered 1 through *n*, should call out his or her rating for each of the eight items listed in the table (cols. B, U, D, A, J, Q, P, W: Each letter corresponds to an item on the questionnaire).

If desired, the effects of consistency information can be tabulated as shown in Table 12.3.

If the main hypothesis is confirmed, the average of the scores for high-consensus items will be higher than that for low-consensus items. The interaction between outcome and event type can also easily be examined. The average of the scores for intellectual/failure items should be the highest, that for the intellectual/success items the lowest, and the averages for the two sets of interpersonal items should be in between.

Analysis of open-ended explanations

The open-ended explanations can be used to test the hypothesis that low-distinctiveness information leads to more person attributions than high-distinctiveness information. The interaction of outcome and type of event can also be examined. However, the first task with any content analysis of open-ended responses is to set up a reliable coding scheme that can be used to classify the data. The coding scheme should be guided by the particular hypotheses under investigation, which in this case require distinguishing between three types of explanation: (1) explanations in terms of the person; (2) explanations in terms of the situation; and (3) explanations involving both person and situational elements. These distinctions are presented in appendix 2, along with examples of each type of explanation. The examples are drawn mostly from a coding manual of explanations for success and failure produced by Elig and Frieze (1975).

Table 12.3. *Raw data entries: effects of consistency*

	High consistency				Low consistency			
	Success		Failure		Success		Failure	
	Intel-lectual (F)	Inter-personal (O)	Intel-lectual (X)	Inter-personal (V)	Intel-lectual (K)	Inter-personal (M)	Intel-lectual (N)	Inter-personal (S)
Student								
1								
2								
3, etc.								

Note: Each student, numbered 1 through n, should call out his or her rating for each of the eight items listed in the table (cols. F, O, X, V, K, M, N, S: Each letter corresponds to an item on the questionnaire).

Discussion

The study was designed to test a range of hypotheses:

1. Did subjects make more situation attributions when presented with high-consensus than with low-consensus information?
2. Did subjects make more person attributions for low-distinctiveness than high-distinctiveness information?
3. Did subjects make more situational attributions when presented with low-consistency than with high-consistency information?
4. Were there interactions between outcome and type of event?

Some other questions that can be examined include whether there were main effects of outcome or of event type, and whether there were any other interactions. These questions can be examined using analyses of variance similar to those described earlier but calculated over all 24 items. Your laboratory instructor can help you with the details. Explanations for any significant effects should be proposed.

It was noted earlier that the procedures used in this study are similar to those commonly used in attribution research. Assuming that the results of the study broadly support the hypotheses, the limitations of these procedures can be discussed. The inadequacy of the particular questionnaire has already been mentioned, but a number of more general questions remain.

The first concerns the presentation of the material. The events were baldly described, but information is seldom received in this way. The bald, skeletal description assumes that an important step in the processes leading to an explanation is unambiguous, such as the definition of the hypothetical event as being a success or as being a failure. This may sometimes be clear enough but on many occasions may be ambiguous. For instance, that John got a particular grade on his paper may be clear, but was it a "good" grade? There are many instances where a person may get high grades but not consider these good because the person expected to do better, and, conversely, cases where average grades may be considered good for a particular individual. Moreover, these problems of the definition of the outcome of the event may be more difficult with regard to interpersonal than with intellectual tasks.

The method also ignores the social context of the question. Why ask "Why did John do well on his history paper?" unless you expected him to do badly? Explanations are usually provided to particular other people in particular social contexts, and the explanation provided is, at least in part, guided by the assumptions the speaker makes about the knowledge and expectations of the questioner. These interpersonal factors are neglected by the present approach, and yet they may have operated as subtle influences on the ratings and explanations that were obtained.

The form of the presentation of the information is also debatable. Rather than present the information in a line of print, it is possible to make up visual material with film or video to present the relevant information sequentially. Such a method of presentation would be much more realistic and give us more confidence in the generality of the results.

Finally, although support for the hypothesis tells us about how consensus, consistency, and distinctiveness information is used, it does not tell us about what information a person might *seek*. In the introduction it was pointed out that the general model of the person in attribution theory was of a scientist. Lalljee (1981) has pointed out that the model adopted by Kelley is largely that of an inductivist, who approaches nature with no theories but counts instances of different types of information to arrive at conclusions. Even in the Jones et al. (1961) study of the job interview for the potential astronaut or submariner, the experimenters assumed that two explanations (i.e., personality characteristics versus behaving in a way that will get the job) were the most important. But it also is possible that the candidate changed his mind about wanting the job or behaved in a way that would cost him the job just because he was in a bad mood. These explanations may not be as plausible as the first two, but one must rely on one's knowledge of the world to specify which explanations are plausible (see Lalljee & Abelson, 1983). Scientific method also presents us with a different analogy: that of the scientist as a hypothesis tester. This approach would imply that we usually have some theories about why an event occurred and look for information that will enable us to test them or to confirm them. It would suggest that we may not *seek* information about consensus, consistency, and distinctiveness except when we do not have specific hypotheses about the event. In order to map the process of information search, a different methodology – for instance, inviting subjects to ask questions about the event and analyzing the questions, would have to be used.

References

Abramson, L.V., Seligman, M.E.P., & Teasdale, J.D. (1978). Learned helplessness in humans: critique and reformulation. *Journal of Abnormal Psychology*, 87, 49–74.

Barnes, R.D., Ickes, W., & Kidd, R.F. (1979). Effects of perceived intentionality and stability of another's dependency on helping behavior. *Personality and Social Psychology Bulletin*, 5, 367–72.

Bernstein, B. (1973). *Class, Codes and Control*, vol. 1. London: Routledge & Kegan Paul.

Elig, T.W., & Frieze, I.R. (1975). A multi-dimensional scheme for coding and interpreting perceived causality for success and failure. *JSAS Catalogue of Selected Documents in Psychology*, 5, MS 1,069.

Heider, F. (1958). *The Psychology of Interpersonal Relations*. New York: Wiley.

Jones, E.E., & Davis, K.E. (1965). From acts to dispositions: the attribution process in person perception. In L. Berkowitz (ed.), *Advances in Experimental Social Psychology*, vol. 2. New York: Academic Press.

Jones, E.E., Davis, K.E., & Gergen, K.J. (1961). Role playing variations and their informational value for person perception. *Journal of Abnormal and Social Psychology*, 63, 302–10.

Kelley, H.H. (1967). Attribution theory in social psychology. In *Nebraska Symposium on Motivation*, 15, 192–238.

Kelley, H.H. (1973). The processes of causal attribution. *American Psychologist*, 28, 107–28.

Kelley, H.H., & Michela, J.L. (1980). Attribution theory and research. In M.R. Rosenzweig and L.M. Porter (eds.), *Annual Review of Psychology*, vol. 31.

Kirk, R.E. (1968). *Experimental Design: Procedures for the Behavioural Sciences*. Monterey, Calif.: Brooks/Cole.

Lalljee, M. (1981). Attribution theory and the analysis of explanations. In C. Antaki (ed.). *The Psychology of Ordinary Explanations of Social Behaviour*. New York: Academic Press.

Lalljee, M., & Abelson, R.P. (1983). The organization of explanations. In M. Hewstone (ed.), *Attribution Theory: Social and Functional Extensions*. Oxford: Blackwell.

Lepper, M.R., Greene, D., & Nisbett, R.E. (1973). Undermining children's intrinsic interest with extrinsic reward: a test of the "over-justification" hypothesis. *Journal of Personality and Social Psychology*, 28, 129–37.

McArthur, L.A. (1972). The how and what of why: some determinants and consequences of causal attribution. *Journal of Personality and Social Psychology*, 22, 171–93.

Mischel, W. (1968). *Personality and Assessment*. New York: Wiley.

Nisbett, R.E., & Schachter, S. (1966). Cognitive manipulation of pain. *Journal of Experimental Social Psychology*, 2, 227–36.

Orvis, B.R., Kelley, H.H., & Cunningham, J.D. (1975). A closer examination of causal inferences: the roles of consensus, distinctiveness and consistency information. *Journal of Personality and Social Psychology*, 32, 605–16.

Piaget, J. (1929). *The Child's Conception of the World*. New York: Harcourt Brace.

Piaget, J. (1932). *The Moral Judgement of the Child*. London: Routledge & Kegan Paul.

Robinson, W.P., & Rackstraw, S.J. (1972). *A Question of Answers*, vol. 1. London: Routledge & Kegan Paul.

Schultz, T.R. (1982). Rules of causal attribution. *Society for Research in Child Development*, monograph 47 (1, serial no. 194).

Weiner, B. (1980). *Human Motivation*. New York: Holt, Rinehart & Winston.

Wells, G.L., & Harvey, J.H. (1977). Do people use consensus information on making causal attributions? *Journal of Personality and Social Psychology*, 35, 279–93.

Appendix 1. Sample events for explanation

This study is concerned with how people explain events. The following questionnaire consists of a number of statements that report the occurrence of some event. Following each statement there is in parentheses an item of information that applies to the event reported. The study consists of two parts, and the instructions for the second part will be dealt with after the first part has been completed.

Part 1

In the first part of the study your task is to decide, on the basis of the information given, what you think probably caused *the event* to occur. Please write down your explanation in your own words in the space below the information. Please read each item carefully before answering.

EXAMPLE: EVENT: Dr. Smith praised Joe's paper. (Information: Dr. Smith praises most people's papers.)

EXPLANATION FOR THE EVENT: that is, why do you think Dr. Smith praised Joe's paper?

A. EVENT: Julian failed to gain Steve's respect. (Information: Julian did not fail to gain the respect of many other people.)
EXPLANATION FOR THE EVENT:

B. EVENT: Henry did well in history exam. (Information: Henry did not do well in his other exams.)
EXPLANATION FOR THE EVENT:

C. EVENT: Robert succeeded in impressing Paul. (Information: Few people succeeded in impressing Paul.)
EXPLANATION FOR THE EVENT:

D. EVENT: Nick did badly on the anagram test. (Information: Nick did not do badly on other tests.)
   EXPLANATION FOR THE EVENT:

E. EVENT: Peter failed to win a prize on the radio quiz. (Information: Most people failed to win a prize on the radio quiz.)
   EXPLANATION FOR THE EVENT:

F. EVENT: Howard successfully completed the crossword puzzle. (Information: Howard usually succeeds in completing the crossword puzzle.)
   EXPLANATION FOR THE EVENT:

G. EVENT: Richard failed to encourage Ed. (Information: Few people failed to encourage Ed.)
   EXPLANATION FOR THE EVENT:

H. EVENT: David succeeded in impressing Jim. (Information: Most people succeeded in impressing Jim.)
   EXPLANATION FOR THE EVENT:

I. EVENT: John got a high mark on the geography paper. (Information: Most people got high marks on the geography paper.)
   EXPLANATION FOR THE EVENT:

J. EVENT: Chris did well on his history exam. (Information: Chris did well on his other exams.)
   EXPLANATION FOR THE EVENT:

K. EVENT: Tom successfully completed the crossword puzzle. (Information: Tom seldom succeeds in completing the crossword puzzle.)
EXPLANATION FOR THE EVENT:

L. EVENT: Edward failed to win a prize on the radio quiz. (Information: few people failed to win a prize on the radio quiz.)
EXPLANATION FOR THE EVENT:

M. EVENT: Roy succeeded in arousing Brian's interest. (Information: Roy seldom succeeds in arousing Brian's interest.)
EXPLANATION FOR THE EVENT:

N. EVENT: Frank did badly on his biology lab test. (Information: Frank seldom does badly on his biology lab test.)
EXPLANATION FOR THE EVENT:

O. EVENT: Hugh succeeded in arousing Graham's interest. (Information: Hugh usually succeeds in arousing Graham's interest.)
EXPLANATION FOR THE EVENT:

P. EVENT: Douglas did badly on the anagram test. (Information: Douglas did badly on other tests.)
EXPLANATION FOR THE EVENT:

Q. EVENT: Charles succeeded in reassuring Andy. (Information: Charles succeeded in reassuring many other people.)
EXPLANATION FOR THE EVENT:

R. EVENT: Bill got a high mark on the geography paper. (Information: Few people got high marks on the geography paper.)
EXPLANATION FOR THE EVENT:

S. EVENT: Martin failed to dominate Ron. (Information: Martin seldom failed to dominate Ron.)
EXPLANATION FOR THE EVENT:

T. EVENT: Michael failed to encourage Jeffrey. (Information: Most people failed to encourage Jeffrey.)
EXPLANATION FOR THE EVENT:

U. EVENT: Alan succeeded in reassuring Gerry. (Information: Alan did not succeed in reassuring most other people.)
EXPLANATION FOR THE EVENT:

V. EVENT: Tony failed to dominate Dick. (Information: Tony usually fails to dominate Dick.)
EXPLANATION FOR THE EVENT:

W. EVENT: Ronald failed to gain Larry's respect. (Information: Ronald failed to gain the respect of many other people.)
EXPLANATION FOR THE EVENT:

X. EVENT: Arthur did badly on his biology lab test. (Information: Arthur usually does badly on his biology lab test.)
EXPLANATION FOR THE EVENT:

Part 2

PLEASE DO NOT READ THESE INSTRUCTIONS UNTIL YOU
HAVE COMPLETED THE FIRST PART OF THE STUDY.

In the second part of the study we would like you to rate each event along a
7-point scale in terms of the degree to which you think the event described
was probably caused by characteristics of the situation and the degree to
which you think it was probably caused by characteristics of the person.

1	2	3	4	5	6	7
Caused entirely by the person		Caused about equally by person and situation			Caused entirely by the situation	

Beside each event on the questionnaire is a circle. For each event we would
like you to indicate, by entering the appropriate number, the degree to
which you think the event was probably caused by characteristics of the
person or characteristics of the situation. Thus, if you think event A was
caused entirely by the person, then enter the number 1; if you think it was
caused entirely by the situation then enter the number 7; and if you think it
was caused partly by the person and partly by the situation, indicate your
judgment about the causality of the event by entering the appropriate
number, from 1 to 7. Please do this for each item on the questionnaire.

Appendix 2. Explanations code

Person explanations

This code category refers to explanations that stress characteristics of the agent and do not refer to the situation.

EXAMPLES: He is an intelligent person.
He tried hard.
He was in a bad mood.
He was afraid of failing.
He is interest in people.

Situation explanations

This code category refers to explanations that stress the situation, including characteristics of the stimulus and of the circumstances, but do not refer to characteristics of the person.

EXAMPLES: The test was very difficult.
He had been badly taught*
He was lucky.†
The room was hot and stuffy.
The other person was easily impressed.

Person and situation explanations

This code category refers to explanations that make roughly equal reference to characteristics of the agent and characteristics of the situation.

---

*If interpreted as part of the *person's history*, being "badly taught" could be coded as a PERSON EXPLANATION.
†If interpreted as an enduring characteristic of the person ("He is a lucky person"), this could be coded as a PERSON EXPLANATION.

EXAMPLES: He knew the material well.
                 He didn't get along well with the teacher.
                 They were friends.
                 The task was too difficult for him to do.
                 They were equally opinionated.

"Not ascertainable" category

This code category refers to explanations not compatible with the three
established categories.

13   An aspect of prejudice

Glynis M. Breakwell

Summary

The exercise concerns the experimental investigation of intergroup dynamics; it focuses on that aspect of prejudice that leads to the devaluation of an out-group's products and how this is affected by the manipulation of group memberships. The experiment tests the impact of crossed-category membership upon the bias in evaluation in in-group and out-group performance.

Introduction

Conflicts between groups are common occurrences. The sorts of groups involved range from whole nations to coteries of four or five people, and the hostility takes many forms, from overt physical violence to subtle propaganda. It is therefore difficult to produce a single, all-encompassing social-psychological explanation for conflict between groups. However, over the last 20 years, two competing explanations have evolved.

The first essentially *social* psychological explanation of intergroup conflict came from Sherif (1966). Sherif argued that hostilities between groups occur as a result of a conflict of interest. When two groups want to achieve the same goal but both cannot have it, hostility develops. In contrast, when two groups work together to achieve a mutually desirable goal that neither would achieve without cooperation, hostility will be avoided. Sherif provided support for this very pragmatic argument from field studies in summer camps for boys in the United States. His studies had three or four stages. In the first stage, boys would arrive at the camp and be allowed to grow accustomed to the place and make friends; at this stage the boys comprised a single large group. The second stage involved the arbitrary division of this initial group into two, and the resulting activities. After these two groups had settled into their distinctive routines, the third stage involved the introduction of competitive activities. This involved sporting events in which teams from one group were matched against teams from another group. Sherif hypothesized that these competitive games, because they introduced a goal (presumably victory) that both groups wanted but only one could have, would instigate hostility between the groups. In fact, this was exactly what happened: verbal and physical attacks were made by both groups on their opponents, and these extended beyond the arena of the athletic activities (for example, raids were made in the middle of the night into the opponents' territory, creating havoc). In some of the studies, the initiation of conflict was followed by a fourth stage that was expected to eliminate the intergroup hostility. This involved the introduction of what Sherif called a "superordinate" goal – a goal that both groups wish to achieve but neither can achieve without the cooperation of the other. For instance, the boys were faced with the choice of pooling their money to rent a movie to be shown at the camp; neither of the groups had enough money to rent the movie alone, and if they were to get to see the movie, both groups had to cooperate in the enterprise. Sherif's hypothesis was to some extent supported: intergroup hostility did decline after the groups had cooperated to achieve a series of superordinate goals, but they were not eliminated.

After Sherif's work, several researchers began to question whether a conflict of interests was a necessary precursor of intergroup hostility. Sherif had shown it to be a *sufficient* cause for hostility, but he had not shown it to be a *necessary* cause. To put it another way, when a conflict of interests occurs, hostility follows, but hostility *can* occur in the absence of a conflict of interests, and, if it does, another sort of explanation is necessary.

The second sort of explanation of intergroup hostility came after a series of experiments had shown that hostility can develop where there is no conflict of interests. These experiments involved the creation of artificial "minimal groups" in the laboratory. Membership in these minimal groups was assigned randomly (sometimes explicitly so), and communication among the members was impossible; an individual in the group would not know the identity of other members, and no group goal or purpose would be established. Such groups were in reality totally arbitrary; they had no purpose or practical reason for being. There was no conflict of interest between groups created in this way, yet such groups still were shown to motivate intergroup discrimination. Faced with the task of allotting rewards to members of their own group and members of the other group, subjects in these experiments gave preferential treatment to members of their own group (Tajfel, Billig, Bundy, & Flament, 1971). Prejudice in favor of one's own group and bias against the out-group, in this situation, cannot be explained in terms of conflicts of interest between the groups; there was no objective conflict of interest. The mere fact of categorization, by simply creating two groups, seems to activate the potential for prejudice. The burning question is obvious: Why should this be so? Prejudice in this context serves no objective purpose; the individual receives no objective benefits from discriminating against the out-group. However, perhaps it can be explained in terms of subjective, psychological benefits.

Tajfel and his coworkers (see Tajfel, 1978) have developed an explanation for prejudice that centers on its psychological benefits. They argue that a person builds a social identity out of group membership, and that a person will want a satisfying social identity. In order to create a satisfying social identity, it is necessary to belong to groups that have a positive image. But groups gain a positive image only through comparison with other groups. An individual knows how well her or his group is doing by comparing it with the performance of other groups (a process similar to the individual social comparisons that Festinger, 1954, described). Emphasizing the distinctions between groups and focusing on those that enable one's own group to come out on top is an essential part of creating a satisfying social identity. The drive toward a satisfying social identity is therefore seen to be at the root of prejudice. It seems that prejudice bolsters self-esteem (Veblen, 1958; Gergen, 1971) through bolstering group esteem.

Now that we have looked at the possible general causes of prejudice, it is time to look at the ways in which prejudice can be expressed and the factors that influence its strength.

Prejudice can be shown in many ways. Obviously, it can involve physical attacks on another group, but it is often more subtle. It might involve minimizing contact with the other group; preventing its members from gaining access to important resources (like employment or housing); and the use of propaganda against them. Propaganda is itself a complex phenomenon, but it normally acts to deprecate the other group and to justify the in-group. Criticizing the out-group often involves the development of a negative stereotype of its members. It also frequently involves saying negative things about the skills or abilities of the out-group and devaluing anything its members have had a hand in producing. It is this last aspect of prejudice, the devaluation of the products of the out-group, that will be explored in this exercise.

There have been a number of studies of the devaluation of out-group products. Sherif, Harvey, White, Hood, and Sherif (1962) showed that after competition between groups in the boys' camps, members of one group would underestimate the talents, capacities, and skills of members of the other group. Blake and Mouton (1962) explored this phenomenon in the laboratory with artificially created groups that were asked to produce group solutions to a problem and then asked to rate their own solution and that of another group. Subjects knew that the two groups were in competition and consistently claimed that their own group's solutions were better than those of the other group. Ferguson and Kelley (1964) queried whether explicit competition between the groups was necessary for this sort of intergroup prejudice to occur. They designed an experiment where groups were not in competition and found that subjects still discriminated in favor of their own group's product. They found that a group member did not even have to be involved in the process of production to show this prejudice. They concluded that "attraction to the group is the crucial factor behind the bias." Merely being a member of the group encourages the individual to prefer the products of that group. This finding fits nicely with the predictions of self-esteem explanations of intergroup prejudice: the value of the group's products reflects on the value of the group itself and so must be seen as better than those of other groups, if the individual's social identity is to be satisfying.

Of course, various circumstances are known to influence the extent of in-group bias. Deschamps and Doise (1978) showed that in-group bias is actually reduced when individuals have to think in terms of more than one membership simultaneously. In their experiment, subjects were either assigned to a single category and then asked to evaluate members of their own category and members of an opposite category (for example, males rating males in contrast to females), or they were assigned to a "crossed category" involving, simultaneously, two memberships and asked to rate members of their own and other crossed categories (for example, young men had to rate young men as compared with old men or young men in contrast to old women). When crossed categorization was used, individuals responded in terms of more than one membership simultaneously. Subjects assigned to a single category showed greater in-group bias than those in crossed categories, for whom bias was virtually eliminated. The implication is that multiple memberships act to limit prejudice.

A second factor known to influence the extent of prejudice has to do with the objective nature of a group's products. In some situations it is obvious that the in-group's products are objectively inferior to those of the out-group, and the distinction cannot be totally ignored. Lemaine (1974) examined how a group would deal with this. He asked two groups to build huts that would then be evaluated by the experimenter; the winning group would be rewarded. He provided both groups with materials to build the huts, but one group was deprived of some essential components for a good hut. The hut produced by one group was therefore objectively inferior. He then found that members of the disadvantaged group produced a little garden around their hut and claimed that this should be taken into consideration in evaluating their hut. They were trying to alter the criterion of evaluation. Knowing that they could not gain points for the group on the existing criterion, they tried to substitute one on which they could. Lemaine called these redefinitions of the criterion acts of "social originality." Objective inferiority motivates a group to change the rules of the game. Given the opportunity, groups will choose dimensions of intergroup comparison that allow them to come out on top.

Aims and hypotheses

The objective of this exercise is to take two themes from the research just described and mold a single experiment around them. These themes are (1) the devaluation of an out-group's products, and (2) the tendency of crossed categorization to lessen in-group bias.

The form of crossed categorization used here is not directly comparable to that used by Deschamps and Doise. The design involves bringing representatives of two groups into the laboratory. These groups should be ones that occur naturally and have a meaning for the subjects. Once in the laboratory, one-third of the total in each of the natural groups will be required to leave their original groups and form a third "mixed" group. Each of the three groups will have to make some kind of object, and each subject will be asked to rate the three products on scales provided by the experimenters.

The primary hypothesis is that subjects in the new mixed groups will show less intergroup prejudice than members of the other two groups. This hypothesis is based on the assumption that members of the mixed group will have dual loyalties – one to their original group and one to the new group. It is also based on the assumption that they would not criticize groups that they are soon going to return to, since that would reflect badly on their self-esteem. A subordinate hypothesis might be made about the use of rating scales. Following Lemaine, it could be hypothesized that group members will choose to inflate the scores of their own group on scales that refer to qualities that they particularly identify with their own group. This subordinate hypothesis should become clear as the method is described, since it depends on the rating scales adopted.

Method

Preparations for the experiment include

- Choice of groupings to be used
- Choice of task
- Choice of cover story
- Preparation of rating scales
- Gathering of materials for the task

The running of the experiment should take no more than 1 hour. It falls into six stages.

Stage 1. The cover story

Most experiments use cover stories. They are the false explanations for the experiment that subjects are given to prevent them from guessing its real purpose. Here the choice of cover story will depend on the sort of groups taking part and the type of task they are asked to do.

The choice of groupings can be a matter for debate; any two opposed groups will do, though it is preferable that they should arouse strong loyalty in their members. The two groups could be set up on the basis of sex, academic background (liberal arts versus science majors), membership in fraternities/sororities, or residence (off-campus versus dormitory). The ways in which subjects (Ss) can be split into two groups are innumerable. For the sake of illustrating the method, it will be assumed that Ss are divided into two groups – arts majors and science majors – on the basis of their academic background.

The task set for the groups can also be discussed. As long as it involves a product that can be evaluated later, any task can be used. Of course, the practicality of the task should be considered. It should be interesting, not too time-consuming, and should not involve inappropriate equipment. The task should also be relevant to the dimension around which the groups were created. For instance, the arts and science groups could be asked to produce a tower from certain materials (like paper, Scotch tape, wire, etc.) provided.

Once you have chosen the groupings and the task, you need to create the cover story. The main point to keep in mind is that it should be realistic without giving away the real purpose of the experiment. If, for example, the task is to construct a tower, you could tell the subjects that the purpose was to find out whether liberal arts and science groups engage in different forms of communication when involved in a creative tasks. The cover story could then be supported by having experimenters observe the interactions and appear to record them on record sheets specially prepared.

Stage 2. Focusing on the two groups

The two groups should comprise equal numbers of Ss, and the number in each should be divisible by three. After they have been given the cover story, Ss should be told that the two groups are very different and are recognized to be different by the experimenters. The object is to make the idea of their membership of these particular groups stand out in the subjects' minds. For instance, in the case of the arts/science majors, you could say that people from these two backgrounds seem to have different kinds of creativity, and you could develop some rationalizations for this statement.

Stage 3: Creation of the mixed group

One-third of the Ss from each of the two initial groups should then be chosen at random to form the mixed group. Experimenters should decide whether they want to find another cover story for this or to just do it without explanining. It is better to explain, since Ss are sure to query this further division. In the example of the arts–science groups, where the initial cover story was that the experiment was set up to explore communication patterns, there is no reason why this original story should not be extended. The creation of the mixed group could be said to be necessary in order to examine communication between members of the two types of academic background when faced with a communal task.

Stage 4. The task

The three groups thus established would then be introduced to the task, given the necessary materials and instructions, and asked to do it. They would remain in the same room but would be asked not to communicate across group boundaries. No explicit instructions to compete should be given. An arbitrary time limit of 15 minutes might be set for the task.

Stage 5. Evaluation of the products

You will need to select criteria and rating scales for the subjects to use in evaluating the products. The exact nature of the scale will be a function of the task, but 5-point rating scales might be most appropriate. A number of criteria said to be relevant to the product could then be chosen, and each subject would rate each of the three products (i.e., those of the in-group and the two out-groups) for each criterion. A sample rating form is provided in the appendix; it uses the criteria relevant to evaluating the towers produced by arts/science/mixed groups.

When the subjects have finished rating the products, they should be asked to rank order the criteria on the rating form in terms of how important they believed their group would consider each criterion to be. The information on ranking will be used, along with information on differential usage of the criteria, to test the second experimental hypothesis.

Stage 6. Debriefing

At the conclusion of the experiment, Ss must be told of its real purpose. They should be provided with an opportunity to comment on the procedure. They might be specifically asked if they had guessed the experimental hypotheses.

Results

Collation of data

Collation of data should take no more than 15 minutes. Rating forms should be collected from subjects, keeping the forms from each of the three groups separate. For ease of description, the two initial groups will be called A and B, and the mixed group X. The teacher should collate the data. A grid, like that in Table 13.1, can be used to summarize the data. For example, Subject 1's ranking of Group A's product on the first rating criterion (which might be "beauty," for instance) would be entered in the grid at the position marked k on Table 13.1. The entire grid would be filled in this way, so that it summarizes all the raw data.

Data on the rank ordering of the criteria in terms of their importance to the group must also be recorded. The mean ranking that each criterion receives from members of each group in turn should be calculated. This is a way of establishing the group's ranking of the criterion.

Analysis of the data

The data can be subjected to analyses at various levels of complexity. Whatever analysis is chosen, it should be designed to test the original hypotheses. These were that

- The mixed group would show less in-group bias and out-group devaluation than the other two groups.
- Rating-scale usage would reflect how important each criterion was perceived to be to the group; criteria believed to be unimportant would not be used in order to differentiate between groups.

Table 13.1. *Collating the data*

Groups	Subjects	Scales	Scales	Scales
		Group Products		
		$1\ 2\ n^a$	$1\ 2\ n$	$1\ 2\ n$
A	1	k		
	2			
	3			
	4			
B	1			
	2			
	3			
	4			
x	1			
	2			
	3			
	4			

"The number of scales will vary. The fewer the scales, the simpler the analysis.

A simple way of looking at the data is to examine mean ratings of each product by each group. Mean ratings can be calculated by taking each rating made for each of the criteria by each of the subjects in a group, adding them, and dividing by the number of subjects. There would then be nine means in all:

> Group A on products A, B, and X
> Group B on products A, B, and X
> Group X on products A, B, and X

These means could then be represented in a graph, as in Figure 13.1. The mean ratings in Figure 13.1 were invented for the purpose of demonstration. They represent the pattern that might be expected from the results if the hypothesis that the mixed group shows less bias was confirmed.

The patterns in Figure 13.1 are based on two assumptions:

- that group X does not differentiate between the three products and that the ratings of all fall roughly in the middle of the scales. Actually their ratings may fall at the bottom of the scale or collect at the top. The actual level of the ratings is less important than the relative ratings of the three products.
- that groups A and B do not discriminate as much against the product of group X as they do against the products of each other. This is an assumption that the experiment will test.

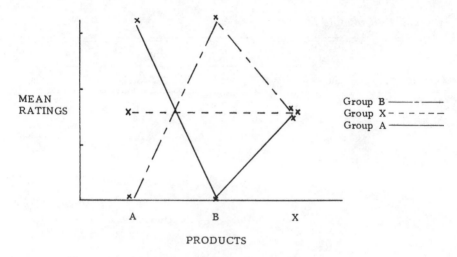

Figure 13.1 Mean ratings of the three products.

Another type of graph that could be used to represent the results might be worthwhile making if it is suspected that different criteria are used differentially by the three groups. For instance, if group A is a bunch of arts students and group B a bunch of engineers, and the criteria include one rating of aesthetic properties of the product and one rating of aerodynamic stability, perhaps arts students will use the aesthetic dimension to differentiate between the two groups' products but ignore the aerodynamic properties. For the arts students, aerodynamic properties are unimportant, and the product that their group creates does not have to have more of these properties than anyone else's product. Graphs representing mean ratings for each criterion independently would show differences of this kind in usage. Figure 13.2 shows what the pattern might look like. It shows group B treating the criterion as unimportant, group A considering it a good dimension for intergroup discrimination, and group X considering it important but not engaging in in-group bias. These types of graph for each criterion would provide some test of the second hypothesis. Of course, data on the ranking of criteria of importance would enable the experiment to predict what patterns would occur for each criterion.

Before going on to a general discussion, one warning should be given about the simpler sorts of analysis. Mean ratings can be misleading unless they are considered in relation to the standard deviation involved. For instance, a mean in the middle of a rating scale can be an artifact produced

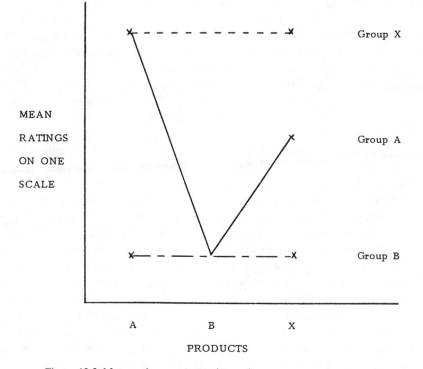

MEAN

RATINGS

ON ONE

SCALE

Group X

Group A

Group B

A   B   X

PRODUCTS

Figure 13.2 Mean ratings on one rating scale.

by an even split among subjects whose ratings are really bimodally distributed. Data should be examined for this kind of artifact.

A more complex analysis is, of course, possible. Given the nature of the
data, the most comprehensive test of these hypotheses would be provided
by subjecting the data to a 3 × 3 × 3 analysis of variance, with repeated
measures on two factors. This analysis is described in Kirk (1968, p. 299).
It would effectively allow the analyst to assess what effects group membership, the origin of the product evaluated, and the criterion used had upon
ratings. It would also pinpoint the effects of interactions between these
three main factors.

The simple 3 × 3 (groups times products) analysis of variance, with
repeated measures on one factor (products), might be conducted if the
differences between criteria were ignored. This would involve taking the
sum of ratings made by each subject about each group's product across all

criteria. This would treat the criteria as if they were merely a cumulative means of rating the product. It would mean that differences between ratings on different criteria would be lost. However, it allows statements to be made about the effects of group membership and the product evaluated on the ratings, and includes information on the ways in which these two factors interact. This analysis is described in Kirk (1968, p. 249).

Discussion

In method, this experiment is typical of an entire genus of experiments. It examines group dynamics in a highly simplified and controlled way, which is both its advantage and its weakness. It involves the creation of artificial, short-term changes in group structures, allows a limited range of activities and modes of expressing allegiance, and is perfectly tailored to the experimenter's needs. Moreover, it involves only small groups (four or five), though they may be drawn as representatives from larger groupings, and it permits only individuals to express intergroup discrimination (groups as a whole do not produce ratings or opinions; the individual is the fundamental source of data). There are obviously severe limitations on the generalizability or realism of results from such circumscribed situations. Nevertheless, this method of choosing one variable, manipulating it, and holding other variables constant while the effects are recorded is the central feature of the experimental method. Its strength is that it may indicate something of the power of the variable manipulated to change behavior; it can pinpoint correlational relationships, even if it can never establish causal ones. These small-scale experiments do have a value as long as they are seen to be what they really are. They should not be treated as the foundation for huge generalizations about international relations. Each well-constructed experiment contributes something to our understanding of group dynamics. Taken together and bound into some semblance of order by social psychological theory, they may have something to say about international relations. So far they are silent.

There are other methodological problems in this type of study besides that associated with generalizability of results. It is always difficult to know whether the subjects have perceived the experimental manipulations in the way in which they were meant to. In this experiment, the manipulation works only if the subjects placed in the mixed group feel that for them a new grouping has been created. If no new allegiance has been created for them, it is unlikely that the hypotheses will be supported.

This particular problem with the experimental manipulation brings into focus an issue that has been deliberately avoided throughout the description of the exercise. Central to the exercise is the whole troubled issue of what constitutes a "group." There are several comprehensive considerations of this issue in the literature (Cartwright & Zander, 1968; pp. 46–8; Dean, 1969, pp. 217–42); suffice it to say here that the term is shrouded in mystery. It seems that all sorts of groups can exist, along a continuum ranging from the completely concrete (groups with fixed hierarchies, goal structures, and communication patterns) to the totally conceptual (groups that exist only in the concept systems of those who believe that they belong). All types of groups seem to have the power to motivate allegiance and intergroup discrimination like that described earlier. On this basis, there is no reason to suppose that the manipulation creating a new group in the experiment by bringing together representatives from the original groups should not work. As long as those allotted to the mixed group believe themselves to be members, it should operate as a full-fledged group.

If the hypotheses were supported, the mixed group should show less intergroup discrimination. This could be a result of one of two things: either the mixed group is less critical of others, or it is more critical of itself. Either way, it implies that creating mixed groups has advantages. It may reduce prejudice across group boundaries, and it may reduce the chances of "groupthink" (Janis, 1976). The damage done by prejudice is well known, those of groupthink less so. Groupthink is what happens when a group begins to believe that it is invincible and its ideas infallible. Most frequently, this is a totally unrealistic perception of the situation and can lead to serious mistakes (Raven & Rubin, 1976, describe how the Nixon group showed all the signs of groupthink during the Watergrate period). A mixed group that has resources of self-criticism may avoid the perils of groupthink.

Of course, in looking at the implications of the results, an important rule must be kept in mind. The results can be understood only *in context*. It may be totally inappropriate to jump to the conclusion that because a mixed group in this experiment showed less intergroup discrimination, all mixed groups will do so. The effects of mixed grouping will obviously depend on the exact conditions of mixing, the history of the "parent" groups, and the context in which discriminations might be made. It is also obvious that other experiments can be designed to shed light on these issues.

Conclusion

Students doing this exercise should gain some knowledge of the social psychology literature on intergroup relations; they should derive some understanding of the limitations and strengths of the experimental methods applied in research on group dynamics; and they should begin to understand that the same data can be subjected to analyses at various levels of complexity in order to test the same hypotheses.

It should become clear during the exercise that an experiment of this sort has a stage structure. Experimentation is a little like gardening: it involves planting, transplanting, pruning, watering, and harvesting. It should be viewed temporally, and the different stages should not be taken out of order. The stages of the experiment construct the social phenomenon that is to be explored in microcosm.

The other clear lesson the exercise has to offer is that all experiments of this kind involve a choice of how much room to give the subjects. The experimenter has to decide how much freedom subjects will have to choose the arena of activity, the medium of expression for opinion, and the audience for those opinions. In making that decision, it is often easiest for the experimenter to include only freedoms that can be encompassed by the existing theoretical framework. In this way a theory can be tested in a narrow fashion, but it is possible (by restricting the subjects' freedom) to prevent unforeseen responses or reactions. Important data that lie outside the bounds of the theory are therefore never collected, and the fundamental tenets of the theory go unchallenged. Experiments that offer the subject minimal freedom of response may test a theory, but they are unlikely to advance it.

References

Blake, R. P., & Mouton, J. S. (1962). Overevaluation of own-group's product in intergroup competition. *Journal of Abnormal and Social Psychology*, 64, 237–8.

Cartwright, D., & Zander, A. (1968). *Group Dynamics*, 3rd ed. New York: Harper & Row.

Dean, D. G. (1969). *Dynamic Social Psychology*. New York: Random House.

Deschamps, J. C., & Doise, W. (1978) Crossed category membership in intergroup relations. In H. Tajfel (ed.), *Differentiation between Social Groups*. London: Academic Press.

Ferguson, C. K., & Kelley, H. H. (1964). Significant factors in over-evaluation of own-group's product. *Journal of Abnormal and Social Psychology*, 69, 223–28.

Festinger, L. (1954). A theory of social comparison processes. *Human Relations*, 7, 117–40.

Gergen, K. (1971). *The Concept of Self*. New York: Holt, Rinehart & Winston.

Janis, I. (1976). Groupthink. In E. P. Hollander and R. G. Hunt (eds.), *Current Perspectives in Social Psychology* (4th ed.). Oxford: Oxford University Press.

Kirk, R. E. (1968). *Experimental Design: Procedures for the Behavioral Sciences*. Monterey, Calif.: Brooks Cole.

Lemaine, G. (1974). Social differentiation and social originality. *European Journal of Social Psychology*, 4, 17–52.

Raven, B., & Rubin, J. (1976) *Social Psychology*. New York: Wiley.

Sherif, M. (1966). *Group Conflict and Cooperation*. London: Routledge & Kegan Paul.

Sherif, M., Harvey, O., White, B., Hood, W., & Sherif, C. (1962). *Intergroup Conflict and Cooperation: The Robber's Cave Experiment*. Norman, Okla.: University Book Exchange.

Tajfel, H. (eds.) (1978). *Differentiation between Social Groups*. New York: Academic Press.

Tajfel, H., Billig, M., Bundy, R., & Flament, C. (1971). Social categorization and intergroup behaviour. *European Journal of Social Psychology*, 1, 149–77.

Veblen, R. (1958). *The Theory of the Leisure Class*. New York: Mentor Books.

Appendix. Rating scale for products

Note: This suggested format for the rating form is based on certain assumptions:

1. That the subjects, when placed in a group, were given a name for that group by which they could identify it
2. That only five criteria are used (actually, any number can be used)
3. That rating is done on a 5-point scale
4. That subjects have just completed the task of building a tower out of material provided (actually, any sort of task can be set)

The language in the rating form can be made more or less complicated, depending on the audience to whom it is directed.

Rating form

Which group did you work with? _____
Consider the three towers that the groups have produced. Now say how good you think they are in terms of the five qualities listed below. Rate each tower in terms of each quality. Use a 5-point rating scale: 5 means that the tower possesses the quality in abundance, and 1 means it does not have it at all, so 3 means the tower has that quality to an average extent. Put your rating in the appropriate column.

Qualities	Group A's Tower	Group B's Tower	Group X's Tower
1. Beauty			
2. Stability			
3. Unusualness/originality			
4. Usefulness			
5. Uses materials efficiently			

Now think about the five qualities. Consider what your group would think were important qualities for the tower to have. Rank order the five qualities in terms of how important your group would think them to be. Put down the most important first, the next most important second, and so on.
Most important   _____
                    _____
                    _____
                    _____
Least important   _____

14   Crowd panic: competing and cooperating in groups

Robin Gilmour

Summary

This exercise will introduce you to a number of important features of the experimental approach to social behavior, on the basis of an experiment by Mintz (1951). More specifically, it is concerned with cooperation and competition among members of a group on an experimental task (extracting cones from a bottle) and permits the examination of a number of variables influencing performance. Following Mintz, it is possible to look at the effect of varying the reward structure by setting up a system of rewards and fines. Similarly, the effect of interfering with communications in the group can be studied, as well as the influence of emotional arousal.

Preliminary Note

This exercise requires at least two groups of 5 or 6 subjects, plus 2 or 3 experimenters per group. It is best to use outside subjects, but if not, some of the class members can act as subjects. If you do this, the students acting as subjects should be selected now, and only the students who are going to be running the exercise as experimenters should read through the exercise for the time being. If there is a large number of available subjects, a third group can be run with the help of 6 to 10 assistants to the experimenters, or groups can be run with 10 or 12 subjects.

Introduction

This exercise is based on the studies by Mintz (1951) attempting to simulate crowd panic reactions in a laboratory situation and to examine the factors influencing such behavior. The particular problem to be investigated is why, under some conditions, members of a group behave in a seemingly "irrationally" competitive way (that is, panic) when a cooperative response

279

would be more rewarding. Possible explanations that have been offered include the effects of changing the reward structures, of disrupted communication, and of emotional arousal, and these will be the main focus of the exercise.

The number and nature of hypotheses to be investigated will depend on what resources are available, remembering that each factor to be examined will require at least a group of five or six subjects and two or three experimenters. As a starting point, it is suggested that the effects of reward structure and communication be investigated, so that the initial experimental hypotheses are

1. Groups show significantly more panic behavior when they operate under a reward structure than without one.
2. Groups show significantly poorer performance when verbal communication is inhibited.

If resources permit, an additional hypothesis would be that conditions of emotional arousal have no significant effect on group performance.

Background

The general background to the exercise comes from work on crowds and collective behavior (for example, see Milgram, 1977). Theories of crowd behavior often tend to look at mobs and riots as examples and to focus on what appears to be the irrational way people act in such situations. Thus the heightened state of emotional arousal that some crowds show may be seen as somehow interfering with "normal" rational action.

This ties in with the way the general public typically sees crowds as behaving in an unpredictable and uncontrolled fashion, with a potential for harmful or violent outcomes. One example was an incident in Cincinnati in 1979, when a crowd lining up for tickets to a rock concert stampeded, trampling 11 people to death and injuring many others.

A similar focus can be seen in Mintz's study of crowd panic. Mintz (1951) was concerned with the way groups of people in certain situations appeared to panic and behave in ways that seemed to be irrational and dysfunctional. The particular illustration he used was that of a theater fire in which, instead of remaining calm and leaving the building in an orderly manner – which could have been done quickly and efficiently, so that everyone escaped safely – people panicked and blocked the exits, with the result that a number were trampled or burned to death. Earlier explanations of such behavior would, he argued, have stressed the emotional excitement of the situation interfering with rational adaptive responses. However, it is possible to suggest a more "rational" model of participants' reaction in terms of their perception of the reward–cost structure of the situation. If everyone remains calm, this orderly, cooperative behavior produces a satisfactory payoff for the individual (i.e., escape); if, on the other hand, some people stop cooperating and start trying to force their way out, then the reward–cost structure for the remaining individuals changes, and they may see the best chance of their own survival in individual competitive action ("If I don't fight my way out now, others will block the exits, and I will get burned"). In addition, as disorder increases, communication is likely to break down, preventing the reemergence of cooperative action.

Mintz set out to examine the influence of reward structure and communication on group panic by setting up a laboratory experiment in which a group of subjects were given the task of extracting a number of cones from a glass bottle that had a narrow neck, so that the cones could only come out one at a time (see the "Method" section for further details). Unless cones were extracted individually, they tended to jam in the neck of the bottle. Thus Mintz attempted to construct an analogue of the theater fire in which cooperative behavior would produce a successful outcome, and panic and competition would be nonadaptive. The effects on the subjects of rewards and fines for performance could be experimentally studied, and so could the influence of communication and emotional arousal. In keeping with his initial hypotheses, Mintz found that emotional arousal had little effect in producing "traffic jams" in the experiment but that significant effects were produced by changes in the reward structure.

Methodologically, the Mintz experiment is particularly interesting. It is an attempt to apply an experimental approach to a complex social phenomenon and to bring an instance of a large-scale social behavior into the laboratory. Such a simulation – creating an analogue task that tries to model significant features of the original phenomenon – is one extensively employed in social psychological research, and the Mintz example provides a useful basis for examining this methodological approach, since there is apparently such a large difference between the behavior under investigation and the situation actually being experimented on.

Method

To give a general summary first, the exercise involves having groups of subjects perform an experimental task of extracting a series of cones from a glass jar within a specified time. Each group has two sets of 10 trials, the first a competitive one with rewards and fines, the second a cooperative one without the reward structure. An additional condition involves having one group perform in the competitive situation in silence, and a further condition, involving a group's performing in the presence of an emotionally arousing "mob" can be added. Some assistance from a few class members in running the exercise is needed, with the rest of the class acting as subjects, or the exercise can be carried out using outside subjects, with class members acting as experimenters.

Resources

Space. It is best if each experimental group works on its own, which requires at least two fairly small rooms or a larger room that can be divided up into separate areas. If more groups are being run at the same time, further space will be required. Each group will need a clear area of floor (preferably uncarpeted), with a table and some chairs at the side.

Subjects. Class members can themselves be the subjects for this exercise. Each experimental group requires 5 or 6 subjects plus 2 or 3 experimenters, so the number of groups to be run and the number of experimental conditions will vary depending on the size of the class. With a very large class, subjects can be run in groups of 10 or 12.

Alternatively, if there is ready access to outside subjects (for instance, if class members can be relied on to bring along suitable people), these can be used with class members running the experiment as far as possible, which gives a useful element of practical research experience. The exercise can be run successfully with a variety of subjects, from children to undergraduates.

Equipment. Each group will need a heavy glass jar with a relatively wide base and a narrow neck (see Figure 14.1).

These can easily be obtained from chemistry equipment suppliers (or perhaps borrowed from a chemistry department). With each jar there should be about 15 cones made out of some convenient material such as wood or aluminium and constructed so that the base of the cone is a little narrower than the neck of the jar (i.e., so that the base of one cone and the tip of another will jam the neck: see Figure 14.1). A hole should be drilled along the length of each cone and a long waxed string attached.

One variation that Mintz used in his experiment involved having water poured into the bottle to add more pressure to the task, since subjects had to keep their cones dry to avoid being fined. If you want to copy this, then a jar with an appropriate inlet will be required (again readily available from chemistry suppliers), together with a suitable water reservoir, such

Figure 14.1 Glass jar and cones.

as a plastic bottle with tap and connecting tubes. Then it is easy to arrange a water flow by placing the reservoir on a table and opening the tap. When this condition is used, it helps to have a small sponge pad stuck to the base of each cone to show whether it has been kept dry or not.

In addition to this equipment, each group will need a stopwatch, a note-book to record results, cloths or paper towels to mop up spilled water (where water is used), and some system of rewards and fines. It would be possible to try simply awarding points here, but this raises an important issue concerning incentives for subjects. If rewards are fairly small, subjects may treat the experiment as a game, with a different kind of involvement and producing different behavior from a real situation, where incentives are perceived as real and substantial. Mintz used sums of money, and if you can afford to give reasonable amounts as rewards, this would be a good solution – for instance, by setting up a points system with a substantial reward for the group with the highest number of points over the whole experiment. If you do not have enough money to offer subjects significant cash incentives, either small amounts of money or some substitute such as candies could be used. These will still generate interest and involvement, but you should be again alert to the possibility that subjects' behavior is somewhat limited to the experimental situation and may not generalize readily to real life – another aspect of the methodological issue that was raised at the end of the introduction.

Time. The exercise can be carried out within a single 3-hour period.

Procedure

First, decide how many groups will be used in the exercise and what conditions are to be examined, given that each group task involves the removal of 10 to 12 cones from a jar, so that each group should consist of 5 or 6 subjects with two cones each, or – with a large class – you can have 10 or 12 subjects with one cone each. As suggested earlier, you should try to have at least two sets of conditions, one comparing the presence with the absence of a reward structure within each group, and the other looking at differences between groups when verbal communication is limited in one of them. Thus, minimally, the exercise requires two groups of 5 subjects, although it is better with two groups of 6; and, depending on the numbers available, you can arrange for two larger groups of subjects, and/or repeat the basic procedure with further groups, and/or add further conditions to the experiment. To simplify the rest of this discussion, it will be assumed that the exercise uses two groups of 6 subjects.

Each group of experimenters should decide (after consulting with other groups, or with the instructor if necessary) which conditions it will be running. Subjects can then be scheduled, allowing time for experimenters to become familiar with procedure and equipment beforehand, which will take between 40 minutes and 1 hour. Where possible, subjects should be scheduled so that they are assigned to groups randomly and so that people used to working with each other are not in the same group.

For each experimenter, group roles should now be assigned as follows: One person acts as coordinator and is responsible for giving instructions to subjects and timing trials; a second scores performance, noting the number of cones extracted by the subjects in the time allowed for each trial, or the time taken to extract all the cones; and a third holds the glass jar down on the floor to keep it from getting broken and unjams the cones when necessary. If numbers are limited, the first two roles can easily be combined.

Having done this, the equipment should be set up, with the glass jar in the center of the floor space to be used and 12 cones sitting on the bottom of the jar with their strings coming out of the jar and spread around it on the floor. Experimenters should then run carefully through the rest of the procedure to make sure they are familiar with how the exercise runs and especially with their own part in it, before the subjects appear.

When subjects arrive, they should be taken to where the equipment is laid out and introduced to the exercise as one on group performance. The following instructions should then be given:

The experimental task here is to try to get cones out of the jar in 20 seconds. In doing this you can win or lose rewards in the form of points [money, etc.]. For each cone safely pulled out within the time limit you will get 2 points, and for each one remaining in the jar after 20 seconds you will lose 1 point. To start with, each of you will be given 4 points to cover any initial losses. Wins and losses will be added up at the end of each trial, and if you go into "debt" this will be noted and set against future winnings. At the end of the experiment the group with the highest number of points will receive _____ dollars.

There will be a number of trials. When I say "go," try to get your cones out of the bottle. At the end of 20 seconds, I'll say "Stop now!", and then you have to stop just where you are. Please try not to pull too hard on the cones because they are pretty fragile.

The "no communication" group (if this condition is being used) should also be told not to talk with each other.

After ensuring that subjects understand the instructions, a clearly visible note should be made on a suitable board of each subject's name and initial "bank" of rewards or points. Subsequent gains or losses are then marked on the board for each subject to see. Subjects should then be told to take hold of the ends of the strings attached to the cones and wait for the start of the trial before lifting cones off the bottom of the jar. The signal to start can then be given, and the trial can be ended after 20 seconds are up or all the cones are out of the jar. At this point, you should note down the number of cones out of the jar or the time taken to get them all out; then each subject can be rewarded or fined accordingly. After this has been done, all the cones should be put back into the jar by one of the experimenters, to avoid giving learning cues to the subjects, and the trial is repeated.

After 10 trials, subjects should be stopped and given new information for the cooperative condition; in this case all groups get the following instructions:

The next set of trials is different. There will be no rewards or fines, and what we will be interested in is the performance of this group as a whole compared with other groups doing the same thing, so you should try to co-operate to get as many cones out as possible.

There should be no restrictions on any of the groups now, and again each group will be given 10 trials, and the number of cones extracted or time taken on each should be recorded. At the end of the second series of trials, subjects should be given their rewards, have the purpose of the exercise explained to them, and be thanked for their participation.

Variations in procedure

One variation than can be used in the competitive condition involves having water pouring into the jar during these first 10 trials so that subjects have to keep cones dry as well as extract them, putting the subjects under somewhat greater pressure (and extending the analogy with a theater fire to a small extent).

For this, the additional equipment noted earlier is required, and instructions have to be modified so that subjects are given a different reward structure: For example, 2 points for each cone extracted during the trial and kept dry, 1 for each cone extracted in time but wet, 1 lost for each cone not extracted but kept dry, and 2 lost for each cone not extracted and wet. Procedure, too, is slightly more complicated. Water flow has to be started at the beginning of each trial and stopped at the end by the person giving instructions to the group. It must be noted whether cones are wet or dry (the sponge pad on the base of the cone helps here), and at the end of each trial cones need to be dried off, the jar emptied of water, and dry cones put back into the jar. Inevitably some water gets spilled and has to be mopped up, so a suitable floor needs to be used. However, the water input does seem to add more interest to the task and so may well be worth the extra trouble.

Another variation in procedure mentioned previously is to add a third "emotional arousal" condition to the competitive trials. Here groups perform in the presence of class members who attempt to produce an emotionally charged atmosphere in order to examine the effect of this on performance (following earlier explanations of crowd panic). For this a few class members need to be selected and coached in advance. Their function is to create an emotional atmosphere in some way – for example, by cheering, booing, making a noise, and so on – during the first 10 trials, but it is extremely difficult to do this in a convincing way, and certainly some practice will be required. At the very least, students involved in this should learn just how difficult the role of experimenter's accomplice can be. Given the nature of this experimental condition, a separate room will be required to run it in.

Results and analysis

At the end of the experiment you will have available two sets of data for each group: the results of each set of 10 trials, in terms of the number of cones extracted by the group in each trial or in terms of the time taken to get them all out. Initially these data can simply be tabulated by group and by trial (as shown in Table 14.1) and inspected to note improvement over the trials (learning effect); difference between each set of trials; and differences among groups. Typically, in the reward–fine (competitive) condition, groups show some learning-effect improvement in the course of the trials but a very marked improvement in performance as soon as they switch to the second set of trials without a reward structure (see Table 14.1), thus supporting the first hypothesis. Typically also, performance in the "no communication" group is markedly worse than in the "reward–fine only" group for the first 10 trials and improves significantly to comparable

Table 14.1. *Sample of group performance on Mintz-type experimental task*

		Reward/fine only group		No-communication group	
	Trial number	Number of cones removed	Time (seconds)	Number of cones removed	Time (seconds)
Reward/ fines imposed	1	3	20.0	2	20.0
	2	5	20.0	0	20.0
	3	8	20.0	2	20.0
	4	10	20.0	0	20.0
	5	6	20.0	1	20.0
	6	12	18.0	0	20.0
	7	8	20.0	0	20.0
	8	10	20.0	1	20.0
	9	12	19.0	1	20.0
	10	10	20.0	1	20.0
No reward structure	1	12	8.5	10	20.0
	2	12	6.0	12	11.0
	3	12	5.5	12	8.0
	4	12	3.7	12	6.5
	5	12	4.4	12	4.5
	6	12	5.3	12	4.0
	7	12	3.8	12	4.0
	8	12	3.6	12	5.0
	9	12	5.9	12	4.0
	10	12	3.1	12	4.5

levels in the second set of trials (see Table 14.1), in accordance with the second hypothesis.

An interesting question now arises with regard to analysis and presentation of the results. The data gathered are rather crude, in measurement terms, since they switch from relating to number of cones extracted per trial to a duration measure of time taken to extract all cones, so performance cannot really be compared over trials in any precise way. Besides constructing a table like Table 14.1 to show simple differences by inspection, the only other way of presenting these results would be to draw rough learning curves of performance over trials for each group.

However, the lack of a sophisticated statistical analysis does not spoil the exercise: Even the rough data produced usually show a clearer difference over the various experimental conditions than many more sophisticated experiments. What it does do is raise some important questions about measurement and analysis that are well worth exploring. One set of questions relates to ways of improving measurements used so that a more sophisticated statistical analysis is possible. All scores might be converted to the same basis, such as number of cones or time measures, in some fairly arbitrary way, but this would distort results. Alternatively, procedure could be modified to produce more manageable results – for instance, by running the experiment using only a time measure and ending trials when all cones have been pulled out of the jar. This would give more "usable" data and also would approximate more to Mintz's original experiment, but it has the practical drawback of making trials too long, and sometimes too frustrating, for subjects (who have been known to break bottles in their attempts to get cones out).

Another possibility would be to repeat the experimental conditions with a second set of groups. Then the results could be analyzed using nonparametric methods, such as Friedman's two-way analysis of variance (see Siegel, 1965, for details).

None of these points detracts from the value of the exercise or from the significance of the results. These questions are raised to draw attention to important general issues in research that could usefully be followed up in class discussion, starting from the situation produced by this exercise, where data emerge that are obviously and clearly significant but that cannot easily be proved to be with the more rigorous quantitative analyses usually employed as part of the scientific approach to social psychology.

Discussion

Generally the results of the exercise should show in a crude but clear way the significant effects of reward structure and communication conditions on groups' performance on the experimental task, in keeping with the initial hypotheses. This is also to some extent in keeping with Mintz's original findings, although he lays less stress on the effects of communication than on reward structure.

Thus results can be seen as suggesting that some apparently nonrational behavior can still be given a more rational explanation: that panic may be more a function of perceived changes in reward structure or of communication breakdown than emotional contagion (emotional arousal conditions in the exercise usually show little effect). Insofar as the experimental situation created here relates to larger groups in a natural environment, then these too can be seen as affected by similar factors and as subject to a similar kind of analysis. Consideration can be extended from the somewhat limited instance of theater fires to other socially relevant situations, such as stock-market panics, or panic buying of commodities like gasoline, or runs on savings and loan companies, all of which can be seen as sharing the same essential characteristics.

If desired, discussion of the exercise can be broadened by referring not only to Mintz's work but also to different accounts of crowd behavior to be found in general social-psychology texts (e.g., Forsyth, 1983, Chapter 11).

Methodologically, there are things to beware of in reviewing and reporting the exercise. Although the findings might suggest the significance of reward structures in group behavior, the exercise – and Mintz's original experiment – are not completely clear on this. The difference between the two sets of trials for each group is not only in terms of the presence or absence of a reward structure; it may also reflect a difference of expectation or "set," induced by other aspects of the situation such as the instructions, which would seem to provide a competitive set followed by a cooperative set, quite separate from the use of rewards. It might be useful to discuss how the procedure could be changed to examine more carefully the importance of reward structure by itself – for example, by altering instructions for subjects.

Experience of running exercises like the one described here suggests that limiting communication may well have a greater effect than Mintz claimed, and again, you could consider how the exercise could be redesigned to separate out clearly the independent effects of communication and reward structures.

A further aspect worth mentioning about the design of the exercise concerns order effects. Groups are run first in competitive conditions and then in cooperative conditions, whereas normal good procedure would suggest counterbalancing order, to separate out learning effects over trials. However, for this exercise it was felt that experience first of successful performance in the cooperative situation was likely to carry over so much that it would mask the influence of other factors.

Finally, it should be noted that the exercise carried out here, and the Mintz experiment it follows, raise important issues of research in social psychology, particularly the issue of whether it is possible and worthwhile to attempt to bring complex social behaviors into the experimental laboratory, and how it might meaningfully be done. On the face of it, pulling cones out of a glass bottle seems to be too far removed from a panic-stricken crowd in a burning theater for behavior in the one situation to tell us much about the other: As Milgram (1977, p. 266) put it, the Mintz experiment "stands in relation to actual panic as the game of Monopoly does to high finance." Yet experience of actually participating in this experimental situation may well give a different perspective. Subjects tend rapidly to become involved: the experiment seems to have a fair amount of psychological impact or "experimental realism" (see Lewin, 1979). So it may well be that criticisms of experimental approaches to social behavior as artificial are not always appropriate and that even large-scale social psychological phenomena such as crowds can be usefully studied in the laboratory by setting up a simulation that *models* significant features, rather than trying to copy the actual behavior.

References

Forsyth, D. R. (1983). *An Introduction to Group Dynamics*. Monterey, Calif.: Brooks Cole.

Lewin, M. (1979) *Understanding Psychological Research*. New York: Wiley.

Milgram, S. (1977). *The Individual in a Social World*. Reading, Mass.: Addison-Wesley.

Mintz, A. (1951). Non-adaptive group behaviour. *Journal of Abnormal and Social Psychology*, 46, 150–9.

Siegel, S. (1956). *Nonparametric Statistics for the Behavioral Sciences*. New York: McGraw-Hill.

15   Norms and roles in the small group

Peter B. Smith

Summary

This exercise provides an opportunity to study the norms of the actual class group with whom you are taking this course. It is intended to show how concepts such as conformity, role, and norm can be translated into practicable and simple data collection procedures. The procedures proposed will enable you to collect potentially sensitive data in a manner that preserves the anonymity of respondents. The data you will assemble will provide a picture of certain aspects of the group to which you belong. This picture may be of value both in reconstructing why the group has developed in the way it has so far, and also in seeking to influence its future course. The chapter illustrates both qualitative and quantitative approaches to data analysis.

Introduction

Perhaps the central problem in social psychology is determining how people's behavior is affected by the reactions of others. When interacting with strangers, we must necessarily base our behavior on generalized assumptions about how others would react to any particular behavior on our part. These assumptions may be internalized within ourselves, in the form of feelings as to what does or does not feel like appropriate behavior in a given setting, or they may be externalized as feelings that one wishes to please, or to displease, particular others whom one encounters. When a group of people continues to meet one another for some time, opportunities arise to test out these generalized assumptions and to adapt them to the reactions that others in the group do actually have to one's behavior. In many groups these reactions may not be spelled out very clearly, so there is plenty of scope for misunderstanding and misperception. Still, with the passage of time, any group that continues to meet develops an increasingly unique set of norms about how the member's should behave in each other's presence.

This exercise seeks to investigate this process in the context of a course designed to introduce students to research methods in psychology. Two specific questions are addressed:

- What is the level of normative consensus in this group?
- What is the relationship between the level of normative consensus and the demographic structure of the group?

The value of the exercise is that it focuses on some very basic central concepts of social psychology, and does so in a way that makes it easy for students to find connections between the exercise and their everyday experience of being in the class.

Laboratory experiments

Most research by social psychologists concerning group norms has been formulated in terms of the process of conformity. Many researchers have followed the lead of Asch (1956) in seeking to demonstrate that group norms are created through the majority of group members imposing their views on the minority, who may initially have different views. In Asch's experiment, small groups were assembled in a laboratory and asked to make judgments of physical stimuli, such as the relative lengths of various lines. All but one of the members of each of these groups were actually collaborating with the experimenter, and on certain trials they all gave the same incorrect responses. The naive subject was asked to respond last, and it was found that quite often he or she did indeed conform to the incorrect previous judgments made by the others. This occurred even though it was actually very easy to make the correct judgments. Although this study provides one of the major landmarks in the development of social psychology, it is easy, 30 years later, to see that it avoided more questions than it answered.

The Asch study and its numerous subsequent replications are often cited as "demonstrating" conformity. In fact, in the original study, about 35% of the judgments made by naive subjects moved toward conformity with the stooges' false judgments, whereas the remaining 65% did not do so. Thus one could make just as good an argument that the experiments demonstrate *independence* from social pressure. A further critique of the Asch study has been advanced by Moscovici (1976), who argues that even in the 35% of cases where conformity did occur, the effect is caused not by the fact that the majority outnumbered the individual but by the fact that the majority responded *consistently* with one another. According to Moscovici, in deciding whether or not to accept a viewpoint we are not much influenced by how many others hold it, but we do pay a lot of attention to whether the viewpoint is consistently maintained. There is some evidence within Asch's own work that supports this view – for instance, the finding that the amount of conformity obtained was unaffected by how many stooges were used. In order to test his hypothesis, Moscovici set up studies in which a *minority* group of two stooges gave incorrect but consistent judgments as to the colors of lights on a screen while the larger, majority group of naive subjects made their judgments. He found that the consistent minority did indeed influence the judgments of the majority.

Moscovici's findings imply a major reconceptualization of the manner in which a group's norms can be expected to develop. Asch's model implies a unilateral process of influence, whereby the most widespread viewpoints in the group will prevail, and those who dissent from them must either change their views or leave the group. Moscovici, by contrast, envisages a more fluid, two-way process of influence. The group's norms will arise out of the persuasiveness and consistency with which various views are advanced. Moscovici's view also makes it easier to imagine the possibility that in some groups there might be no consensus but rather a state of continuing conflict.

The assumption that consensus in a group or in a society is the normal state of affairs, whereas conflict is either unusual or pathological, has crept into the thinking of many theorists, including Asch. Indeed, his choice of experimental procedures picks out a field – judgment of physical stimuli – in which that assumption is hardly questioned. Except for the small minority who do not trust what they see with their own eyes, our daily experience of the physical world is solidly built on the consensual assumption that others see it the same way that we see it ourselves. However, the norms that develop among a small group of people are rarely concerned with judgments of the physical world. More typically they concern the values and actions of group members, and their reactions both to each other and to others outside the group. Allen and Levine (1968) set up an experiment resembling Asch's that concerned both physical judgments and social values. They found that the conditions resulting in greatest conformity on physical judgments were not the same as those resulting in greatest conformity on social-value judgments. In particular, on physical-judgment tasks, the addition of a subject who gave correct answers practically eliminated conformity to the majority stooges' judgments. On social-value judgments, the effect of the additional subject depended upon the position that this subject took. In other words, the experiment supported the

commonsense view that whereas we do expect others to share our perceptions of the physical world, we do not necessarily expect them to share
our social values. In this respect also, then, the Asch experiment may have
given an unfortunate impetus to research in this field, by directing
attention toward that small and atypical area in which objective consensual
judgments are relatively possible.

Field experiments

Each of the studies discussed so far has used the traditional format of
the laboratory-based psychological experiment, with subjects who are
strangers to one another, manipulation and deception by the experimenter, followed by measurement of change in the dependent variable,
which in these studies was the amount of conformity. Field studies of the
development of group norms and conformity have come up with somewhat
different results. Perhaps the best-known study of this kind was done in the
so-called Bank Wiring Observation Room, which was part of a factory at
Hawthorne, near Chicago, in the 1930s. A particularly valuable reanalysis
of the data was done by Homans (1950), in his classic book *The Human
Group*. The workers in this room – and in the rest of the factory – were
wiring telephone banks of the type then used. Basically what was found
was that the workers' productivity was astonishingly consistent over time.
Workers at the front of the room completed around 6,600 connections
per day, whereas those at the back achieved 6,000. These figures scarcely
varied over the 9 months that the study lasted. In contrast to the laboratory
experiments, there is no "objectively correct" norm against which these
figures can be compared. Management's motion study experts apparently
regarded 8,000 connections per day as about right, but in interviews
workers repeatedly said that the present norm represented a "fair day's
work for a fair day's pay." Although some subsequent empirical work has
reported on work groups who proved not to have such productivity norms,
everyday experience underlines the fact that such norms are widespread,
not just in factory work groups but within all types of organizations,
including schools and universities. Just as was the case in the original
Hawthorne study, such norms usually specify not only how much work is
too much, but also how much is too little.

 Homans argues that the best way to understand the creation of these and
other norms in the group is through a "systems" theory. In other words,
one does not simply note the level of the productivity norm and of consensus to it and then seek to explain it by postulating some causal variable.
Instead one treats the productivity norm as both a cause and an effect of

the system. Homans differentiates an external system (the structure and history of the firm, the economic situation, the physical layout of the work) and an internal system (the activities, values, and sentiments of the group members). Initially the external system "causes" a particular pattern of development of the internal system, but, in turn, the evolution of the internal system has powerful effects on the external system. For instance, the existence of the productivity norm affects the company's prospects of profitability, its ability to predict future productivity, and so forth.

According to this line of reasoning, the type of norms that arise in a group and the amount of consensus concerning them will be a product both of the context of the group and of the history of relationships within it. This position is more reminiscent of Moscovici than of Asch. Conformity is not seen as something inevitable but as something whose explanation must be sought within the specific situation of the group. Homans also provides a valuable discussion of the relation between the norms of a group and the roles taken up by each member. Having defined norms as behaviors that are expected of group members, he goes on to discuss the possibility that some group norms might apply to only one or a small number of members of the group. Such norms would ordinarily be considered as role prescriptions. In this manner Homans makes clear that social psychology has no great need to keep separate a conception of role and a conception of norm. A norm is simply a role prescription that applies to all members.

Defining norms and roles

Before one can make a study of the *norms* and *roles* in a group, we need to clarify their definitions. The definition of norms by Homans that was just cited involves an ambiguity that was present in many early definitions. In speaking of behavior that is "expected" of the group member, there are two possible meanings to the word. "Expected" could mean behavior that is *anticipated* of another, or behavior that is *required* of another. For instance, in a class it might be said that since Jane took an active part in the class last week, I "expect" that she will do so again this week. In this case one is simply extrapolating from past behavior and predicting or anticipating future behavior, without any implied evaluation. On the other hand, if I, as the teacher, announce that reports on the previous experiment are "expected" to be handed in by Friday, I am using "expected" in the sense of "required" rather than "anticipated," and there is a clear implication of disapproval of those who do not do as required.

Most recent researchers would prefer to define norms and roles in terms of *required* behaviors. A further important point is that the presence of roles and norms in a group should be investigated, rather than assumed. Gross, Mason, and McEachern (1958) have pointed out how many theorists have assumed that consensus exists in society as to the behaviors required of the person performing a particular role. Thus one might discuss the role of students, parents, bus drivers, or policemen and incautiously assume that consensus exists in society as to how the people who fill these particular roles are required to behave. At a rather general level, there clearly *is* a certain amount of widely shared agreement as to what occupants of different roles should do. Nevertheless, where empirical studies have been made of particular roles (for example, that by Gross et al. themselves), a great deal of conflict has been revealed as to how the people performing the roles ought to behave on specific issues. This line of reasoning is again reminiscent of Moscovici's view. The data collection procedures to be employed must leave open the possibility of conflict rather than consensus, since conflict is just as much a "normal" characteristic of groups as is consensus.

The exercise

The mode of investigation to be employed is correlational rather than causal. No formal hypothesis is to be tested. Data are to be collected as to how members of the class evaluate each of a list of behaviors, considering separately one's own evaluations and one's perceptions of the group's evaluations. These data will yield a series of indexes reflecting the level of normative consensus in the group. Further data will also be available concerning the demographic structure of the group, and an exploratory study will be made of the relationship between these variables and the level of normative consensus. Both the list of behaviors to be rated and the demographic variable(s) selected can be subject to the control of the class, thereby ensuring that the study is concerned with issues that the class members are interested in and are willing to make public.

In some ways these research procedures resemble the "action-research" model employed by consultants to large organizations. In action research, the collection of data is collaboratively planned between consultant and client. Once collected, it is fed back to the client for the purpose of considering whether or not any change is desirable in current practices within the organization. If the need for such change does emerge, further collaborative planning is done to find out the best way to make that change. In a similar manner, a survey of class norms may (or may not) reveal a situation that class members would like to change.

Methods

Groupings

The precise form of the project to be employed may have to be adapted slightly, depending on the prior history of the class group. The guiding principle should be that the study is focused on the group, or groups, in which class members spend most of their class time together. In other words, if the class is relatively small (up to 15, say), and a good deal of time is spent with the total group together, then the total class would provide the group to be studied. If the class is bigger and, as a result, is for much of the time broken up into smaller groupings that conduct their studies and discuss their findings separately, then these subgroups may provide a more appropriate focus. If subgroupings are employed but they vary in composition from week to week, then the total group must be the focus.

Procedure

The project can readily be carried through within a single week's class meetings, including most of the required data analysis. A single room is required, and the only necessary materials are the questionnaires to be described shortly. The first stage comprises the selection of a suitable range of behaviors that can provide the basis of the norms of the class. Obviously it is not possible to specify in advance which behaviors may become the most salient ones within a particular class. The first half hour or so of the period is to be devoted to introducing the project and selecting suitable behaviors. What is required is a list of the 12 behaviors that are most salient to members of the class. This list of 12 behaviors is to be arrived at through class discussion. Appendix 1 provides 21 possible candidates for the list, and these will be written on the blackboard in advance or issued as a handout. The final list is to be arrived at by selection from the list of 21, amendment of items on the list of 21, and addition of new items suggested by members of the class. It is important not to rush this stage in the project, since the validity of the findings rests on the selection of items for the list that do have some relevance to the group's previous history. The criterion for accepting an item on the list should be that the event described is one that people would respond to with various levels of approval or disapproval. If the exercise is to be done in subgroups, then each subgroup will need to select their own list of 12 items.

When the process of selecting 12 items is complete, check that the items are on the blackboard in their correct form or else that class members have amended the list issued to them to match the final version. Whichever of the original 21 items have survived, whether amended or not, should be referred to by their code letters *A* through *U*, as in appendix 1. New items should be assigned code letters from *V* onward.

Before the actual data collection starts, one further decision is required, namely the selection of an appropriate demographic variable whose relationship to the norm structure will be studied. What is required is a salient dimension of what Homans called the "external system" of the group – that is, aspects of the structure that are fixed before the group has ever met. Possible dimensions would be sex, age, race, or nationality. The dimension selected should be one that divides the class reasonably equally, rather than spotlighting some small and potentially self-conscious minority. Most often the sex variable is the most useful, or in a class that has a reasonable number of mature students, the age variable. Whichever variable is selected, all that is required is the differentiation of two discrete categories. If age is selected, this can be mature students versus others; if race, then white versus nonwhite.

Data collection

Data collection can be accomplished quickly by completing a questionnaire. A suitable version of the questionnaire is given in appendix 2. It should take about 15 minutes to complete. It will be useful for each student to have two copies of the questionnaire. When both copies have been completed, one can be used to collect the data anonymously, while the other is retained for later comparison with the class means. The questionnaire asks for three types of evaluations of the list of 12 behaviors developed earlier. The first of these is concerned with *perceived group norms* – that is, how each group member perceived the group's usual responses. The second evaluation will be used to derive a measure of the group's *actual norms*, if norms are considered as the sum of individual members' evaluations. The final question is focused not on norms per se but on each person's preferences concerning how they themselves behave.

There is no logical reason why the data deriving from these three questions should not be closely correlated. In practice there is usually considerable divergence, and a richer and more valid picture of the group can be obtained by collecting all three sets of data. The principal reason why perceived group norms are likely to diverge from what are here called "actual norms" is that the actual-norm measure assumes that each group member's evaluation of behavior carries equal weight in the determination of the group norm. In practice some member's evaluations will be more influential than those of others, and this will be reflected in the perceived group norm measure. A divergence can also be anticipated between the personal preference question and the perceived group norms. The breadth of this divergence is likely to show the degree to which the group is currently meeting the needs of its members.

Note that the first question asks for ratings of how much each behavior is approved or disapproved, whereas the remaining two questions ask only for a ranking. The ratings are to be used in a qualitative analysis of the data, to be discussed shortly. For purposes of subsequent quantitative analysis, these ratings will then be converted into rankings.

When you complete the questionnaire, it should be clear that you are asked to do so anonymously but that the responses will be shared publicly, in a way that makes it impossible to know which set of data comes from which person. When questionnaire completion is finished, fold your questionnaire once and hand it in to the professor. When all questionnaires are in, they should be visibly shuffled and a start made on qualitative data analysis. This is to be done by tabulating responses to question 1 on the blackboard. This tabulation should not be started before all responses are in; otherwise the anonymity of late responders will be lost.

Data analysis

Descriptive statistics

The primary purpose of the qualitative data analysis is to determine which of the 12 behaviors on the list attracts enough of a concensus for them to be considered group norms. There is no agreement in the research literature as to how strong a group consensus must be before a norm is considered to be present. Bates and Cloyd (1956) made a study of roles and norms in student discussion groups. They judged a norm to be present where at least 75% of group members throught that 75% of members would agree with it. Lieberman, Yalom, and Miles (1973) studied the norms of student encounter groups. They accepted as norm-governed all behaviors that were described as "appropriate" by 67% and all behaviors described as "inappropriate" by 67%. However, these are relatively arbitrary cutoff points.

This analysis will follow the less complex approach of Lieberman et al. The data should be tabulated in the form shown in Table 15.1. For convenience in the later quantitiative data analysis, the data from males and females (or whatever other category split is used) should be grouped

Table 15.1. *Tabulation of responses to question 1*

Behavior code	B	C	E	F	I	K	M	O	Q	R	S	T
Category of subject												
F (Female)	4	3	3	3	3	2	4	4	3	1	4	2
F	3	2	2	2	4	2	3	4	4	2	4	3
etc....												
Sum of ratings	70	50	53	51	72	40	69	80	72	33	82	49
Rank order of summed ratings	8.0	4.0	6.0	5.0	9.5	2.0	7.0	11.0	9.5	1.0	12.0	3.0

together. When the data are tabulated, it is easy to determine the presence or absence of norms. Examine each column in turn, and count whether the number of 1 and 2 ratings exceeds 67%. In a similar way, determine whether the number of 4 and 5 ratings exceeds 67%. In a long-established class group, it may turn out that half or more of the 12 items do satisfy the definition of norms.

Some time may now be taken in discussing the results with the class. Issues that could be explored include whether or not the norms shown by this data analysis to be most strongly held do indeed feel like the salient norms of the group; why these particular norms have developed; why the group does not have more (or fewer) norms; and how far these norms resemble those found in other class groups that have done this study. Past groups have, for example, shown norms favoring K, L, Q, and T, and opposing H, M, O, and S.

If you want to make most use of the qualitative data generated by this project, then the responses to questions 2 and 3 should now be tabulated in a similar way. In these cases, what are available for tabulation are the ranks assigned to each behavior, rather than ratings. This means that it is not possible to use the data from questions 2 and 3 so precisely for determining the presence or absence of norms. However, the data do make it possible to obtain an overall summation of which behaviors are ranked highest. It is the possible divergence between these ranks and those from the question 1 data, as tabulated at the bottom of Table 15.1, that is of interest. Identify the behaviors that show the greatest divergence between the data derived from question 1 and that derived from questions 2 and 3. You can now discuss the probable explanations of these divergences. Assuming that the divergence found is large enough to *require* some explanation, there are two main possibilities. The first is that the question 1 data have been influenced by some kind of pluralistic ignorance in the group. In other words each group member assumes that most of the others disapprove of a certain behavior – such as appearing too studious and scholarly, whereas they themselves do not disapprove of it. The *perceived* group consensus is not a consensus at all, but the group has failed to discover this. This situation is most likely to arise in groups whose members have kept rather distant from one another, thereby minimizing opportunities for discovering one another's actual feelings and values.

The second possible explanation for divergences in the data is that there is indeed a group consensus about how a certain behavior is evaluated but that this consensus does not represent the sum of individual members' preferences. This state of affairs would arise where some members of the group were much more influential than others. Perhaps some members of the class are much more highly verbal than others, and their opinions come, over time, to be seen as the group norms, whereas others' views are less heard.

The discussion of these and other possible explanations for whatever divergences are found may be used to provide an opportunity to review within the class or sub-groupings of the class the way in which their social structure has so far developed. The data should not be treated as a set of definitive "answers" but as a vehicle for opening up the discussion in whatever directions class members find interesting.

If you want to place more stress on quantitative analysis of the data, the procedures outlined in the preceding three paragraphs can be omitted, to save time and to enable the main hypotheses of the project to be tested.

Inferential statistics

The first step in the quantitative data analysis is to obtain a more precise estimate of the level of normative consensus in the group. This can be accomplished through the use of Kendall's coefficient of concordance (W). This is a statistic for testing the degree of agreement between a set of rankings of the same objects. In order to use the test on the data in Table 15.1, it is necessary to transform each row of ratings into a ranking. This is done by ranking the sum of the ratings in each column. As is the case in the example in Table 15.1, there may sometimes be ties in the rankings. However, this does not invalidate the procedure, so long as the appropriate correction for ties is employed. In assigning ranks it is important to remember that tied ratings are assigned the *average* of their tied ranks. For instance, if two ratings tie for top place, they are assigned a rank of 1.5 each, not 1.0. Full instructions for the calculation of W are given in Siegel (1956).

The value of W obtained will reflect not only the presence or absence of norms, as defined in the prior qualitative data analysis, but also the level of agreement or disagreement about the evaluation of each one of the 12 behaviors on the list. This means that the value of W may be substantially affected by which items the group chooses to include on the list. If something is included about which the group is strongly divided, or if something is excluded about which most of the group agree (for example, approving of being friendly to one another), the value of W will be depressed. The W value is useful not so much for comparing it with values for other samples but to serve as a baseline for further analysis within the present sample.

Earlier it was mentioned that the level of normative consensus in the group would be a reflection of its "external" or demographic structure. A preliminary test of this idea can be made by calculating separate values of W for the data from the males and females in the class (or whatever demographic category was selected). Time can be saved in class by having some members compute the overall W, some the male W, and some the female W. Since the values of W are not all derived from a similar number of judges, they must be compared in terms of the significance levels that each achieves. These can be computed as indicated by Siegel (1956), using the procedure for large samples.

A variety of findings is possible. If there is greater consensus within either or both of the single-sex categories than in the total class, this can be taken as indicating that the demographic variable selected is indeed an important one in relation to the level of normative consensus within the class. If there is little difference between consensus in the single-sex groups and the total class, this would indicate that there *was* a shared perception of how behavior was evaluated in the total group. This would still leave open the possibility that those evaluations were more acceptable to one subcategory than to the other.

A fuller testing of the general hypothesis is possible through drawing on the responses to questions 2 and 3. What is required is a measure of the degree to which members of each subcategory concur with the perceived group consensus indicated by the data from question 1. To put it another way, what is the match between each individual's views and the views of the group as a whole?

You should now refer to your own rankings, of which you should have kept a record. Two rank order correlation coefficients are to be computed. One is between the ranking of perceived group norms obtained from question 1 (to be found on the bottom line of Table 15.1) and your own response to question 2. The other is between the ranking of perceived group norms and your response to question 3. The preferred correlation coefficient is Kendall's tau (Siegel, 1956). If you are already familiar with

Spearman's rho, this could be used instead, but it does not deal as well with ties. In any case, all members of the class must use the same test. When these correlations have been made, you should write the two values of tau (or rho) on a slip of paper, making clear which is which; add a statement of your sex (or other relevant characteristic); and hand the slip to the professor. Preserving anonymity as before, the professor should then write the obtained values of tau (or rho) on the blackboard. The significance of the difference between male and female scores on each of the two correlations can now be established. The best way to do this is with *t*-tests for independent means, using the values of tau (or rho) as scores.

The amount of time required for this project will depend on the length of the discussions of the qualitative data and how familiar students are with Kendall's tau and Kendall's *W*. If insufficient time remains, the *t*-tests could be computed afterward, although this would prevent any final discussion of the findings obtained. It is important that such discussion occur at some stage, because the findings may well show that one or the other sex (assuming sex is used to dichotomize the group) does not gain a full hearing for their views and values in the group. If you find such a situation, you have some responsibility to explore ways of changing it.

Discussion

The various options outlined within this chapter make it possible to emphasize qualitative approaches or quantitative approaches to investigation or to sample some of both and to contrast what can and what cannot be accomplished by each approach. The qualitative study is structured in such a way that people are likely to find it interesting and to see connections between what it shows and their experience within the class. Somewhat in the manner of some of the early experiments by Lewin, it uses group participation both as a research method and as a method of motivating people's interest in the findings. It is considerably more structured than the methods employed by contemporary action researchers in the field of organizational consultancy, but it gives a flavor of that approach. Its weakness lies in the lack of cumulativeness of the findings. Systematic recording of the class discussions of the findings might provide illustrations from the history of a particular group supporting one or another theoretical model of conformity processes. For instance, it might be found that, in line with Moscovici's view, the norms had arisen from what was initially a consistently held minority position. But such findings would be a matter of chance rather than design, and there would be no way of measuring the frequency with which they occurred.

The quantitative study seeks to relate the internal normative system to the external constraints acting upon that system. The form of the data makes it easier to compare different sets of findings, but there is little expectation that the elements of the external system acting on a group will always have the same weightings. In one group, age may be a crucial variable, whereas in another it could be sex. The goal of this type of study is thus not to contribute to a search for generalized laws or explanations concerning conformity but to provide a more precise estimate than that provided by the qualitative study of the interrelatedness of the group's internal and external systems. Neither system is seen as "causing" the other: They act and react upon one another. There is a substantial intuitive element in this type of research. For instance, the researcher must make an appropriate selection of an external system variable related to the group being investigated, if there is to be any hope that the research will be useful.

The "laws" of social psychology mostly concern processes that occur between people without very much conscious attention on the part of the people concerned. Thus one forms impressions of strangers, one attributes traits to individuals, one comes to expect that a group will or should behave in a certain way. Social psychologists have investigated much less fully what happens when one encourages someone to pay attention to these processes. The evidence that we do have comes from research in such fields as psychotherapy, education, training, and consultancy. In each of these areas there is evidence to support the view that enhancing someone's awareness of a social process in which he or she is engaged will increase the probability that the person will seek to change that process. Some tentative formulations are available (for example, Smith, 1980) as to the circumstances under which such change attempts are most likely to be successful. If one accepts this argument, then this exercise may be useful not only in studying the class norms but also in possibly changing them. Where such changes are effectively accomplished, they provide a vivid demonstration of the manner in which social norms are at the same time both socially patterned in lawful ways and also subject to change through human agency.

Report guidelines

The reports that you write on this project will differ somewhat depending upon how much emphasis your group has placed upon the descriptive or the interpretative aspects of the data.

In all cases you will need a section outlining the field to be investigated, followed by a description of the methods used. Your results section would then focus either on the range of group norms identified or on your study of the different subgroups within the class. A qualitatively based report might then consider aspects of the group's history or present situation that were identified in class discussion and that might bear upon why the class has the norms that it currently does. A quantitative report would lay more stress upon the values and meaning of *W* and tau that were obtained. In either case, the report should close with an evaluation of the particular research methods that were employed.

References

Allen, V.L., & Levine, J.M. (1968). Social support, dissent and conformity. *Sociometry, 31*, 138–49.

Asch, S.E. (1956). Studies of independence and conformity: I. A minority of one against a unanimous majority. *Psychological Monographs, 70*, (9), whole no. 416.

Bates, A.P., & Cloyd, J.S. (1956). Toward the definition of operations for defining group norms and member roles. *Sociometry, 19*, 26–39.

Gross, N.E., Mason, W.S., & McEachern, A.W. (1958). *Explorations in Role Analysis: Studies of the School Superintendency Roles*. New York: Wiley.

Homans, G.C. (1950). *The Human Groups*. New York: Harcourt, Brace, Jovanovich.

Lieberman, M.A., Yalom, I.D., & Miles, M.B. (1973). *Encounter Groups: First Facts*. New York: Basic Books.

Moscovici, S. (1976). *Social Influence and Social Change*. New York: Academic Press.

Siegel, S.E. (1956). *Non-parametric Statistics for the Behavioural Sciences*. New York: McGraw-Hill.

Smith, P.B. (1980). *Group Processes and Personal Change*. New York: Harper & Row.

Appendix 1. List of behaviors that can provide the basis of class norms

A. Someone is absent without explanation.
B. Someone always argues with the teacher.
C. Someone becomes dissatisfied with the study of psychology.
D. Someone shows in discussion that he or she has done a lot of reading about the topic.
E. Someone jokes all the time.
F. Someone remains silent during discussions.
G. Someone shows keen interest in the topic.
H. Someone "invents" data rather than collecting it.
I. Someone hands in all the required reports on time.
J. Someone expresses difficulty in understanding the statistical tests required.
K. Someone offers to help another student understand something that is puzzling him or her.
L. Someone criticizes a study the class is doing as "artificial."
M. Someone fails to do his or her share of the task on a group project.
N. Someone criticizes the teacher behind his or her back.
O. Someone keeps the discussion going when others want to leave.
P. Someone tries to manipulate the group to get his or her own way.
Q. Someone proposes that the group have greater control over which projects are to be done.
R. Someone behaves in a friendly manner toward others.
S. Someone frequently interrupts others.
T. Someone helps keep the group focused on what needs to be done.
U. A group member organizes the work of the group.

Appendix 2. Behavior rating form

Class group [for example, "Wednesday morning class"]
Category [for example, "female"]

1. You are asked first to indicate how you think *this group would react* if
   a member behaved in each of the ways on the list of 12 behaviors that
   the class has constructed. For each pair of boxes below, place in the
   upper box the code letter of one of the behaviors and in the lower box
   your view of how the group would react to it. In recording your views,
   choose whichever of the following categories is most appropriate:

   1   Everyone would approve of this behavior.
   2   Most people would approve of this behavior.
   3   Some would approve of this; others would be indifferent or would
       disapprove.
   4   Most people would disapprove of this behavior.
   5   Everyone would disapprove of this behavior.

   Now complete your ratings:

   Behavior code

   How you think
   group would
   react

2. Now think again of the list of 12 behaviors. This time you are asked to
   rank them in order of how *you personally would feel about someone
   other than yourself* doing each of these behaviors in this group. Place
   the behaviors you would most approve of highest. If you find that you
   cannot differentiate between how much you would approve of some
   of the behaviors, you can use tied ranks for them. Write the codes
   of the behaviors in the order you wish to rank them. Make sure to
   include all 12 behaviors.

   Rank order: 1 _____   7 _____
                 2 _____   8 _____
                 3 _____   9 _____
                 4 _____   10 _____
                 5 _____   11 _____
                 6 _____   12 _____

3. Finally, think once more of the 12 behaviors. This time rank them in order of how you would feel about behaving in each of these ways *yourself*. Place the behaviors you would most approve of highest. Be sure to include all 12 behaviors.

Rank order: 1 _____   7 _____
             2 _____   8 _____
             3 _____   9 _____
             4 _____ 10 _____
             5 _____ 11 _____
             6 _____ 12 _____

Index